IF YOU FALL RUN ON

Caroline Owens

Dedicated to

My parents
Johnnie and Margaret Owens

And to Derry's mothers,
fathers, sons, and daughters.

Preface

Whether we turn to them with fondness or disdain, our childhoods have made an indelible imprint on the hearts and minds that we have become. Curiously, all that is great about who we are is as much to do with the irritants, frustrations, hurts, scrapes, and falls of our early life and times, as it is to do with our pleasures and loves. Who we are now and the quality of our contribution in the world is rooted in our early childhoods and the legacy of our parents and previous generations. Just as we have been imprinted and shaped by what has gone before us – we continue to leave our mark on the world and the people in it – therefore, each one of us is making a contribution to the destiny of the generations yet to come. With this in mind, we have a responsibility to live and love well, and living and loving well will not be free of mistakes and misdemeanours. Living and loving well involves taking time to reflect on who we are and who and how we want to be in the world. Who we are now is the story of who we were before and where we have been.

We all have a story…

This is mine.

Acknowledgements

The decision to write this book and eventually have it published has not been straightforward. From the initial conception to its birth, many times it seemed that it just wasn't going to happen, as I had either lost faith in the book or in my capacities as a writer. My labour has involved much soul searching about my own motivation for delivering such a book into the public domain but I am deeply grateful to my family and friends, whose faith in me and my endeavour have helped me recover from times of doubt, and whose encouragement and support just to keep going has made this book possible.

My parents, Margaret and Johnnie Owens, you are in my bones and deep in my heart. My book is a tribute to you and your lives and to the way that you kept on loving and kept on doing your best for our family and our community. I have carried you both within me throughout my life.

My daughters, Kerrie and Meghan, thank you for making room in your hearts and minds for this new baby. I am very aware that whatever life this book goes on to have in the world – you have to live with it too. Your curiosity in me and my emotional and cultural history have been a powerful source of inspiration. Thank you too for your trust and for providing me with some of my greatest life lessons in mothering.

The pages of this book contain the names of real people, all of whom have made a deep impression on my life and me; otherwise, they would not have been mentioned. Where possible, I have contacted many of the characters featured and gained their permission, without which there would be no book. The generosity of spirit of all of those who have agreed to have my memories of them and their lives included within these pages, even when my memories may not have concurred with theirs, has overwhelmed me. It became very clear to me that those who have given their permission shared my own need and motivation in telling my story, and I think that in doing so; they have helped put into words what was often unspeakable, unspoken, and misunderstood all those years ago. Therefore, together, I hope that we have contributed to a deeper understanding of what it was like to grow up in Northern Ireland through one of the most significant periods in modern Irish history. Whether this is a period referred to or remembered as "a war'" or "the troubles", it profoundly imprinted a generation and shaped the future of generations to come. So this has been the spirit in which those featured have given their permission. An example of which was plainly but emphatically expressed by Sandra Cullen, "Caroline, get it published because your story is our story too."

I am indebted to my childhood friends, in particular, Sandra, Majella, and Moya, whose continued friendship and love has provided sustenance throughout my adult life and through this protracted labour. You have continued to make a big imprint on my heart and mind and remain a constant source of inspiration; I am blessed to have you as treasured friends.

I am indebted to my eldest brother Tommy who has tirelessly and steadily encouraged me over the years by keeping the faith in this project when it seemed that mine was lost, holding my hand when I'd lost my balance, and helping me rise from many a fall. Tommy has also read sevral drafts and eventually found himself in an editorial/advisory role. I owe you bro' and yes, I do need to brush up on my grammar.

My brother Sean, a force of nature, has observed my every step along the way and has been my most severe critic. Yes, Sean, you were constantly on my back and I didn't always want to hear what you had to say, but I'd have lost my head without you. You did all you could to protect me from compromising others and myself in the telling of my story. Sean, being Sean, has project managed and coordinated the publishing and marketing and is responsible for creating the book cover design. No end to your talents, bro'.

Throughout this endeavour, my brother Mark, whose enthusiasm for the project remained steadfast and whose knowledge and expertise has made a deep imprint on its content, has closely debated and considered the themes and ideas within the book. Mark, you are still making magic out of muck!

The early drafts and manuscript weren't fit to see the light of day but my close friends, family, and colleagues were subjected to misspellings, grammar mistakes, and unformed themes. I am indebted to you all for your generous feedback and for seeing the potential in what I was hoping to achieve.

My sister Donna and brothers David and Liam, and extended family who have been less closely involved in the process of producing this book, you have been close in my heart throughout, and I am deeply appreciative of your continued trust in me to tell a story, which brings into the public domain your history and your names.

Finally, taking the decision to publish now has been in large part due to the encouragement and generosity of spirit of my close friend Johnnie Dammone, whose email about the merits of online publishing was the beginning of the final push into getting this book to market. Thanks Johnnie for keep-

ing me linked in... you're a star. The Dammone family in Leeds has taught me much over this past thirty years about "the power of now", about living and loving well, and has reminded me that an investment in the quality of my own personal and professional growth is an investment in the world around me.

To all of my colleagues and friends who have helped me decide on the cover and whose support and confidence in my story and me has kept me going through the final push. I can't thank you all enough.

This book would not have been published for this deadline had it not been for the considerable effort and support of my extended family in Mullingar, Co. Westmeath. I am overwhelmed by your generosity of spirit and willingness to remain closely involved with the project at the eleventh hour.

Names and defining information about some of the characters in this book have been radically altered where it would not have been appropriate to reveal the person's identity and/or when I have been unable to contact the individual to gain their permission. Sadly, many characters within the story have since passed away; however, I am deeply grateful to each and every one and hope that I have treated your name and memory with honesty, dignity, and respect.

The Story within these pages has emerged from my memories. Memory of course, is subject to many influences and may not always provide us with a reliable account of events. With this in mind, I have tried hard to truthfully represent my history and the people and events within my story. Nonelethe-less, this is my version of my life and times and as such, it is my truth.

Chapter 1
IF YOU FALL RUN ON

"SORRY to say that it's not good news. Unfortunately, the lump is highly suspicious and indicates a malignancy. There is, however, a ten to fifteen percent chance that it may turn out to be benign; I do hope that we're wrong, sometimes we do get it wrong but I need to inform you that it doesn't look good at all."

The specialist registrar, a short man in his early thirties with lots of little potholes on his cheeks that looked like oil-filled puddles, was sitting at his desk whilst talking to me and busily writing something down about me on a form containing boxes, which he proceeded to tick. It was only yesterday when the mechanic at the garage who, with his black face and filthy overalls, was struggling to hold his gaze and uncomfortably moved his posture from hip resting to arms folding, could hardly bear the obvious discomfort of giving me the bad news.

"Sorry to say it's not good news," he said, with big brown, tired, but kindly eyes. "But you're going to need a new exhaust... sometimes we can repair them, but I'm really sorry I'm afraid I just can't save it, and your electrics are knackered!" He paused, looked at me directly, and continued.

"I'm really sorry but I think that your car has run its race. There's no other way of saying it but I think that this lovely little thing is dying."

In contrast, the doctor routinely continued to explain the detail of the examination and the state of my left breast, as though he were telling me that I might be losing a tooth that I didn't need in the first place. This little man may as well not have been in the same room as me or even on the same planet. He didn't matter anyway. I was already somewhere else.

Having suddenly gone deaf, I wasn't listening to him. It was as though a part of me had stepped out of my body and was numbly standing by, watching a scene of someone else's movie. Another part of me, in defiance of this seemingly heartless little oily man, was swallowing a bucket of tears, which seemed stuck, held up, and waiting at the back of my throat because there were no kindly eyes willing to witness the hurt. I tried to get a grip... contain myself... hold myself together.

Chapter 1 IF YOU FALL RUN ON

I finished dressing and followed instructions to proceed to the waiting room where I would be called for more tests. Dizzy, dazed, and drunk with anxiety, the gradual dawning of what was happening assaulted my barely woken up mind at seven thirty on a dark winter's morning in that sleepy and awakening hospital breast clinic. I was in desperate need of my mother's hand. But she wasn't there. She could not have been there – how could she be? There was no one there except the woman who was coming towards me wheeling a trolley of rattling teacups and two big fat silver pots. "Here you are love... tea or coffee?" she smiled. I asked for tea, and no sooner had she poured it than she was gone.

Sitting back in the hard and uncomfortable blue plastic waiting room chair, I glimpsed a picture from a magazine on the coffee table beneath me showing a vivid colour picture of Salvador Dali's 'The Persistence of Memory', the one where the clocks are melting and time drips onto a weird, bleak desert nightmare land. Me – the parts of me, my breast, and this friggin' cup of weak tea may as well be sitting in the middle of that mad picture because this was a nightmare. No way could my time be up. I had too much to do. But what in God's name would I do? Nowhere to run and nowhere to turn, I clung on to the hot cup, pinned to that blue plastic chair. Closing my eyes in an attempt to escape, a shadowy vision of my mother's concerned face emerged. The warmth of her was close by, now resting beside me. I nestled my hurt in the hearth of her soft safe breasts and stayed there for a while. Wanting to cry 'not fair' tears, my head was stroked and soothed by her deepest sense of love for me and that she would kiss it all better.

Yet how could it be made better? "It does not look good," he had definitely said that. Christ Almighty, what if it really is not good, what if I am going to die – soon? If I wasn't going to be around, who would be there for my two daughters? Who would hold their hands and love them as I do? I could see parts of their lives in front of me, and I ticked through a checklist of what they would miss and what they would need if I wasn't going to be around. What and who could they rely on to help them through? I briefly allowed myself to mourn my loss of them and to consider what I didn't want to miss of their lives.

The winter weeks that followed were dark and bleak, and I fought and battled with thoughts about the pointlessness and preciousness of life, pulling me in and out of not wanting to do anything at all, and yet being driven by an urgent desperation to seize every moment. For a while, I went about my life and work only partially engaged. Like a camera, I filtered my world in slow motion, as merged pictures of time past and time present developed and hung around the dark room walls of my mind, reminding me of my childhood, my life and times – where I had come from, who I had become, and of the fear of not knowing how it all might turn out.

It was hard to keep my mind on anything because nothing mattered and yet everything mattered. I had a wobbly feeling of being on the edge... neither in life nor out. My head was either full or empty, and thinking about something and nothing was dragging me into a dark hole – as if I was being sucked into my own coffin. But within the still of that blackness, a shaft of hope reached down into me, and I was awoken back to life by the sound of my mother's voice, as she whispered. "If you fall, run on!"

"No bread in the house again! It's like feeding the five thousand!" Mamai was getting ready to make the tea. Seven weans to feed, five of them boys who ate like horses. We were "all steps of stairs" she would explain when introducing her weans. Tommy, ten years old was the eldest; Liam nine; then me, eight – my birthday one day after Liam's. I used to think that he was a day older than me. And I was only eleven months older than my sister Donna, who was seven years old. We were 'the four biguns'. I could add Brendan Henderson, Tommy's best friend because he was always in our house and considered one of us. Brendan was the youngest of thirteen children from a musical family that sold and repaired pianos but whose father died shortly after he was born. We had unofficially adopted Brendan, and I wonder if he had somehow filled the gap made by the still birth... Kevin, who had been born just after Donna, who was followed by 'the three weans': Sean, Mark and David, four, three, and two years old. "All steps of stairs" Mamai would explain about her troop and like the Von Trapp family, we would line up for photos and take our rightful places... oldest first.

I spent most of my early childhood thinking that my mother was fat. It was in the days when women didn't have sex, instead storks and angels came to hospitals or to bushes in the garden. It was not 'the done thing' to explain the facts of life to children and that babies were growing inside their mothers' bellies. A Catholic code of conduct was that you could do 'it' as long as you were married but never talk about 'it' because 'it' was sacred but at the same time, unspeakable and shameful. So it became a sad fact of life that my mother could not be comforted and supported through the long nine month stretches by knowing the joy and warmth of her young children's curiosity in, and care for the contents of her belly.

"I don't know where you all put it," Mamai continued in reference to how bread in our house just seemed to disappear. "I need someone to go a message," she said. The boys dived out of the front door, not wanting to go to the shops.

"Caroline, you're old enough now. Run down to Pollock's and buy a loaf, not that Mothers' Pride elastic rubbish... get an honest crusty sliced loaf." Standing at the ready, I reported for duty, and there was, as you may imagine, plenty of duty in our house with seven weans, 'the troubles' brewing, and a father with a mental illness and a drink problem. My mother never seemed to stop and didn't have a minute to spare. In fact, in the whole of my life I don't ever remember her just doing nothing. Even when she was sitting down, she was either knitting, sewing, cutting out pompoms for her latest knitted fashion creation, working out some complicated dressmaking pattern, or working out her finances... or lack of them. She had so many vegetables to prepare and potatoes to peel that she would often collect the pans and bags of spuds, bring them into the living room, where she would sit down and continue to prepare the meal whilst tutoring us through our school homework. So sitting down for Mamai never seemed to be a rest.

Opening my hand, Mamai bent down and instructed me with the seriousness of a commanding officer requesting a special mission. A half crown was placed in my hand, and she folded my fingers over the coin, pressed hard, and anchored the instruction into me. "Ask for a crusty white loaf. Watch crossing the road, don't be there until you're back, and don't come home without the change – it's all I've got, and if you fall, run on!"

Mamai was forever nursing the cuts and bruises of our scrapes and falls, as we ran, climbed, and crawled our way through childhood. She could always magically kiss the hurt better before rubbing it with a bit of butter. On this assignment, I was sure not to fall and only too glad to go a message, as I had just turned eight years old and soon would be going to the 'big girl's school' so I was feeling honoured to be trusted with the mission. With an air of confidence and pride, I set off remembering the Green Cross Code: "Look left and right then left again and if all is clear – quick march!"

I walked down Broadway – my street with the big fancy American name – with my mind on the job until I came to the walls at the bottom of the street. These were an oval of walls about four feet high that didn't seem to serve any purpose: a kind of minimalist installation. It was as though the builders had red bricks left over from the houses and just built this strange round of walls around a couple of oak trees. They were known as 'The Red Walls'.

Well, these walls weren't just any old red walls – for many years after, they made me sick even at the thought of them because of what happened that day, when suddenly my pride was punctured by panic, as I approached them. I had been skipping along when I noticed a big hyperactive dog and a pack of fierce looking weeboys waving big sticks about and popping up from behind the walls. Terror struck, and I stopped in my tracks. One filthy, freckle-faced weeboy demanded,

"Hi weegirl, you can't come past here." He commanded, "Get ready to fire!"

As he raised his arm high above his head, two or three of the wee brutes popped up from behind the walls with bricks and stones in their hands aimed at me. About three yards away from the line of fire, I froze in my clear plastic 'jelly bean' sandals. There were about five weeboys; some looked older than I did. There was no way round it, and I had to pass the walls to get to the shops. I couldn't go back home without the bread so seemingly without any thought at all, I proceeded.

Limping on and dragging my leg behind me as though my foot was falling off, I contorted my face and made my eyes go squinty, giving the impression that I was a 'spastic' child. I was so engrossed in playing the part with my eyes all squinty that I couldn't see where I was going, tripped over the pavement, and fell hard to the ground. I wanted to cry straight away with the stinging pain in my knee, which was cut, but I didn't have time because the big dog was running towards me, and I was mortified that the wee brutes had witnessed and watched my fall. I can almost hear my heart pounding now as I think of how I was trying to spring up from the fall and at the same time, remember what leg I was meant to be dragging behind me, when now I had a real limp. I didn't know what way to walk but I battered on and I neared the wall with my legs all over the place, looking like they were having a fit. The ringleader shouted, "Hold fire... let her pass!"

I didn't dare look at any of them in the eye but sensed that they were either guiltily watching or dumb struck by my performance. And I was worried sick that my squinty eyes would stick like that forever.

I don't know how I kept my guts inside me; they were heaving, and I thought that my lungs would combust, as I gasped for breath when the thought occurred to me that if the weeboys had worked out that I was pretending to be disabled, I would really be in for it. But I continued dragging my left leg behind me until I was well past the walls. I daren't stop in case they were following, but even I myself almost believed that I was disabled and God forgive me, I thought, for doing it, for mocking a poor spastic wean. If the weeboys didn't get me then the devil would, and how, I ask you, would I tell this in confession? I managed to turn a corner just beyond the walls when I then bumped into Mrs. Campbell who lived opposite our house.

"Caroline, what in God's name are you doing? Are you okay... you look like you're not half reared?"

Remembering that I was in fact not disabled, I then had to reckon with shame; an emotion particularly hard to stomach and not so easy to manage because like a worm, it tends to slide deep down under the nearest thing that it can hide under and it wriggles about, rearing itself when you least expect it. So thank God for Mrs. Campbell who appeared and thank God for my pride that reappeared, pushing my shame deep down under some mucky place inside of me – a place where I didn't have to know it was there.

So I puffed myself up and proudly announced that I was going a message for Mamai, to get a crusty white loaf. Mrs. Campbell, a beautifully spoken southern Irish woman, looked at me kindly and patted me on the head.

"You're getting to be a great big girl doing jobs for your mother." She winked and told me to run on and so I did, relieved to see the shops, which were not far now from the red walls. I tried to forget that the weeboys had ambushed me. I didn't want to notice the rotten wee brute feelings of fear, shame, and guilt that had started to give me a hammering from inside my belly before I had reached the shops. God forgive me! I thought. So there I was going a message for a loaf of bread and running into a whole commotion where I was ambushed by the cheeky wee brutes at the walls, and I was left fighting a battle inside myself, believing that I would have to tell the tale to the priest in confession – all because I was trying to buy a crusty loaf of bread for my mother!

Over time, I came to know the various treats and tribulations of 'going for messages'. It was normally the job of our Tommy or Liam, as they were the eldest, but they got fed up going and only were happy to go if they got to keep a 'ha'penny' for a 'dainty' – a chewy caramel toffee sweet, which seemed to last in the mouth forever. Now that I was eight years old and next in line, I was only too keen to take up the mantle of 'message go getter!'

I learned about 'the book', which was the 1960's version of a store card but without the glamour and glitz. The bald headed Mr. Pollock, in his tan-coloured shopkeeper's overall seemed to perform a kind of social work, as he would discreetly make an entry in the book for goods that were to be paid for later when the money came in or when the welfare cheque was cashed.

Pollock's shop was dark and dim inside and seemed quieter than the other shops. An extended counter from one side of the shop to the other was a barrier separating customers from the shelved goods on the other side. Yet the shop managed to convey a warm and welcoming atmosphere, which was underpinned by an air of reverence and confidentiality. It gradually dawned on me that Mamai would never have had 'a book' in any of the other shops where everyone knew our business and nosey parker women would hang around gossiping. Mr. Pollock was to be trusted, and this was certainly an accolade because pride was my mother's most trusted friend.

I waited in the queue, tasting the contents of the large jars of sweets with my eyes, as I watched the person in front order a half pound of brandy balls, a quarter of liquorice, and an ounce of snuff. With a wonderful sense of drama and theatre, the scene both mouthwateringly tantalized and entertained me. A stepladder was wheeled across to the tall jar of brandy balls. Mr. Pollock climbed up, dug out the jar, descended the ladder, and unscrewed the lid in an anticipatory opening scene to the pouring out of sweets, as they clinked into the shiny silver scales. Two or three sweets too many were popped back into the jar. They were tipped into the small brown paper bag, which was then ceremoniously and expertly swung round leaving two twisted up bag ends.

Chapter 1 IF YOU FALL RUN ON

I just about reached the counter, my fingers folded over the edge, as I was stretching myself up so I could see all that was going on. Mr. Pollock noticed me and my intensive observation of him and the grocer shop drama. Just as he had measured out the liquorice and was tipping some of the over poured contents back into the jar, he reached over the counter and handed me a huge piece of liquorice. Shyly but most gratefully, I reached up, took the liquorice, and popped it into my mouth. It tasted every bit as good as it looked. I loved liquorice... it was my favourite sweet. When my Granda Murphy was alive, he would give each of us a tanner on Sundays to go to the shops to spend on sweets and if we returned with liquorice, he would give us a thri'penny bit for one piece of liquorice. I would then run back down to the shop and buy some sherbet with liquorish dip and a comic, usually 'The Bunty', which I preferred to 'The Mandy', Donna's favourite.

It was now my turn to ask for a crusty sliced loaf and I was a bit embarrassed to say it, as my mouth was fully occupied with the liquorice.

"Who are you then?" asked the bespectacled Mr. Pollock.

"Caroline," I replied.

"That's a lovely princess name. Do you know that there is a young Princess Caroline of Monaco and she's about your age?"

I nodded that I didn't know.

"Well, she probably doesn't know who you are either. So you are Caroline who?" he added.

Sucking back the juicy saliva, I dribbled, "Caroline Owens."

The black of the liquorice now lacing my lips ensures my place in Mr. Pollock's memory. "What can I do for you Miss Owens?"

I requested a crusty sliced loaf, and Mr. Pollock reached into the baker's tray and with a long pole, he pulled out a great big loaf, which smelled like a slice of heaven itself and placed it in my two small hands. I offered the half crown up to Mr. Pollock and keen to proceed home and complete the mission, I thanked the kindly man, put the loaf under my arm, and walked off.

"Princess Caroline," he shouted. "Don't forget your change."

Mr. Pollock lifted the hatch of his counter, walked out towards me, and placing the change into my hand, gently and seriously, he reminded me to hold it tight and not to lose it.

Outside the shop, it was now raining, and various people were milling around. I set off purposefully, putting my mind to how I would manage the Red Walls and the wee brutes, when I was aware of a lot of shouting and panic across the street with men running fast. Bang! Bang! Bang! A noise like I'd never heard before.

"Jesus Christ, weegirl," someone shouted. "Get down! Lie down!"

The gunshots continued, and I was encased in fear, frozen to the spot, the plastic sandals nearly melting into my feet with the heat of my terror. I could hear people screaming and shouting and being commanded to lie on the ground. Deeply shocked that grown-ups were actually lying on the ground looking frightened, I couldn't move and in the next moment, I was swept off my feet by the force of some man's hand pushing me hard on to the gravelly ground. The bread burst out of its packet and scattered onto the wet pavement. The money, which by now had been carved into my hand with fear and determination that it would not be lost, was sprayed across the road. I attempted to get up to gather the money but was further flattened into the ground by the man, who yelled,

'For Jesus sake weegirl, do you want to get yourself killed? Stay down!'

I didn't attempt to move again, and lay there on the wet ground with rain pouring down my face, and I watched it soak into the bread, now blackening with the mud from the ground. The worry of the ruined bread and the lost change was seemingly more important than the horror of the shooting around me. It was as much a commotion, as I could cope with, and I was suddenly oblivious to the terror that I had been caught in cross fire.

To this day, I don't know who was doing the shooting or who was being shot at but whoever the frigg it was, they had ruined my bread, spoiled my mission, and I was left defeated, as I lay there thinking that I didn't know that grownups played Cowboys and Indians 'cos I had never seen grown-ups lying on the ground like this before; why were they playing Cowboys and Indians?

Following the gunfire, the man who pushed me down to the ground helped me up and brushed my knees and hands that were now bleeding.

"Are you all right weegirl?" he asked, "What's your name and where do you live?"

Desperately fighting back the tears, I managed to say something incoherent from my trembling, bloody, and black liquorice lips, about needing to find the change that had been scattered on the ground.

Mr. Pollock came rushing over and tried to persuade me to come back into the shop. He said he would give me another loaf but I only wanted to pick up what I could of this loaf – my crusty white loaf – the one that I had bought, and find the change, and go home to my mother, who would probably kill me anyway for bringing home half a filthy loaf and for losing the change because it was all she had.

I proceeded home with a battered and bruised loaf, knees, and face, and just past the Red Walls, the sight of my mother in her apron running down the street filled me with a mixture of relief and worry. Grabbing me with a frantic panic, she wiped my bloody face, dusted down my sore and cut knees, lifted me up into her arms, and carried me towards home whilst my tears, which had been held at bay until now, came flooding out. I tried to tell her that I was sorry and that my knees and hands were stinging with the hurt. Mamai stopped sat me down on a neighbour's garden wall, which my dadai had built, and as she examined my wounds, I noticed her happy sad face, as she kissed my hands and knees, held me tight, and told me that I was a great big girl. In that moment, I knew that everything would be all right and that my mamai had kissed it all better.

So there I was, an eight-year-old child doing my best to get a straightforward job done but running into the line of fire without any recognisable warning. I never knew that going a message for a crusty sliced loaf of bread was such a dangerous and stressful carry on! Those wee brutes made me do something I had never done before and it didn't feel right to be doing it: acting and pretending to be something I wasn't but it saved my neck. I was not to know that this pretending would become a skill that I would develop and that it would ultimately serve me well through my life, as I would learn to use my imagination and vision to think myself forward out of trouble and into new territory. But back then, I could not have known this nor about what was to unfold before me, my family, and our community in our streets and in our town, and that it would involve lots of falling and as many run-ins to various lines of fire. Mamai was keen to turn on the TV to hear the news that evening to find out if anything had been reported about what had happened down at the Beechwood shops and to find out what it was all about, but nothing was reported. She checked in the newspapers that evening and the following day, but nothing was reported. It was as though it had never happened. But worse things were going on it seemed because a black man in America had been shot dead! I thought that at first he was a black king, king of the black people in America, but later learned that his name was Martin Luther King. He wasn't even a baddie... he was trying to help black people get jobs and homes. The people on the TV were screaming and crying out with anger about his death. As well as in America, there was trouble on other Irish streets too, and there was a big riot in my own city centre. It was something to do with the police banning a Catholic civil rights march, and the 'B specials', a kind of special arm of the Protestant police force, were battering Catholic demonstrators with their truncheons. It seemed to be something to do with housing and the fact that a young single Protestant woman with no dependants was allocated a council house over a large Catholic family who had been next on the list.

I went to bed that evening not wanting to think about shootings, beatings, or riots nor about goodies being killed but about the bread and about my mother's mantra 'if you fall, run on'. I was preoccupied with the notion that someone could actually run on if they had fallen. Surely, it was only possible to run on if you managed to get up first?

Chapter 2
MAMAI

MAMAI fished out her best headscarf that wafted the smell of her as she confidently spun it high over her head like a little parachute that settled on to her short dark curly hair and then tied it under her chin. A five-foot tall powerhouse of a woman, my mother was mostly dressed for comfort and wore tabards and aprons to protect her clothes from the soils of servicing seven weans. She would very occasionally dab some powder on her forehead, cheeks, nose, and chin from a compact, which lived in her handbag that only saw the light of day on Sundays for Mass and contained a mostly empty purse, a white cotton handkerchief with her initial M embroidered on a corner, and a lipstick. I would watch with my lips puckered, as she painted on the tiniest hint of the lightest shade of coral pink. I often wanted Mamai to be more glamorous or exotic looking like our neighbour Mrs. O'Hara who looked like a film star and seemed never to be without perfectly applied make-up. I was sure that Mrs O'Hara must be the sister of Maureen O'Hara, the Irish Hollywood star, and I had to remind myself that Mr. O'Hara was not in fact John Wayne. Sometimes, when I called in for her daughter Pauline who went to the same school as me, I secretly hoped that Mrs. O'Hara would open the door just so that I could get a look at her. And sure enough, when she did open the door, it was as though I had stepped into a Hollywood set and there I was standing right beside a stunningly beautiful star who probably – definitely used – 'Camay Soap with Moisturising Cream'. I was captivated every time I saw her. How could she be Pauline O'Hara's mother or anybody's mother, never mind being a mother of a big houseful of weans? I could only look straight at her face and for far too long for it not to be bad manners.

There was plainness about my mother's looks, and although she only wore perfume on special occasions, she mostly smelled of that wonderful and comforting mixture of economy 'Lifebuoy Soap' combined with her own bodily scent – the kind that every child recognises as being uniquely of their mother alone. But her smiley, sparkly eyes and friendly personality made her an attractive woman and sometimes when she was laughing or singing, I would allow myself to know that she was the most beautiful woman in the world and the best thing since an honest crusty loaf.

When my mother was coat buttoned and head all tied up fashionably, I was fastened together with a sense of security and silent giddy pride because my mamai was proudly walking me to my new school. So I would get to know the route, we both pounded the streets together for the first week of term on our way down to St. Eugene's Middle School. I cherished these mornings having Mamai all to myself, with the unfamiliar intimacy of feeling her warm hand wrapped around my little, big-girl hand. Mamai had so many hands to hold that when the opportunity arouse for my turn, I felt as excited and indulged as the most special 'only child' in the world.

But after that wonderful first week, I had to make the journey by myself. It felt like the longest hike in unfamiliar territory because from Beechwood onwards right down to the school, I was walking what I understood to be 'better off' streets. What I mean is the adults who lived there had jobs that paid enough for them to either rent or buy their homes, and many of them weren't even Protestants. At eight years old, I did not understand that I was living in a council house. Couldn't the builders just build nice houses for everybody? Why couldn't we live in a nice house like these with the big grand bay windows? I asked myself.

Trekking along this fancy street, I wandered into my mind, which would become my private and secret den. Here was the place where I would build my world from my own bricks and mortar. I discovered this mind place was a good place to be. It was my tree house where I could hide and play, privately reveal, invent, and distort my world; a home where I could make things happen – a house from where I would look out onto the outside world – and it was my very own space that I didn't have to share with anyone.

The novelty of looking at the houses in Beechwood and wondering who lived in each one was a lovely distraction to the worry about going to a new school without my mother by my side. I fantasised about what kind of person or persons lived in a house like these, and I was certain that they definitely wouldn't be like me nor would these houses be crammed full of weans like the houses in Creggan where I came from. I became a kind of estate agent, critiquing the aesthetic merits of each house and their levels of relative kemptness and cleanliness. Even as an eight-year-old child, I was acutely aware not just that there was a difference between these houses and the houses in the council estate but worked out that the difference was to do with quality of life. I don't ever remember anyone ever talking about the difference either in the houses or the people who lived in them. It was just something that I came to understand and at times, deeply felt. It was a difference, which didn't feel very nice, and it was to do with a gradual understanding that people who lived in the council houses seemingly had little or no choice but to live there and if they were Catholic, they should be lucky to even have a council house. I was sure that someday I would live in a house like the ones in Beechwood but in the meantime and over the next two years, I became intimately acquainted with this new territory: from number Eleven, Creggan Broadway, Derry City, Northern Ireland, down past the Redbrick Walls, down Beechwood hill, past Marlborough Terrace with the huge 'really fancy' houses, across the park, past the corner sweet shop, across the road to the cathedral, down the hill, and in through the huge gated entrance to the cathedral and a kind of pre entrance to St. Eugene's Convent School: 'The big girls' school!'

The big girl feeling seemed to ebb away, as I tried to ignore a feeling of loss that my mother – my guide and my companion – was no longer by my side. I seemed very far away from home in this big old convent school for girls only. Our teachers were mostly nuns who wafted around the school with their long black veils and huge floor length skirts tightly fastened around their waists, floating around and behind them like puffed up parachutes. With the hem dragging on the floor, the skirts swept and polished as they moved along, attracting bits of dust and fluff that settled on the rim. Nuns: sometimes curious, mysterious, and scary creatures; no hair showing, no hair at all perhaps; no make-up, just a powdery pale pallor; small, tall, thin, fat, and wrinkly, and one or two with faces like angels. They were not all old but something about the contrast between the black habit and the grey white skin gave many of them the appearance of age and sickliness. Even the ones with rosy cheeks appeared slightly ill, as the starkness of the black habit seemed to magnify every vein and pore.

Some of them looked like angels and were kindness itself, but others would frighten the life out of you if you happened to turn around to find one of them as though having appeared from nowhere, standing still, looking towards you. And on top of all that, we had to cope with the constant gaze of the various statues, which were a benign presence at times but depending on my state of my mind, they could scare and persecute the life out of me. Yet the nuns were Christ's wives with stained free souls, and they all wore the rings to prove it. So I aspired to be a good holy girl with a sparkling whiter than white soul with no stains whatsoever just in case I might want to be a bride of Christ one day.

Often late for school, I became accustomed to offering my hand out to have it sharply and stingily slapped by Sister Bernadette, who, like a sentry, guarded the front entrance of the school. The big school turned out to be a big nightmare with wee small periods of relief.

"I'm sending Caroline to a lovely wee school down the town." Mamai would explain that St. Eugene's would provide me with a good education. Education was important to Mamai. I remember her talking about reaching her Higher Inter Cert, which was some kind of rite of passage to a higher education that Mamai didn't manage to take up as she was too busy having babies and rearing weans. But she was determined that we would make something of our lives and have good jobs, and that we would have to work hard to make something of ourselves.

Tommy, the eldest, was expected to go to university like Mamai's brother Liam who became a young professor of physics and chemistry at Bradford University in England. Not too many of those came from the Creggan Estate, and we would tell anyone who would care to listen about how well our uncle was doing. I heard Mamai telling our next-door neighbour, Mrs. McLaughlin that he had even gone to Rome to visit the Vatican and that his girlfriend wasn't allowed in because she was wearing her skirt too short! Well, I wore his name as a badge of honour in my own mind. So there were brains in our family, and education was important.

On Saturday nights, Tommy and me, being the eldest boy and girl, were often able to stay up late keeping Mamai company whilst she sat by the fire knitting or sewing. Once, around the time of the bombings of power stations, there were frequent power cuts throughout the province, which meant that we had nights without light in our streets and homes, and I was full of excitement to light candles in our house.

I was busy at the coffee table with my scrapbook, and Tommy, who was obsessed with origami, was sitting at Mamai's feet and had been trying to make a paper bird following the instructions from the origami book he had borrowed from Brooke Park Library. Tommy was an avid reader, and he had reams of books that I think he had squirreled well past their due back date. The three of us were sitting peacefully and contentedly involved in our endeavours accompanied by the ambient sound of the clicking knitting needles and the sparky, flickering flames of the turf and coal fire, which smelled of warmth and contentment. The brass pendulum was swaying and ticking inside the tall grandfather clock in the background adding to the hypnotic mood, which was occasionally interrupted by Tommy's sighs of frustration and exasperation that it just wasn't working out, as he tried to manipulate the bird's tail to activate its flapping wings. Mamai's interest in what he was doing; her ability to keep her eyes on him as she clicked and clacked the needles together whilst pulling the strand of wool from its shrinking ball prompted him with occasional words of encouragement, which seemed to help keep his interest, as he failed tried again and failed better. Eventually, after what seemed like an hour or more, Tommy elated held up his bird,

"I did it! Look Mamai... look Caroline, I did it!"

Tommy' smile was as wide as his whole head. Mamai continued knitting and the look of pride in her face was her gift in return to him.

"I've been sitting here watching you for the past hour and I knew that you'd do it. Let that be a lesson that you never forget, work hard at everything you do, never give up on something if it's worth doing because if you never make a mistake then you'll never make anything at all. Don't be afraid to chance your arm and try new things. You too, Caroline, never be afraid of taking your chances and if you fall you, run on because whatever happens, you have your own two feet to stand on."

I looked down at my feet and noticed that they weren't the baby feet that I'd come to know. They were no longer the feet with the wee toes that had gone to market and the ones that stayed at home, these were 'big girl's' feet and I had just noticed that they had grown. I breathed in all the excitement, apprehension, and wonder about what the world had to offer, where my feet would take me, and I drifted into a candlelight dream about when my chances would come and what I would do with them because in that wee small moment, I knew that anything and everything was possible because our Tommy could make a moving bird out of paper and I had two lovely feet.

Just at that moment, the lights came on and I was kind of disappointed that our special time had been interrupted.

"Let's see what's going on in the world," Mamai said, stuffing her knitting needles down the side of the armchair and proceeding to turn on the TV. There was a lot that I couldn't get my head round on the news. Stuff to do with civil rights riots and protests around the world. Something was reported again about trouble in Belfast and there was talk of a war between Catholics and Protestants. It seemed to be linked to the fact that Catholics didn't have good enough housing and something to do with Catholic and Protestant armies or gangs threatening to have a war on the streets of Belfast because there weren't enough houses or enough votes for Catholics. All I knew was that I didn't understand it all but what I did understand was that I was a Catholic and that we had a house, and thank God, we didn't live in Belfast, so I thought that we should be alright.

'The lovely wee school' for big girls aged eight to eleven was cupped within the grounds of the city's cathedral and located below a beautiful grotto of Our Lady and St. Bernadette. The white marbled St. Bernadette kneeling on the ground and praying to the apparition of the Virgin Mary became a source of courage to me, as I would kneel down make a quick prayer and finish by stroking the back of St. Bernadette's marbled veil. Sometimes I was drawn to look up behind me towards the parochial house to find that the kindliest, sweetest smiling face of the old bishop, who was sitting at his window, was greeting me. He would tilt his head and wave as though encouraging me to proceed on into class and I would bless myself, breathe in some spiritual comfort from St. Bernadette, the Virgin Mary, and the bishop before proceeding towards the school gates to face my punishment... just a few steps from holiness to hell.

I think that this was her first teaching post. She was young, tall, with curly short blonde hair. She was a dolly daydreamer, and although her body was in the classroom, she often appeared to be somewhere else, as she would stand warming her hands by the big fat pipes that ran up the walls. Holding on to the pipe and occasionally stroking it, Miss. Dunne, my teacher, was definitely far away. In fact, she wasn't from Derry and had to travel some distance from up the country somewhere. I often felt as though we children were intruding upon her private space. She had long fingernails, and I was equally fascinated and disgusted by the way she would pick at her ears without perforating her eardrums, dig out the waxy contents, and flick it onto the floor. She burrowed around in there, seemingly oblivious to the fact that the children she was teaching were not blind and in fact, had stomachs like mine, which were 'easily turned'. Surely, a person might engage in this activity only if they were alone.

I really didn't become close friends with anyone in that class apart from Roma Downey, and I wonder now if the odds were stacked against me in the popularity stakes, as Miss Dunne made sure that I was regularly and severely humiliated.

"Caroline Owens. Have you done your homework?"

With a sickening nod, I indicated that the homework had been done. Never admitting that my mother had spent half the night trying to teach me and eventually had given in, and in response to my desperation and her frustration, she just did the sums for me. Sometimes when mother had been working late at the hotel where she occasionally had spells as a waitress for weddings and functions, I would leave my homework out for her to check. Knowing that I had struggled, my mother would attempt the homework in the wee small hours and in the morning, the sums were corrected and completed as though the fairies had been. Dunne, however, was on to it and would hold my book up to the class and make a daily spectacle of me.

"Look at this, girls! Caroline Owens has got all of her sums right. Come up to the board and show us how you managed to do it."

I would attempt the task with all the brains and courage I could muster but my brains, the Virgin Mary, St. Bernadette, the bishop, or my mother couldn't help me now. I died a slow torturous death in the weekly public shaming. Initially the children were encouraged to laugh at me, as she would giggle whilst looking out at the class and continue sadistically to ask me what I thought I was doing, knowing full well that I hadn't got a clue.

Over time, however, the children no longer laughed at me and seemingly tried to ignore the wretched and painful pantomime. The most unforgivable sin of all committed by Miss. Dunne was that she would make me stand there in front of the uncompleted and messed up sum over lunchtime whilst everyone else either had gone off on the bus to the canteen a few miles away or to the 'packed-lunch' room. Sometimes I was hopeful when I had been released on time only to see the bus set off for the canteen without me and my empty belly.

I was on free meals because my father was on sickness benefit and as a 'have not'; I was given a pink meal ticket, whilst the others, 'the haves' whose fathers were working, had green tickets. But not only was I a 'have not' but I did not get to have the 'have not meal' but got to have the 'have not' easily identifiable ticket, which left me with nothing, no pride, and no meal. I would throw the friggin' pink ticket on the ground on math days when I was finally released from the blackboard. After the bus had left for the canteen, Miss Dunne would send me off to the packed-lunch room, where I sat and watched others chat over their nicely packed and nutritiously balanced lunches. Sometimes I was so hungry that I would have to ask someone for a piece of their food but mostly I just ate the sickening plateful of shame and humiliation and tried to make myself disappear. The deepest feeling of outrage filled my starving stomach but I felt helpless to do anything about it. I couldn't tell my mother because I didn't want to get her into trouble for doing my sums and in any case, I was having her think that I had understood the sums and her corrections so I didn't want her to go mad with me.

Hell was just about survivable because of Roma, a beautiful girl with the longest black hair and the face of an angel who became my most cherished friend. Roma never seemed influenced by the teacher's view of me and if she was, it was by responding with kindness and concern for me and eagerness that we have fun. I don't know how we first became friends; I think that it was something to do with my mother being a friend of Roma's mother. They had been friends together in the pantomimes when they were younger and worked together for a time in the shirt factories where they were both bookkeepers. I rarely looked forward to going to school but I looked forward to Roma.

Our mothers had arranged that we should walk together to school and that I would call in for Roma on my way down from the Creggan estate as Roma lived in one of those posh terraced houses at the top of Beechwood.

I made a habit of getting there early, as Roma's mother often had a plate of toast and jam ready and greeted me so enthusiastically. She was a gentle and quietly spoken woman who my mother told me had been a star in the local armature musicals. I was embarrassingly envious at times, as I felt as though I was intruding on this beautifully intimate scene when Mrs. Downey took great care, slowly brushing Roma's long glossy hair and putting it into two perfect plaits.

It seemed to be in such sharp contrast to the frantic, noisy, and busy mornings in the Owens' household. My mother had seven heads to prepare and when it came to her girls, she was a great one for high plaits. My sister and I not only had a fresh hairstyle every morning as our hair was often so tightly scraped back with a comb which had been dipped into sugar and water, but it was tied so tightly that it had the added effect of giving us a non-surgical face lift. We were often yelping out in pain as the brush dragged through our heads and made even less bearable by my mother's lament, "Pride feels no pain."

Well pride may well not feel the pain, but Caroline and Donna are in agony here, in case you haven't noticed, I thought through gritted teeth.

We were never allowed to 'turn a word' in my mother's mouth that meant that we were not allowed to talk back so it was difficult to protest, and a lot of protesting went on just inside a clenched and puckered mouth.

Down at Roma's house the pace was much slower and more peaceful. The toast and a hot drink were great but I feasted on the stories that Roma's mother would tell about the shows and the pantomimes. I was struck by the feeling of space even though Roma's house was smaller than our house, it wasn't crammed full of children, just Roma, her brother, mother, and father and stories about old times and musicals.

Roma and I earned some money for sweets when we charged other children a penny or tup'pence to sit on my school case as though it were a sleigh and slide down to the bottom of Beechwood hill. It was an ingenious way of managing the embarrassment of my wooden school case.

My father was a great man with his hands and although a builder by trade, he was a fine carpenter. Our house was full of his constructions and creations. He made a lot of furniture: bookcases, wardrobes, dressing tables, and built all sorts of cabinets and special features into our house. So with my father's hands and my mother's eye for style, our house looked pretty nifty eventhough it was a council house. I don't know where my father got the time but he also made a lot of our toys. I came home from school one day to find in my bedroom the smell of varnish and a big wooden contraption. Dadai proudly announced that it was a loom and it was for me. Brilliant, I thought, feeling excited, but what the heck is a loom?

He handed me two wooden instruments, and my mother gave me the wool and taught me how to weave.

I was hooked and spent many hours weaving mother's leftover bits of wool. I produced aprons, hats, scarves, tablemats, anything as long as it was square or rectangle shaped.

My father also made wooden puppets and go-carts for the boys and beautiful dolls houses and cradles for Donna and me for our dolls. The finished article was sometimes complete with intricate carvings, beautiful transfers, and italic writing. There is no doubt about it, he was a gifted craftsman but I don't know what possessed him to make wooden school cases for my sister and me. Like men's tool boxes complete with lovely hinges and fastenings, they were received with a mixture of gratitude, surprise, and uncertainty. Mine was bigger than Donna's because I was older. Our initials, C.O. and D.O., were exquisitely hand painted in white right in the centre of the mahogany stained 'attaché' case. They came with matching pencil cases and weighed a ton even without the books inside.

With a hint of self-importance and a sizeable portion of uncertainty, I tentatively explained to inquisitive onlookers that my father had made it for me and invited the other children to have a look explaining that it was an 'attaché' case!' Well I had done a pitiful impression of provoking envy as there seemed only to be a momentary hint of anyone being impressed and I soon realised that the other children were giggling about it, only too glad that they did not have to carry such a weight to school. Roma, seemingly aware of the potential for a wounded ego, rescued me and my father's name by disguising the fact that there was an issue here to be worried about.

"Ah but it is not just any old attaché case." She demonstrated, "It turns into a wee seat when you need a wee rest." As Roma sat on the 'wee seat', I could see that she had another idea, "And it turns into a sleigh."

Roma positioned herself on the case, held on to the sides, and invited me to take a seat behind her. I put my arms around her waist and together we slid down the hill in hysterical laughter. Suddenly the wooden attaché case was a triumph, and weeboys and girls would shout over to us, "Hey wee girl, can I have a go on your 'apache' case?" In Derry, at that time, children were more familiar with the notion of an apache Indian, as we'd regularly watch the Sunday Cowboy and

Western films on television but an attaché case would have been not so familiar an article.

Roma and I charged a fee to the other weans who were queuing up for a ride down the hill on the newly named apache case, and we made enough money to buy Rainbow Drops at the sweet shop just by the school and earned a considerable quota of street cred into the bargain.

The Miss. Dunne situation was a chronic constant but she didn't manage to contaminate my appreciation of the girls in my class whom I suppose I turned to as a comforting distraction by way of shutting out the misery and upset. Most girls in my class came from families whose parents were professionals.

Take, for example, Grainne McAteer, whose father was a high profile Nationalist MP. My parents always voted for him until John Hume led the SDLP and it seemed that Hume was the new man to be backed. Grainne was a tall, hard working, lovely quiet girl with rosy cheeks like her father and a sweet smiley face. She lived just down the road from Roma in a big house with a great big hallway, and they had hundreds of books on shelves around the walls. To my surprise, there were seemingly loads of children living in this house, and I supposed that it was only right that it be filled.

Another lovely girl in our class puzzled me. Rosemary Quigley, whose father was a dentist but curiously, Rosemary, a giant of a girl had huge prominent teeth, even bigger than mine, and she soon left our class to go to a boarding school. I didn't understand anything about boarding schools and it didn't make sense to me. A bit like the attaché case scenario, it sounded like a good thing and to be going to boarding school, especially the idea of escaping from the dreaded Miss. Dunne sounded too good but in my mind, I had constructed a sad reality that Rosemary was being sent away and that it might have been something to do with her teeth.

Another girl, Andrea O'Hare had beautiful red curly hair and a freckly face. Her hair was a dramatic defining feature and I had always thought of her as 'Andrea O'Beautiful Hair'. Andrea was a budding artist, and her work was often held up as being exemplary. Her father's corner chemist shop was just opposite Roma's house, so she was another one of the Beechwood Beauties.

We did have some beauties in our school that came from the Creggan Estate. Take Marion McGrellas, for example, who I always thought looked like a mermaid, because she had the thickest, creamy, long yellow blonde hair, and I was happy to sometimes walk home with her, together with Pauline O'Hara and Geraldine Doherty who lived just around the corner from me. Now this is no joke, but Geraldine Doherty was exquisitely and unassumingly, Irish 'coleenly' beautiful. She had the dreamiest blue eyes, glossy black, wavy hair, and was another quietly spoken and giggly girl with a gentle nature who wouldn't hurt a fly. Captivated by the beauty around me, I saw myself in such sharp contrast and emptied myself of any beauty that I may have possessed, deposited it in to the other girls, leaving myself with little to feel good about.

I was very small for my age, a freckly faced child, and although I would inform others that my freckles were a sign of beauty, I myself was not convinced, and I don't think that I managed to convince them either. Skinny too, with blonde brown hair and big prominent teeth – but not as big as Rosemary Quigley's – and with having gained something of a reputation for being a dunce, I didn't seem to have a lot going for me apart from the fact that I had two lovely feet and a great head of long thick blonde brown hair that grownups often kindly remarked on. In any case, I had a feeling that it was not a good thing to think of myself as being good looking, it was something that I had read in the bible, I think. But secretly I allowed myself to love my feet, which were porcelain white and I had thought that they were as perfect as feet should be... and I had two of them.

The dunce reputation was something of a shock to me, as in my first school, The Holy Child's; I was confident, happy, and pleased as punch with myself.

In the days leading up to starting my first day at infant school, I thought that I would explode with excitement, as my anticipation fizzed up inside me like a dose of Andrew's liver salts. On my first day, with my long blonde curly hair tied up in two beautifully arranged ringlets, my white ankle socks, shiny patent shoes, and perfectly fitted pinafore dress, I stood in the assembly hall, and as my name was called, I ran out to be put in line for my new class. I was smiling so much with pleasure that my face could easily have set in perpetuity, until I became a wee bit unnerved and unsettled by the many sobbing children around me who were crying for their mothers. What did they know that I didn't? A wee bit put off, I scanned the back of the hall in search of my mother and was reassured by the sight of her smiling face, dressed in her best coat and headscarf, as she smiled and nodded encouragingly towards me, and at once I was convinced that I would be okay.

I had a treasure of a teacher, Miss. Brown who was a dead ringer for the American actress Mary Tyler Moore, with her short brown swingy-out bobbed hairstyle, beautiful big brown eyes, and a mouthful of the straightest, whitest teeth, and when she smiled, which was nearly always, she was quite simply radiant. She would often stand me up on the broad classroom window ledge and request a rendition of 'on the good ship lollipop'. Miss. Brown loved children and loved teaching, and I had the sense that she enjoyed us so much that she would have paid to come to work.

One time, when a particularly difficult and disruptive boy in the class was chatting and unsettling the others, Miss. Brown, in a frustrated tone, responded, "John, will you please be quiet so that we can get on with the lesson?"

"But I haven't finished Miss... I was just telling something to Peter," he replied with his five-year-old sincerity.

Hould your whisht John, if ye don't want to get scolded, I thought. He would be in trouble for sure. I looked towards Miss. Brown to see what she would do.

She looked at him seriously and thoughtfully and continued, "I'm so sorry to have interrupted you John. Could you please finish what you're telling Peter. We will wait for you, and we can then get on with the lesson."

John quickly finished the telling of his tale and continued with the lesson, and Miss. Brown smiled towards him, fondly acknowledging his response, and I smiled to myself that this was the best place in the world to be.

The school day however was over too soon because we were on the 'Dual System'. This was some kind of arrangement that the school had with the education authority arising out of the need to accommodate twice as many pupils as other schools – something to do with too many weans being born in Creggan. So for the first three years of our schooling, we only attended half days and after lunch times, our class went home and the other class came in for the afternoon.

The visiting priest had me down as a nun in the making, as I was well able to recite my prayers. I won a holy book because I was able to tell him that upon receipt of Holy Communion, one puts the bread into ones mouth and one says, "Dear Father in heaven, now that you have come into my soul, please let me come into yours."

I didn't forget it because I loved the idea that I could put God – something more good than goodness itself – inside me, and my stained soul would be cleansed and that he in return would receive me into the safety of his bright shiny soul – a fluffy warm place that smelled like my mother's skin, and I would never be alone or sad and where my hurts would always be kissed better.

After the priest had left the class, Miss. Brown was uncharacteristically slightly annoyed and gave us a sharp talking to because she felt disappointed in the overall class performance and concluded, "Caroline Owens was the only one who remembered what she had been taught."

Miss. Brown called me up to her desk, opened her purse, and handed me a shiny sixpence, which I kept for the longest time in my musical box bought to me by my Godmother, Aunt Margaret, Dadai's sister. I would often open my wee box, watch the beautiful ballerina spin around, pick up my shiny sixpence that was like my soul, and savour the heavenly moment of achievement and acknowledgement. My confidence was strengthened further when I was made to sit beside Lee Barlow, who I had decided was my boyfriend, and the teacher had put him with me because she thought that I would be a good help to him. Strangely, Lee kept running away from me even when I told him that he was my boyfriend and even when I was older and at the convent school, I would still see him going to the boy's school, and he would try to escape my predatory gaze because I still thought of him as my boyfriend.

Yes, I did love my first school and longed to be back there with my long blonde hair, angelic freckle free face, and shiny soul, sitting beside Lee Barlow, and looking at my lovely teacher, Miss. Brown who looked like Mary Tyler Moore, and who thought that I was the best thing since Shirley Temple.

At St. Eugene's, we were a class of music lovers and had some shining stars. Roma, our brightest star won many a talent contest and often directed us in impromptu singing contests when the teacher had left the room. Some of the girls had their own signature tunes. Fionnulla Houston, a tall, jolly, easy going and funny girl's tunes were 'On white horses, let me ride away', and 'Wooden Heart'... treat me nice, treat me good, treat me like you really should, I'm not made of wood and I don't have a wooden heart...'

I wish it had been my song for Miss. Dunne. Fionnula had a beautiful voice and sang her song so passionately. I could imagine her galloping along in her snowy white horse to a land of far away dreams; I only wished that she would take me with her.

Derry was a city of music and culture. Many of the girls in my class went to The McCafferty School of Music. I would have loved to go there but it was cheaper to have Irish dancing lessons, so my sister, Donna and I went to Mary McLaughlin's School of Dance. The yearly singing, dancing, verse speaking, and music competitions, at Feis Daoire Colmcille, in the town hall, were practiced for all year round, and seemed to provide something of the warp and weft of the complexly woven cloth of Derry culture. For many of us not actively pulled into the various factions of Republican armies, Derry's cultural activity gave us something of an alternative act of protest against the view that as Catholics, we were somehow second-class citizens. So our singing, dancing, poetry, and music made us feel connected to something important and it was as though we were keeping something alive whilst others were doing the killing.

The likes of Mary McLaughlin and the McCafferty family and the many others who were committed to teaching, tutoring, and giving Derry's children a different song to sing other than the one of fighting and killing really did help hold us together by encouraging the experience of standing up and being counted and putting our best feet forward. Even when battles raged and bombs blasted, the city never cancelled an annual Feis, which was the annual festival of music and culture.

Roma was a McCafferty singer and her two signature tunes in class were 'Happy Talk' from the film South Pacific, and she would sing her heart out and make little bird shapes with her hands as though they were birds talking, "...you've got to have a dream, if you don't have a dream, how you gonna have a dream come true..." The theatre of it all enthralled me and the way Roma convincingly sang about the possibility that dreams could come true. She also sang a duet and I sometimes got to fill in when Roma's partner was unable to practice. Roma was dressed up in the male's costume singing to some girl whom I wished was me.

"Darling go home your husband is ill..."

"Oh, is he ill, let them give him a pill.....Come my Dear France, this is no time to dance... I must go home to my dear old man."

This song in particular meant something to me and always brought me back to reality, as I was becoming more aware of my father's illness and that there was lots of talk about him needing to take his tablets.

The girls in our class seemed to become terribly excited and slightly envious of Roma when she was on the TV talent contest, 'Teatime with Tommy', which was a Northern Irish version of 'Opportunity Knocks'. Although deeply proud of Roma because she kept on winning, which meant that she got to be on the TV the following week, I was secretly disappointed too because Roma always seemed so busy with her rehearsals and I don't think that we actually spent much time together after school plus she had lots of friends who lived down in Beechwood. Roma was a special and good friend to me and in my mind she was my best friend but there was a lot going on in her life and I knew that I was only one of her many friends.

Life for me, however, would never be the same again when Roma stopped coming to class. I called for her in the mornings and there was no answer. Roma didn't come to class, and days went by and there was no sign of her. I stared at her empty chair in class and longed for her return.

No longer did I enjoy the singing contests in class and was feeling very alone, when one day when I was getting told off at home for being a pain in the neck and for hitting Donna, my mother sat me down and asked me what had gotten in to me. I told her that I didn't know but plucked up the courage to ask her if she knew about what had happened to Roma, as she wasn't coming to class. My mother had obvious difficulty in explaining, "I am so sorry." She confessed with watery eyes, and went on to say that Roma's mother had died and that Roma wouldn't be coming back to class. I was devastated, and I felt terribly sorry for Roma and her brother. What would they do, how would they cope, where would they go? Who would brush Roma's hair? And her poor, kind, and gentle mother would never see Roma again. Roma would never see her own mother again. I could hardly bear to think of it and was angry that no one had thought of helping me or the other children in the class to think it through. It seems that even though the Irish are good at having wakes and perhaps somewhat romanticize the business of death and dying, there was a big problem in helping children understand and in helping them deal with the aftermath. I did feel sad for Roma, her brother, and Dadai but I am ashamed to say that, selfishly, I felt sorrier for myself, and I wanted to cry every time I looked at the empty chair in class.

One time Fionnulla asked me why I seemed so quiet and fed up and no longer joining in on the fun in class, and I tried to explain that things didn't feel the same without Roma. Fionnulla tried to be helpful but couldn't understand it and said, "But you weren't Roma's best friend!"

I thought that this was probably, sadly true and that even if I wasn't to be Roma's best friend, at that time, she was my dearest and best friend, and no-one but my mother seemed to understand or care.

I wasn't to see Roma much after that because she passed her eleven plus exam and was accepted into grammar school.

I remember the tension building up as we awaited the results of our exams and on the morning that the letter was due, my mother called me to say that the letter had arrived. There was a stampede in our house, as we all ran to the hallway where my mother was standing holding the letter. I sat at the top of the stairs unable to face the outcome but desperately hoping and praying that I would make it to the grammar school. Mother opened the envelope to a chorus of "Did she get in? Did she pass? " Looking up at me, Mamai smiled, trying to swallow her disappointment, she told me not to worry, that St. Mary's was a good school and that I could walk there in ten minutes. I hadn't passed. I smiled and kept smiling but I couldn't stop the tears. Liam taunted, "Ha, ha you didn't pass!"

And my mother opened the front door and pushed him outside, saying "Neither did you, you cheeky article." Tommy, the eldest offered the philosophical consolation, "Just because you didn't pass doesn't mean that you've failed."

I ran into my bedroom feeling the shame. I could see my mother's face as she swallowed her disappointment in order to support me; a face I recognized. I knew that Roma and my other friends would have passed and again, I would know the feeling of being on the outside of something and of feeling excluded.

So for now I was doomed in the dungeons of Miss. Dunne's holy hell, but just as suddenly as Roma's absence, Miss. Dunne also disappeared and she was replaced by Miss. Jackson, an older, big-breasted woman who looked like everyone's mother, except Pauline O'Hara's. There were no more public floggings at the blackboard and no more missed lunches.

When Miss. Jackson regularly and affectionately patted me on the head on my way in to class from the playground, each time I felt as though I was being bestowed with an honorary degree.

All of a sudden, I began to feel as though I counted, like I had a rightful place in the class just like the other girls. I started to get chosen to be in charge of giving out pencils and of collecting books. One day, following an art lesson, Miss. Jackson informed the class that she needed three sensible girls to go down to the washrooms outside at the rear of the school to clean the paint trays and brushes.

The whole class put up their hands, and as Miss. Jackson scanned the classroom, I was desperate for the job. With hand raised as high as a flagpole and straining with excitement, I joined my classmates shouting, "Please Miss, please Miss!" Finally, the honour was bestowed upon Grainne, Marion, and me!

Delighted and giddy with the novelty of this responsibility, which took us out of class, we three trotted down to the washroom feeling chuffed that we were considered such sensible girls. Once in the washroom, we became slightly hysterical with laughter that we had been let loose and began happily and merrily washing the paintbrushes and containers. We wanted to do a really good job and make sure that there was no sign of paint on either brush or paint tray. So we dried what we could on the towels and ventured back into class. Miss. Jackson was impressed with the result and announced that we were to have the permanent job as the art material monitors and cleaners.

We three were smiling from ear to ear, when our classroom door opened to the entry of the gate keeping and hand slapping Sister Bernadette, who's redder than usual red face looked as though it had just been pickled in beetroot. With her hands stuffed into the opposite sleeves of her black witchy and wicked habit, she, finding a smile, enquired politely as to who was responsible for cleaning the paint utensils today. We three raised our hands quickly in readiness for our commendation and were then duly summoned to the front of the class. Slowly and with a measured and restrained composure, the nun proceeded to interrogate us about who did exactly what in the washroom, determined to find the culprit who had messed up the towels. My heart pounded with fear and the embarrassment of it all. Clearly, there was to be no commendation and by the shocked and saddened look on Miss. Jackson's face; it was unlikely that we were going to be dismissed without punishment.

The sickening feeling that my short-lived pride came before a fall turned to outright panic when quick as a flash, we were grabbed together by our plaits, ponytails, and ringlets, and dragged out of the classroom. Chuntering on aloud about the disgrace of these three dirty articles, Sister Bernadette dragged us through the adjoining classrooms for the whole school to see and managed to draw everything to a shocking halt. By now, we were tripping over each other, sliding on the holy highly polished floors, and crying in pain and humiliation. Outside of the classrooms, we were then dragged up the polished mahogany staircase, which had at the summit, a statue of the Virgin Mary. We were told to kneel in front of her and think of our disgusting sins before being taken in to see the head nun. Sister Dolorosa could barely be seen behind her desk, and when she stood up, she appeared no taller than me, looking like a little leprechaun in comparison to the hulk standing beside her, ranting and raving about the terrible sin that had been committed by us three dirty girls, the evidence in her hand was a paint stained towel.

By now us three were wailing with the snot and tears tripping us. The school bell had rung for the end of the day and we could hear the other children leaving, and I was worried that Donna who was now also at the school would be looking for me so that we could walk home together. Sister Dolorosa asked us our names and to explain what had happened. I thought that she would give us a reprieve because she seemed such a sweet and holy wee thing, but she gave us a tissue instead and asked if we were sorry. Of course, we were sorry even though we didn't know that it was a sin to clean the paint trays with a towel.

As a punishment, the softly spoken and somewhat pathetic Sister Dolorosa gave us each a pen and paper and instructed us to write one hundred lines, 'I must not be a dirty girl!'

We cried quietly through the whole episode, my pen hating every word of it. It was the final humiliation worse than a flogging, because I was not a dirty girl! Before we got half way through the wet and soggy page of filthy words, Sister Dolorosa intervened and told us to go home, much to Sister Bernadette's displeasure.

Once out of the school grounds Grainne, Marion, and I made a pact that we would tell our parents and bring them to the school in the morning in order that the beetroot faced, banshee witch would get her dues. I thanked God that Pauline O'Hara was waiting for me outside the school gates, and she managed to counsel and console me all the way home. It was late by the time we arrived home, and again I was fearful that I would be killed by Mamai for being such a disgrace but Pauline had assured me that she didn't think that it was a sin to have made a mess on the towels.

"Jesus Mary and St. Joseph look at the state of you!" I was shocked that my mother was so shocked. I shamefully and tearfully explained what had happened. My mother had been worried sick. She had heard some story from Donna that I had been dragged through the school, and when she saw the state I was in, with swollen bloodshot eyes and hair all stuck up like an Antrim goat, she undid her apron, took me by the hand, and marched me down to the Creggan parochial house to see the priest, Father Carlin. The banging on his door and the pounding of my heart made my head ache even worse, and I was sick with worry that the priest would send me away to boarding school or something because I was a filthy sinner. The door opened to a welcoming "Oh hello, Margaret. What in God's name is the matter?" the baldy headed and friendly priest enquired through his smoky piped mouth.

"Father, take a look at my wean. Have you ever seen the like of it? Take a look at her scalp."

I had never seen my mother so enraged and gradually realized that she was furious on my behalf and not angry with me. I had wished at that moment that I had told her everything about Miss. Dunne too. I never knew that my mother would defend me so fiercely and that she was such a force to be reckoned with. The priest gave me an apple and asked me to wait in the hall while he had a quiet word with my mother so that she could explain what it was all about. Mamai emerged from her confab with Father Carlin looking confident and vindicated in her outrage.

But my school commotion wasn't the only commotion to worry about. On the UTV News that night we watched terrible rioting in Belfast. I knew that Belfast wasn't far from Derry – only an hour's drive away. I was afraid to think about that only an hour away nine people had been killed and a wee Catholic boy who was only nine years old – the very same age as me – was lying in his bed when a tracer flare came through his bedroom window and killed him'stone- dead'! The news showed that hundreds of people had been injured in the riots and that Catholics who had been living in predominantly Protestant areas were being made to move out of their homes with nowhere to go.

Unable to stomach any tea, I went to bed that night with scenes from the news and my school worries banging like a hammer inside my head. At least I still had a head and a home, but I was still sick with the prospect of returning to school the following day. Even though my mother was on my side, I was still worried sick.

Having waved my brothers and sister off to school the next morning, Mamai told me that I was to wait with her because we would go down to school together when she was ready. I couldn't believe that we were going to be late for school on purpose and my stomach was in knots but I was a wee bit excited and a big bit not sure how it would all turn out.

There was no Sister Bernadette there waiting at the gate as it was past ten o'clock and everyone was already in class. I looked up to see if I could see the bishop at the window but no sign of him either. Straight in, my mother marched and turned the handle on the huge oak door leading into Sister Bernadette's classroom. There she was, in her full regalia and glory standing at her podium, preaching something or other to the class. The beetroot face was all at once white and redder than the fire of hell.

"Oh hello, Mrs. Owens," she humbly greeted my mother with the kind of smile that was supposed to have us think that she was pleased to see us but had, "Oh my God, how do I get out of this" written all over it.

"Hello Sister Bernadette, take a look at my child. Can you explain to me what in God's name did she do to deserve what you put her through yesterday? Look at the bruises on her legs and the state of her face."

Sister Bernadette looked down at me, and I nervously smiled up at her. She was reddening by the second and ushered my mother out of the classroom in case she would be shown up in front of her girls. Once outside of the room, my mother continued,

"What exactly were you trying to teach my child, because what she has learned is that mistakes are not to be tolerated. Have you ever made a mistake in your life, Sister?"

Sister Bernadette was going on about the mess made of the towel, as I looked up to find the girls in her class looking out of the windows on to the corridor where we were having our confab.

"It's a sad state of affairs that you are more concerned with a mess made on a towel than you are of the mess you have made of my child."

My mother tugged at the nun's veil and asked her how she would like to be publicly humiliated and be dragged through the school by the hair.

"I don't suppose you would like it would you, and although I have a mind to pull every hair out of your head, in front of all these girls, I would not put you through what you subjected my child to. I hope you go to confession. And I am telling you… don't ever dare put a hand on my child again."

My mother's speech ended to cheers from the surrounding classrooms and to a suddenly meek and mild Sister Bernadette who appeared to shrink right in front of me. Yet I felt strangely sorry for her and didn't want her to be humiliated. Stopping short of pulling off her veil, Mamai seemingly sensed that she needed go no further; she had made her point with dignity and integrity. Mamai then took me by the hand and walked me through the adjoining classrooms into my class at the end of the row of classrooms where Miss. Jackson, apologizing profusely, greeted us. Sister Bernadette never bothered me again, and my mother and I became heroines, as mine was the only parent of the three girls to go down to the school in order that justice was done.

So my mother was a force to be reckoned with and even when the Sister Bernadette story had lost its shine and the St Eugene's schooling memories had faded, my mother's action that day was like a seed of spinach rooted deep inside me, providing me with courage when the going got tough. Of course, neither my mother nor I could have known that what she did that day would have so much meaning for me and my future story. No, as the years went on, my mother was more likely to get messages from me about what she wasn't doing right or what she was getting wrong or about how somebody else's mother was really really 'dead on' (cool).

The thing about looking back and telling stories about our childhoods like this is that we tend to consider our parents through the headline memories and the dramas where we give them Oscars and bouquets for the times that they stood up for us or did us proud. But it seems more difficult to appreciate any value in the times when they let us down, when they didn't or couldn't mop up our frustrations or disappointments and left us feeling aggrieved; these became the front-page unpopular headlines in my adolescence where I would devalue my mother's contribution to my growth and development. Yet behind the scenes, my mother like most good enough mothers did the worry work and the tough decision-making. She was the same person who had become the shore when I had been washed up from the stormy waters of youger life, and now was becomming the wall upon which I would force my will in order to find my limits. What was this all about- how could I have hating feelings towards that same person whom I depended upon, admired and loved? And so my mother had no option but to tolerate my disappointment in and hatred of her. And in doing so – managing and surviving – my mother without knowing it, provided me with a sweet and bitter sustenance that would firmly underpin the scaffolding of my personality.

Chapter 3
OUT OF SIGHT - KEPT IN MIND

IN the summer of 1969, we watched daily reports on the evening TV news that the troubles were worsening. Mamai tried to explain and I was beginning to understand that it had all arisen out of the conflict created by government and police opposition to the Catholic civil rights protesters. These protesters, as I understood it, were ordinary and law abiding people. They were Catholics protesting about religious discrimination that favoured Irish Protestants at the expense of a Catholic community who were governed by an oppressive Special Powers Act. I learned that this was some kind of government law that gave the Protestant police force the powers to discriminate against the Catholic community. Mamai told us more about the good man called Martin Luther King who was the black man in America who had been killed because he spoke out against injustice whilst trying to help the black people who were in an even worse predicament than us Catholics. I understood that Martin Luther King was a king of a man who had been staging peaceful protests, marches, pickets and sit-ins, where he talked about having a dream that black people would have equal rights to white people, and as far as I could understand, the Catholics in Northern Ireland were seeking a similar kind of fairness.

But more important worries took over, as I had a sense that something at home was not okay and then eventually we were told that Mamai would be going into hospital "to have her womb out." A bit like having your tonsils removed I supposed, except Mamai would have to be in hospital for quite some time. I have little sense of where my father was at that time; he may have been working in England or just out drinking himself into oblivion. Mamai didn't appear to be distressed about the prospect of having an operation but then again, we would scarcely have known, as she was skilled in disguising her feelings in order that ours would be spared.

Still I was worried, and the worry seemed to sink down into my stomach – heavy like a lumpy porridge. What if she was not going to be okay? There were times in the past when we had glimpses of her fallibility when she had been unable to shield us from her pain. One time when we were all sitting around the table in the kitchen noisily awaiting our dinner, Mamai was transferring a huge pot of boiling vegetable broth from the stove to the counter and suddenly the handle snapped off the pot, felling mother to the floor, as she screamed out in agony, the sticky scalding thick soup, cooking her belly. Tommy the eldest, quick as a flash jumped off his chair and managed to rip off her apron and clothes whilst shouting at me to run across the road to get Mr. Campbell who would take her to casualty.

Now that was the second time I had seen my mother cry for herself and that was as distressing to me, as was witnessing her being scalded because by now I had been convinced that nothing could hurt my mother because she was strong as an ox. The first time I saw her cry tears of pain was when she came into the living room one evening to sit in the fireside chair after a busy Saturday evening of preparing food for Sunday and getting the clothes ready for Mass the next morning. With exhaustion, she plunked herself down onto the chair only to be immediately ejected out of it in pain, as she had sat on her knitting needles that she kept tucked down the side of the chair in readiness of her next opportunity for a knitting session.

These two memories are filed in my mind under 'mother's injuries' and are linked to a story that she used to tell us about a time before we were born, when as a younger woman, she had worked in the shirt factory. Although she had been a bookkeeper, she would often have a go on the machines, and one day she was sewing away and laughing aloud with her friends when a needle from the machine snapped and sprang up right into her mouth and stuck in her throat, and she was rushed into hospital.

But any anxiety that I may have had about mother's womb being taken out was soon shelved when we were told that Donna, Sean, and I would be going down to Cork in Southern Ireland to spend the summer with our Aunt Theresa, Uncle Martin, and cousins, Debbie, Morgan, and Jacqueline. Well strictly speaking, Theresa wasn't our aunt; she was Mamai's cousin. Mamai was especially fond of Theresa, who was stepping into the breach in order to provide our mother with respite and so we could have a new home that summer.

The journey from Derry to Cork was about seven hours long, made longer by my travel sickness, as I was in and out of the car like a yo-yo throwing my guts up. Aunt Theresa did what she could by supplying us with travel sickness tablets and the thickest 'Jumbo' colouring books I had ever seen, with pictures of elephants and circus clowns, peacocks, children playing in the sand, princesses, and 'dot to dots' and word searches. So Donna, Sean, and I coloured our way to Cork.

Aunt Teresa and Uncle Martin were kindness itself, and we were spoiled rotten. When we arrived in Cork, I felt it in my bones that this was going to be a really great holiday yet something of a strange situation, as we were to spend four weeks here, and we had never ever been away from our family before not even for a sleep-over in someone else's house. Uncle Martin O'Brien was a tailor, and the family lived above their shop in Shandon Street. It was odd – in a good way – for us to live here in the middle of a busy high street surrounded by shops. Our house was directly opposite the baker's shop, and we awoke every morning to the comforting and hunger inducing smells of freshly baked bread. The shop owners soon got to know us and made us feel special by introducing us to customers as, "the little ones from The North," and we were happy to be quizzed about the troubles and asked if we were frightened up there. I even began to enjoy the drama of coming from the troubles. It was one of the times in our childhood when being from a war zone had made me feel proud – like I was a survivor – and I began to think of us Northerners as being brave soldiers of Ireland because the shopkeepers were always giving us sweets and cakes. The best thing though was in being invited to go in to the baker's shop to put the morning's freshly baked loaf through the bread-slicing machine, bag it, and take it home.

In the evenings, as we watched the riots happening in Derry on R.T.E. news, I wasn't feeling so brave. I felt scared, worried, and sad. How weird it seemed to stand back and view our town and the troubles in the North from a distance. Cork was way down at the very bottom of Ireland and Derry was right up at the top. It may as well have been a different country altogether. There was much about the Cork way of life and the O'Brien family, which was just brilliant and a great distraction from the troubles and problems at home.

It was a hot sunny summer, and we revelled in the excitement and novelty of our new territory. The Shandon Bells, an important landmark and tremendous tourist attraction, were high up in a church just at the back of our house. Morgan, Debbie, Donna, and I mischievously climbed the steep and seemingly unending steps to get to the balcony at the top and look out onto spectacular views of the land. The bells rang out over the city at certain times of day, and visitors were able to ring out tunes that would be heard far across Cork. There was something wonderfully comforting and containing about hearing the ring of the big fat breasted bells, which was a change from hearing shootings and bombings ringing out over our own Derry skies. The Shandon tower stood proud of the city: strong, always there, dependable, and stable. Excitedly but perhaps with some sense of anxiety, I urgently pulled back the bedroom curtains each morning relieved to find that the Shandon Bells and the tower were still there, parenting the city like a mother and father combined robustly watching over its children and singing out in celebration and reassurance.

Donna and I went to a wee Convent School nearby the Shandon Bells for a couple of weeks and we couldn't believe our luck when the nuns poured us hot chocolate and offered buns at break time. We sat in the courtyard being pampered by nuns and pupils alike because we were the little special children who came from a war zone. Although Donna and I together giggled that we had found ourselves in a great place altogether, I begun to feel a wee bit ashamed and uncomfortable and thought about the black babies in Africa who had nothing. For as long as I could remember in school, chapel, and at home, we were to think of the black babies and give them our pocket money or collect money for them when we could. I pushed to the back of my mind the unappetizing feeling of shame that people might be feeling sorry for us, like we felt sorry for the black babies, because I just wanted to enjoy the tasty buns, drink, and attention, which we did make a meal of.

Our Uncle Martin and Aunt Theresa were the best! We loved them. But something wasn't right; something just didn't feel right in my heart. I was starting to love them like they were my mamai and dadai and that didn't feel right because they weren't. The way that our aunt and uncle fondly kissed us on the head, tucked us in to bed at night, and spent so much time with us, I sometimes wanted to cry because I wished it were Dadai and Mamai doing these things. I tried not to be too jealous of Debbie and Jacqueline, as my envious eyes watched how their dadai showed his love for them. For starters, Uncle Martin was always there. He was not running out to the pub with his mates spending all of his earnings on drink. He was there, devoted to his wife and children and busy making suits for the shop. I began to feel envious as well that they lived in a place without riots in the streets and were nobody was shot dead. Not surprisingly then, my jealousy of Debbie's happy family was sometimes hard to manage, and so I had sewn the competitive threads of tension between her and me. I had little thought for her that she had to share her parents and home with us and that their family had doubled since we had arrived, as I was far too busy being envious and jealous of what she had that I couldn't care about what she might have to manage with us being there. I tried to hide from the the rotten oul' jealousy and envy by escaping into my mind place where I indulged myself in my own magical thinking.

Theresa and Martin were a great team, and they reminded me of the times when our mamai and dadai were the best parents in the world. Theresa, a tiny wee woman with huge chocolate brown eyes, baked the best fruitcake I had ever tasted in my whole life. There was always plenty to go around, and eating it reminded me of Mamai and her scone bread. Trips to the Ingle Nook social club in Cork were to become a highlight where a children's talent contest was held on Sundays and our Sean, all dressed up in his Sunday best entered the competition and sang, "Build a bonfire, build a bonfire, and put Paisley on the top put Lundy in the middle and burn the bloody lot!"

Aunt Theresa, who had no idea what he was going to sing, didn't know where to put herself but kissed him on the head, "God love him, he's a star turn", she said as she carried him off the stage. Paisley - in the song -had been a notorious staunch protestant MP who had a bulldozing voice that rammed his message through the eardrums of even the most politically deaf of voters, and funnily enough Mamai used to say that Sean had a voice like Paisley and could raise a riot in an empty church.

Whilst on a night out at the cinema with the O'Brien's, I couldn't help but think about the time that Mamai and Dadai took us to our first ever cinema trip when we all got dressed up, and me and Donna, wore our Sunday best dresses and patent shoes, bags, and white cotton gloves. I was six years old, Donna five, and we were setting off to see the Sound of Music. The rectangle boxes of chocolate toffees were a great treat and we had never tasted the likes. This was my best ever, warmest most gorgeous memory of being with my mamai and dadai. The sheer pleasure and delight seemed to never end as our love of the film and the Von Trapps, was wrapped up with the delight of Dadai walking down to the front of the screen at the interval to buy us ice cream and popcorn. We sang all the way home, and Mamai and Dadai were clearly beguiled by the obvious similarities in the Von Trapp family life and our own. Donna and I cherished this as one of our happiest childhood memories.

Aunt Theresa had a lovely wee yellow budgie in a cage, and it reminded me of when our own budgie, Snowy had died. Ours was a beautiful white budgie, and Mamai didn't agree with caged birds; in fact, she didn't really like the idea of a bird in the house at all and thought of them as being bad luck but me dadai thought that it would be good for us to have pets to look after. So we had Janet the golden labrador whom I adored and after Janet died, Prince the black labrador arrived and all the wanes in the street loved him as we had him perform all kinds of wild games, and he was subjected to being dressed up by me and Donna whenever we took the fancy. Any time mamai went out of the house; we would let Snowy the budgie out of the cage and fly around to our frenzied excitement. On one fateful day, however, she flew into the top of a bottle of brown sauce, that was all sticky with the congealed sauce, and suffocated, and that was the end of her. We then buried her in a shoebox in the back garden, and we all stood around and said our goodbyes. Donna was more upset than the rest of us, and so Dadai promised that he would buy her another one.

"No more birds, Johnnie. They're more bother than they are worth and it's not right to have them locked up in a cage anyway." Mamai tried to explain to Donna that birds were never meant to be in cages anyway and that it was cruel.

A few months passed when Donna and me were outside playing 'The Mary Cotton Wool Show' (our version of the Mary Tyler Moore Show) and we could see Dadai coming up the street carrying a big bird cage draped in a black cloth.

We ran towards him in excitement. "Dadai, is it the new budgie?" Donna quizzed jumping up and down with excitement.

"Go'n the two of ye run home fast and sit down on the sofa with your mamai to see what I have got for ye."

Mamai, Donna, and I sat like the three stooges on the sofa and the boys piled in around us. Proud as punch, Dadai, stood in the bay window and like a magician, pulled off the black cloth.

"Aghhhhhhhh! Jesus Mary and St. Joseph and Mother of You Devine what in God's name is it?" cried Mamai.

Donna and I yelped out in shock and surprise, the boys hysterically falling over laughing at our response, and David the youngest, was now screaming, as the big black bird the size of a big Christmas turkey, was flapping like a mad thing in the cage.

"What in God's name is wrong with your head, Johnnie? Take it back to where you found it."

"Come on, Margaret! The wean wanted a budgie."

"Jesus Christ, Johnnie! What kind of a budgie is that?"

By now, the big black bird that wasn't a budgie, with his big orange beak called out, "Jesus Christ! Jesus Christ!"

Now at this point, Mamai nearly passed out, and the boys were practically on the ceiling with laughter and excitement.

"I know it's not a budgie, Margaret. It's better than a budgie, it's a minor bird!"

Dadai, in all seriousness, tried to convince Mamai that it was a great thing and he didn't even have to pay for it.

"Johnnie, there's a square difference between a budgie and that thing sitting in front of us, which no more looks like anything 'minor' than I look like Marilyn Munroe. No wonder you didn't have to pay for it. Whoever gave it to you saw you coming."

The minor bird was part of the family for a wee while but as soon as Mamai could, she palmed it off on some woman who lived over in the Waterside because it cursed like a trooper. Having lived in one of the pubs down the town, the poor bird's vocabulary was as filthy as was its droppings. Never again did we have a bird in the house.

I drifted off into a place where I sucked and chewed on what good memories I had of Mamai and Dadai doing things together and of the family ups and downs. I lay there thinking of how they sang together and of how sometimes, Mamai laughed so much that she would have to run to the toilet. I thought of how we used to all jump on top of Dadai and tickle the life out of him, reducing him to hysterical laughter that sounded like a baby crying, as he became so defenceless, and we were delighted with ourselves that we had so much power and strength that we could turn our big strong dadai into such a jellied mess.

I thought about the times when we practiced headstands against the living room door and Dadai would join in, and we couldn't resist the opportunity to run towards him and grab his exposed tummy and tickle the life out of him again. The thoughts of our parents came thick and fast. I remembered how they cooked together. Dadai was a powerful pounder of potatoes. Putting the huge pot on the floor, he mashed and smashed our potatoes with butter, milk, and eggs, determined that there would be no lumps and that we would have the creamiest mash possible.

I thought of how my father threw himself into the job of resurrecting wrecked, battered, and scuffed shoes, which he polished, spat on, and left to dry in, then brushed, and buffed with old stockings and emerged shiny and highly polished. Fourteen shoes were then lined up in front of the fireplace on a Saturday night whilst Mamai scrubbed us in the bath and spent hours putting me and Donna's hair in strings, which looked like fat sausages hanging from our heads so that we'd wake up with ringlets in the morning when our curly hair would then be tied up in ribbons that matched our best Sunday frocks. After Sunday lunch and the usual aftermath of washing up, our dadai sometimes took us into the countryside on foot so that Mamai had a few hours to herself. We'd happily walk for miles, singing as we went along, with containers under our arms picking blackberries, gooseberries, and raspberries on our way up to Sheriff's Mountain and into the Black Hut – a makeshift shop in the middle of nowhere – that sold cinder toffee, Peggy's Leg, and Black jacks, which we sucked and chewed on the way home, delighted that our mother would make our berries into jam.

I lay there in my Cork bed and tried hard not to think of the worries, the hard times, and of the times that Dadai just wasn't there. Like on a Saturday night when he didn't come home after work or when he came home, got ready, and then went out again, leaving Mamai to bath all of us and manage the bedtime conveyor belt activity of inspecting hair for nits and any hair styling and grooming that needed doing whilst we all sat drying in front of the fire and watching the Val Doonican Show on T.V. No wonder I took a shine to the corny crooner, as he was always there on a Saturday night wearing lovely woolly jumpers, rocking in his rocking chair, and singing about peeping in to say good night and seeing his child in prayer; and a song about walking tall and straight and looking the world right in the eye; and another one about a goat belonging to some man called Paddy McGinty. So Val Doonican was a great help to Mamai on a Saturday night as she got us ready for our beds where she would kneel with us and pray,

"Good night dear God I am going to bed
My work is over my prayers are said
I am not afraid at night
As you will watch 'till morning's light.
And if I die before I wake
I pray my Lord, my soul to take.
God bless, Mamai and Dadai,
Brothers and sisters,
Granny and Granda
Aunties and Uncles
Cousins and all friends and relations and enemies
Amen."

So there we were, glad and thankful to be living in Cork and welcomed in this happy and warm family, and this was a memory that would be filed in my heart as one of my happiest childhood times even though it was a time that I held on to my own family life like it was my favourite satin blanket, wrapping myself in memories and sucking on thoughts of Val Doonican who stepped in to the room in my head on a Saturday night – in place of Dadai who wasn't there – and thanking God for Mamai 'cos she was always there, even when she was faraway.

Chapter 4
THE WANDERERS RETURN

SHINY orange satin trimmed the white sheets tucked around Mamai who was sitting up in her beautifully dressed double bed with the bedding that she, her very self, had handmade.

"The wanderers return!" she smiled, reaching her arms out to greet us.

I so wanted to climb into that bedding with the orange satin bedspread featuring little orange-ribboned bows that Mamai and me had carefully sewn on. I so wanted to be tucked back into my old life. But something wasn't right. A big Scandinavian looking woman with a sculpted hairdo – the kind that looks as though it's just planted on top of the head – guarded the white, fat feathered pillows that supported my mother's back. She was sitting beside my mother immaculately dressed in trousers and an Arran cardigan. I kept looking at that short blonde streaked hairdo; all set to perfection, it looked like it belonged to some other woman and didn't belong to her because she looked like a man. Her name was Eva, and she was introduced to us as Mamai's home help and she would be living with us for a while. A home help was someone who the State paid to come into homes and provide help to vulnerable families or at times of crisis. Mamai was smiley faced and clearly pleased to see us, inviting us to come and sit close by her.

Donna and Sean ran towards her but I felt strangely awkward and unable to look into my own mother's eyes. I didn't want this stranger to be sitting here with us, and I didn't know how to be with my own mother. Although pleased and relieved to see her face and her smile, I felt a sense of estrangement between us, and I just didn't know how to be or where to look, so I just stood beside the bed, stroking the satin bedspread, deaf to what was being said around me.

This was the beginning of a new and different kind of relationship with my mother, full of unspoken expectation. Something stopped me from being able to really look into her eyes. Perhaps I didn't want to see the face of a mother who had had her womb taken out as though she was never going to be the same again. Perhaps I couldn't bear to see in her face what she'd been through, and I didn't want her to see how much I had missed her and of how I just wanted to climb right into bed beside her, nestle into the warmth of her, and suck and lick the orange satin trim of her blanket.

As time went on, I seemed to get into a lot of trouble with Eva who was scolding me every five minutes. I was Mamai's helper, what was she doing here, telling me off about stuff? Just because she was a hard worker, good and kind, and right enough, a great help and friend to Mamai, it didn't mean that I had to like her. So it turned out that she and I didn't really hit it off especially, as she was a great one for throwing us out into the street to play so that we would give Mamai's head peace. I would just try to keep out of her way by spending as much time outside as I could with my friend Sandra Cullen and her cousin Kitty, who just lived across the road from us.

"Red rover, red rover, we want Kitty Young over."

"Red rover, red rover we want Sandra Cullen over."

Like a heavy stone dropping deep inside my stomach sending sickly ripples and waves through my body, the anticipation and fear of not being picked for a team heavily weighed me down when at last Richard Moore called out, "Red rover red rover we want Caroline Owens over."

This is how we picked teams for our games, and I didn't give a monkey's uncle for whose team I was in, as long as I was in a team and as long as I wasn't the last one called over. Richard saved my life from ruin at the moment that he called me over, and I lived another day for mischief and play. We spent hours at the park in a street near by our house and our special pastime was 'playing on the bars', a row of railings, which became gymnastic apparatus, and we competitively spun around, often falling off and receiving painful bloody cuts with little bits of gravel all stuck into the stingy wounds. This was just a small-scale activity park but it never emptied, as swarms of weans like a locus of insects flitted and buzzed around the swings, slides, roundabout, and bars.

We girls sometimes had an audience of children watching us, and we were especially keen to attract the boys' attention. My heart would stop if Lee Barlow passed by or if Richard Moore stopped for a chat. Richard was not like the other boys who wouldn't be seen dead actually talking to a girl. Richard appeared more mature and respectful of girls, and I was especially chuffed when he would say, "Yes, Caroline, what about ye?"

He knew my name and always said, "Yes!" (a Derry hello); therefore, I had decided that he was my new boyfriend and if anyone asked me if I had a boyfriend, I would now announce that I did and that his name was Richard Moore – I got fed up with Lee Barlow running away from me and never saying hello.

Richard had a lovely freckly face and wavy brown hair in a neat and respectable side parting. I think what drew me especially to Richard was the kindliness shining out of his beautiful eyes and that he could look into my eyes when he spoke. This seemed to be in contrast to other weeboys, who were so busy being big shots and tough teddies that they were seemingly unable to tolerate the softness of girls whom they appeared to ignore. Richard was a couple of years younger than me but given that I was small for my age, I was happy to ignore the age difference. Richard never knew that he was my boyfriend; it all just existed in me and my friends' heads, and I was thrilled every time I saw him in the street and if he said, "Yes Caroline, what about ye?"

Then I knew that we were still on.

Donna and I were worst friends and best enemies. Given that I was only eleven months older than her, my birthday was in the end of April and hers the end of March, we were not far enough apart in age to give us a reasonable distance, nor were we close enough to twin us in friendship. With me enjoying something of the benefits of being the first girl born into our family, it all seemed to mean that we were destined to have a complicated relationship. So Donna, at times, would feel overshadowed by me and my position in the family, and I would sometimes give her a hard as I claimed my authority as the elder sister. It is difficult to know how much the tension between us was to do with our wildly different temperaments and how much our wildly differing temperaments were to do with our position in the family and the stories about us that were being told around us and that became our early life scripts.

Yet we spent most of our early childhood playing with each other, fighting, and making up. At Christmas, Donna would get a doll with black hair because her hair was black and I would get one with blonde hair, like my own.

"Day and night, chalk and cheese they are," Mamai would say about us.

Yet she would talk of how she never wanted to make a difference in us and was at pains to dress us in the same clothes, and she was delighted when people would admiringly ask if we were twins. I suppose it was her way of managing the jealousies and rivalries between us – she would ignore the differences and just make us the same.

"I never make a difference in any of the seven of them; I treat them all the same."

This was clearly an impossibility because at the same time, she knew our differences like the back of her hand and was skilfully attuned to our 'ways'.

Donna was a lot quieter than me and seemed to be more favoured by aunties and uncles because she was no bother at all, where as I had a lot more to say and was something of a performer, a wee bit of a clown, and a bit of a nuisance.

Donna was better at working hard at school and would always practice her Irish dancing and know her steps, and I was the opposite. I loved the getting up on the stage and dancing but got fed up with practicing my steps, so Donna would have to give me extra lessons in the kitchen. I soon tired of the endeavour, as my heart wasn't in it so, I'd give up and end up only knowing half a dance and was happy to wing it whilst on stage at the Feis.

Mary McLaughlin, our dancing teacher, always used to say that I had "great poise, points, and carriage," and had the makings of a good dancer if I put my mind to it, and she wouldn't give up on me, especially after I started winning medals. I just didn't feel like having to try that hard and the dances got harder and more complicated and I didn't have Donna's dedication, so after a few torturous years of indecision, I finally decided that I needed to pack it in. Although I felt great relief, I always regretted my decision at Feis times because I wanted to be up on the stage with everyone else. But I couldn't expect the reward if I didn't do the work and was proud of Donna when her medals came pouring in. Donna was able to have something of her own to be proud of, and I didn't mind that she could do something that I couldn't do.

Although we had our jealousies and rivalries, falling in and falling outs, we had a special connection in so far that we were the only two girls amongst the five boys, and when we didn't have our own friends to play with, we had each other.

One hot summer day, Dadai was building a big ranch style fence around our house. Donna and I were dancing up and down the street together in our plastic jellybean shoes, and Donna danced into a three-inch nail, which went right up into the arch of her foot. She screamed out and immediately collapsed and was rushed to hospital, where she remained for many weeks and returned home with her leg in Plaster of Paris. After a few weeks, she complained of her foot hurting and burning and when she returned to have the plaster removed, they found that she had blood poisoning and could have died if they hadn't operated immediately. Not only did she not die but they hadn't given her enough anaesthetic during the operation, so she woke up during it and was in excruciating pain. Mamai contemplated sueing the doctors because she said that Donna had been traumatized as a result of the botched operation but she was advised to leave well enough alone by her greatly respected GP and Mamai soon consoled herself now that Donna was on the mend.

During the whole time that this was happening, I prayed to Our Lady whilst in chapel and at my own May alter in my bedroom that if Donna recovered then I would never fight with her or call her names ever again. I would even give her my loom and all my best scraps for her scrapbook, I would never tell her to go away ever again, and I would always let her play with my friends.

The whole experience of Donna being in hospital and all the fuss made of her left me with the notion that it would be great to spend some time in hospital. So when it came to 'hearing tests' at school, I found myself going a bit deaf.

I had to put on earphones and indicate by tapping if I had heard the noise. So even when I heard the noise, I just stood as still as I could, pretending that I couldn't hear. The upshot of it was that I was sent to the hospital for more tests, and I was being tested with our Mark who really did have a hearing problem. Together, we sat in the hospital waiting room through the excitement of it all, and Mamai was informed that we would have to be admitted to have our tonsils and adenoids removed.

Mark and I were over the moon especially as he was my 'wee dote' and I was his wee mother. He was in a different hospital room from me and in a cot because he was five years younger than me and I was put in a normal size bed. But given that he would end up in my bed, eventually the nurses made him a bed beside mine. The nurses pampered us to the high heavens, and we were so indulged by aunties and uncles and Mamai, and sometimes Dadai who visited us.

But oh my Holy God of Heaven! Following the operation, I truly regretted my antics because the pain in my throat was unbearable like it was stuffed with barbed wire and I thought that I was burning in hell with the heat of the fever.

Mark recovered easily so they moved him out of my room, as they had to nurse me intensively. I thought that I was going to die. I kept throwing the covers off myself exposing my naked body to the world, and Mamai hurriedly tucked me in again and again to protect my modesty.

I vowed that never ever again would I say that I was ill if I wasn't because it wasn't worth the attention and the fuss to have half the contents of my throat and mouth cut out. So when an epidemic of arse boils hit our family, I was determined that I wouldn't get one. Mamai and Dadai made poultices to put on the big throbbing lumps. Tommy was the first to get one... on his rear end! We watched as me dadai poured scalding water into a bowl with bits of bread and coal tar soap and mashed it around in the bowl. Dadai held Tommy as tightly as he could and Mamai slapped the sticky, steamy stew on top of the ugly lump. Tommy screamed his head off, and we all ran out of the room in horror at the whole performance. Tommy however was right as rain the next day, as the poultice had drawn out the poisonous puss and although it was a wee while before he could sit down, he was in much better form. Gradually the blighters went around every one of us weans – mainly bum boils – and after watching too many of the operations, I prayed to God in heaven that I wouldn't get one. I did get one despite the fact that Dadai had set about treating us with his own medicinal concoction. We had all to line up each morning to receive a dessertspoon full of molasses and cod liver oil, which made my stomach wretch, and the piece of bread and sugar afterwards barely helped the medicine go down.

My boil was a great big brute of a thing and just sat there throbbing on my finger. The pain was so excruciating that I didn't care if they chopped off my whole finger – it would have been a lot kinder I thought than having a poultice. I begged Mamai, asking her to promise me that she wouldn't put a poultice on it but she kept avoiding the question until one night my wailing in pain was driving everyone to distraction. Into my bedroom came Mamai and Dadai with the bowl, concoction, towel, and bandage, and I nearly lost my mind at the sight of it all. Just as the unbearable pain of the scalding poultice on my finger got me to fever pitch, I could feel the life drain out of me, and I thought that it could have gone either way and death was a definite possibility. But they were quick, and just as I thought that I was going to the angels, I felt the sensation of the puss oozing out of my finger and relief soon came. Mamai cradled me in her arms and Dadai brought me tea and toast and tucked me into bed. Later on, Mamai appeared with a bottle of lucozade and the Bunty magazine and I felt more loved, cherished, and cared for than I ever could have imagined thanking God in heaven that my mamai and dadai could work miracles.

Chapter 5
DADAI; MY HOPELESS HERO - OUR CHAMPION

"CAROLINA moon, keep shining, shining on the one who waits for me" and "Cara Mia Mi, say you will be mine."

These were the special songs that Dadai affectionately sang to me, leaving me with a sense that I had a special connection to the moon and to him, as I was the one to wait for him and that he would always wait for me. I adored him and the look of him and the smell of his skin even though I would run away from him and scream when he would come to Donna and me, as he tried to give us a 'beardy kiss' when it was just before he needed a shave and the prickly growth scratched at our peachy skin.

Enrico Caruso was his favourite singer and Rigoletto or Pagliacci, the sad clown from the opera Cavalleria Rusticana, Ave Maria, and Santa Lucia were amongst his favourite songs.

"'His Masters Voice', Nobody can produce tenors like the Italians, Gili, Caruso, and Mario Lanza. Only the Italians can breed genius in opera, it's in their blood like their love of family and food," he'd announce, whilst shaking his head emphasizing the Italian accolade. Count John McCormack the Irish tenor was good too, he thought, with his version of Panis Angelicos, and Joseph Locke was good enough but neither of them were a match for Caruso.

Dadai got his love of opera from his father and listening to the songs over and over again, I think made him feel as though Granda Owens was close by. There was definitely a sense of being connected to something solid and steady in listening to the music and songs, and Dadai clung on to them like a child would cling to a favourite blanket. So Dadai handed the tradition down the family line, and he would try to instil an appreciation of opera in all of us, spending many an hour lamenting the merits and differences in the songs and the singers.

Caruso's Palliachi was blaring out of the radiogram downstairs and I could hear Dadai upstairs in the bathroom singing his head off. I loved it when he was in good form and joined in with the singing but Mamai, often in frustration and annoyance, shouted out,

"Sweet God in heaven, turn that thing down, as if there isn't enough to cry about, do we have to drown in some poor clowns tears as well?"

Mamai loved to listen to Jim Reeves and Patsy Cline and the old Irish ballads and although Dadai could enjoy her musical preferences, she didn't have a huge appetite for opera. Even so, she found it hard to resist some of the classics, and sometimes we would catch her as she sang along to her favourites when she was cleaning.

Upstairs in the bathroom, I many a time sat on the rim of the bath and observed every move when my father was shaving. He always wore a vest tucked into his immaculately pressed trousers, and I loved the sight of his big shiny muscles like the Mountains of Mourne solidly rippling down his arms. My name ran through a ribbon that floated out of a big red heart, which was tattooed at the very top of his left arm, and Donna's name was tattooed onto a flower on the right arm.

Fag hanging out of his mouth, he would fill the sink with warm water, adjust the little circular mirror on the window ledge above the sink, dip the funny wee brush with the long pony tail hair into the water then into the bar of soap, and brush it all around his chin and neck, magically making a creamy froth. Clinking the razor into the sink, he would tilt his head to one side and drag the blade across his face, making a cringingly yet comforting sound. Up and down with the sharp razor that was then plunged back into the sink and out again and up under his chin. I'd hold my breath in anticipation when he got to the part with the big pointy lump – the Adam's apple. It was usually around that area that he cut himself or at the side near the sideburns.

I would hand him the towel, which he patted on to his checks and neck. Then I'd hand him the Old Spice that he splashed on to his hands and patted all around his handsome square face. After pulling out the plug, the sink was left with a scummy white surface with wee tiny black bits. Dadai would plunge his giant hands on which Mamai's name was tattooed (across the knuckles: MARG on the left hand and ARET on the right) into the sink and swill the fresh water all around and the sink was now as clean as his face. His face was now as shiny as his muscles except for the bleeding bits, which he covered with little pieces of toilet roll that I had torn off for him and he would stick to the cuts to stop the bleeding.

Handsome to his bones, with curly black hair and a mouthful of beautiful teeth, he took sideways glances into the mirror as he put the finishing touches to his hair with Brylcreem from the pot. Now sitting on the rim of the bath beside me, he allowed me to be the hairdresser, letting me slap the sweet smelling cream onto his hair and give it a wee style. After he put his new clean shirt on, his big strong arms lifted me up from the ground, carried me downstairs where we sat down in the chair beside the fire. Putting me on his knee, he'd ask me about my day and what I did at school and about what I'd been up to. I had everything I could ever want and could do no wrong in his eyes, nor he in mine. I often had my father all to myself and was his happy travel companion when I sat on the back of his bicycle. There was a time when he had a motorbike and sidecar and he would take Donna and me for rides. We used to royally wave out to our friends who were speechless at the sight.

Most of my early memories of my father are of deep fondness, pride, and affection to the point that I used to pray that he would not die before my mother because I couldn't bear to live without him. My mother loved him too. She was an intelligent woman and although clearly attracted to his good looks and charm, the complexity of the man was the big attraction; one of the best boxers of his day in Derry, the classical music and opera fanatic, the brilliant harmonica player, the award winning gardener and vegetable grower, the master bricklayer, the toy maker, the furniture maker, the exquisite italic hand writer, the shoe shiner, and potato masher, and attaché case maker. They met at the Corinthian where me mamai was singing – The Green Glens of Antrim – in the Derry Feis, and Dadai in the audience was captivated by the woman who won the competition – winning a gold cup, a box of chocolates, a pair of silk stockings, and the heart of a young handsome man named Johnnie Owens.

I put to the back of my mind any version of my father that frustrated my sense of absolute unconditional love for him. Yet I shall always remember the time when he was busy building a bookcase to which he had been carving the finishing touches. Tommy, aged nine years, was helping him, passing him nails and tools. Dadai asked Tommy to bring him a chisel and Tommy, I think brought the wrong thing. Dadai went mental, shouted at Tommy, grabbed him, and started shaking him and slapping him. Mamai was hysterical, dragged Tommy off, begging Dadai not to hurt him she cried and pleaded, "Jesus Johnnie, he's only a wean. Leave him alone."

Tommy was silently tearful and I couldn't stand to see him, my big brother so shocked and upset, and I refused to believe my eyes because this was the first and only time I had ever seen my father hit any of us. He lifted the hatchet and chopped and hacked the bookcase to bits while my mother wrapped herself around Tommy, and I stepped far back from the scene. The bookcase finally demolished, my father falls to his knees, crying and sobbing for his dead father. Mother and Tommy step aside, as I instinctively and tentatively, walk towards my dadai. With my seven-year-old hands now stroking his head and wiping his tears, he reaches towards me and holds me close as he sobs into me. Calm settles and Mamai manages to set Tommy and I free to the garden, as she attends to Dadai.

From that day onwards, my father was never to take responsibility for chastising or disciplining us weans. Yet, somebody needed to keep the seven of us in check and Mamai was no soft touch, as she increasingly became a harsh and hard taskmaster.

Bedtime was after the six o'clock news on school days but we were rarely ready to sleep. Tommy, Liam, and the three weans were always up to something, getting out of bed and running around, playing Cowboys and Indians. Donna and I played 'shows' – The Mary Cotton Wool Show , and mums and dads, or schools. We ignored Mamai's warnings that she'd come upstairs and "empty" us, or that she'd "go in and out" through every one of us if we didn't get into bed or that we'd be seeing stars if we didn't settle down. Then sometimes we would have the biggest shock, as she'd suddenly appear as if from nowhere, skelping us around the legs. To be "emptied" was to be dealt with either by a good telling off or a "skelping", a slapping around the legs. I was always confused about who was being emptied, as it looked as though the person doing the telling off or the hitting was the one who was emptying themselves of their anger or frustration but I think that the intention was to empty the offender of the offensive behaviour.

To "go in and out" through us was more clearly to do with physical punishment. Loathing the skelps and the shameful stinging blows to my sense of justice and pride, I tried hard not to think of how much I hated her in those times of punishment. Dadai would never treat us like this, I thought. She was supposed to be our mother. We were never allowed to 'turn a word in her mouth' and definitely not allowed to swear.

The closest we got to swearing was calling each other "pigs", "bitches" or "flumers!", which was a mild alternative to "fuckers". However, when we could manage it without being caught, we went as far as referring to our brothers as "pigs". "Fat pigs, stupid pigs, lazy pigs, ignorant, filthy, rotten dirty pigs or, cheeky pigs," and our brother's referred to us as "wee bitches" of varying varieties.

If Mamai ever caught us name calling, she would empty us by shaking her fist into our faces, "There are no animals in this house. If I hear any of you at that carry on, I'll bitch you," or "I'll kill you stone dead."

We secretly managed to have a hierarchy of bad words. We progressed to the satisfyingly dizzy heights of verbal execution by firing, "You are one 'Get' or 'a Get up the back'," which was even worse, yet I have no clue what it technically meant but to us, it meant that someone was probably a repeat offender of badness. "Big 'Effer" (big fucker) or "bad B" (bad bastard) towards or about the offender was used mainly by the boys. We weren't allowed to say 'shit' or 'shite'. So Donna and I replaced it with 'sugar' and 'shilo'.

Sometimes I would say the hard core swear words to myself under the covers at night just to hear what they sounded like coming out of my mouth but then I would go to confession and confess so that I wouldn't have a stain on my soul.

"Schizophrenia" was the biggest word I had ever heard, and I could pronounce it but it was a sickening word that made me worried and fearful so I tried to change its impact on me by singing it to myself and whispering rhymes about it " schizophrenia - whatyoumeania?!... Schizophrenia Whereyoubeenia?... Schizophrenia areyoumeania?"

Like a ghost, the word haunted my night-time bed and lurked around in the back of my mind like a terrifying shadow, and even when I tried to tell myself that I was a clever girl because I could say such a big word – the big word – it seemed was bigger and more clever than me.

I don't remember how I first learned of the word or if my mother had told us about it. I certainly don't remember anyone explaining it to us but I knew that it was to do with Dadai's sickness. It was something to do with coming home to find me dadai giving away our big antique grandfather clock to some man that he didn't know. It was to do with walking into the living room to find that all of Dadai's highly polished silver, boxing medals, gold cups, and trophies had disappeared. It was to do with our bookcases, which were full of encyclopaedias and hard backed medical books, which had three-dimensional picture pop ups of body parts that we used to look at and secretly find out about sex organs, and old Irish and English hard back classics, all having vanished. It was to do with Dadai being carried home from the pub after having drowned his sorrows in alcohol. It was to do with him working in England with other Derry men and all of their families standing at their garden gates waiting for the Wireman to come on his motorbike and deliver the money wire to everybody else, but ours never arrived. It was to do with him building furniture then smashing it to bits. It was to do with him being an only son in a family of six.. It was to do with him at seventeen years old going to work on a bus with his father, and Dadai – who was not me dadai yet – getting up from the seat beside his father and going down to the back of the bus to sit with his friend. Then the bus crashed and Dadai's father was killed stone dead, and Granda's bloody dead face was staring up at his own. And it was to do with Dadai seeing flashes of the bloody scene over and over again and again every day ever since. It was to do with the guilt that Dadai had moved down the bus and Granda had moved into the seat that Dadai had been sitting in and then Dadai was sick with the guilt that he should have died instead of his da. It may also have been to do with the fact that Dadai's own grandfather, our great grandfather died young too, only a slip of a man, having drowned in the Lusitania ship that sank in the First World War. Perhaps the young Johnnie Owens reckoned that one way or another, he too would be doomed and that his time would soon be up. So my father's history ate away at his nerves and gnawed and chewed at our family for years.

Schizophrenia and alcoholism were Mamai's crosses to bear when she had to turn away from the garden gate because there was no money wire for us. Watching Mamai swallow her pride over and over again made me dare to hate him, 'cos he was just bad letting on to be mad. You see, even when he was well or better and not being schizophrenic and working on the building sites earning good money, he rarely came straight home after work on a Friday. Like many Derry men at that time, selfish, pampered, and leaving their wives and families to make do whilst they spent half their lives down the pub pissing their wages up the walls and down the gutters, then coming home all sentimental about their weans and emptying out of their pockets what was left of their wages to give the weans for pocket money. The mothers then had the damndable job of having to take the money off the weans and put up with their screaming and crying and having to withstand yet again being thought of as the parent who was taking something away from their children.

The part of me that wanted to keep the money just so that we could go to the shops like Kitty Young – whose dad wasn't a drinker – and buy Lucky Bags, comics, and sweets, hated my mother for making us look poor. Sometimes, when my father returned home drunk to obliteration, Mamai and us would attempt to empty his pockets whilst he was asleep and find what money we could so that food could be bought and bills could be paid. When Dadai came round from his drunken stupor, wondering where all of his money had gone, we would tell him that he must have spent it in the pub or given it away, which he often did anyway. Sometimes he wouldn't believe the tale, and we would hear slapping and crashing noises going on behind my parent's bedroom door.

Following one such incident, my mother's face was black and blue but I never heard her speak a word about what went on, and I couldn't bear to think about what might have gone on – and never did ask. It seemed like half of Creggan's fathers were alcoholics or dog fanatics who spent their money on beer or food for the greyhounds before handing in the leftover wages for their families. I recognized many of my friend's fathers down the pub when I was sent down to try to entice Dadai out to come home for his tea.

"Caroline, you're your dadai's number one so you go down to that friggin' den of iniquity and tell him that his tea is ready – he'll listen to you," Mamai desperately but guiltily implored me to go, knowing she couldn't affront him by turning up herself. Mamai didn't drink or smoke and hated pubs but she was clearly tied in knots about sending me down to the pub – knowing it wasn't a job for a wean.

Nevertheless, sometimes my innocent powers of persuasion worked, and the part of me who loved my father was so happy to see him even if he was glossy eyed and full of sloppy affectionate sentimentalism.

"Here she is, my wee doll. Come on over here and sit yourself down beside me, you're my girl, you know that don't you? Here's my girl, isn't she beautiful? Carolina Moon, keep shining…"

"Ah, Johnnie, she's an Owens, she's the spit out of your mouth. Here wee love, buy yourself a lucky bag or some crisps."

I refused the sweaty money even though the thought of the lucky bag was tempting; I knew that was somebody's bread money or milk money.

"Aye she is and she's a good wean, a great help to her mother," Dadai proudly dribbled his words out from his smelly, drunken breath adding to the putrid alcoholic fumes. The place smelled like many of the bars in the town – I'd got to know them all as I'd run in and out of many of them until I'd find him sitting there; a potpourri of piss and alcohol and the stench of drunken men and women too, and some of them seemingly didn't give a damn about going home to their weans.

Presenting me to his buddies - a drunken swamp of wet, dribbly, incoherent, selfish wage wasters and gamblers, Dadai was only just on this planet. There they all were, sitting in a smoky, stinky, beer-stained, whisky swilling pit. A part of me tried but couldn't manage to be flattered by my father's sentimental dribbling so I just tried to keep my mind on the job.

"Dadai, g'on come home, please, g'on Dadai?"

I knew that if I didn't manage to get him home, there wouldn't be enough money left for buying the messages in the morning. Saturday was the day for filling the larders with the groceries for the week.

At least he's better looking than the rest of them, and he has bigger muscles than them too I thought, and I did feel good that seemingly I was able to use my innocent powers of persuasion. The part of me who loved him and loved Mamai and wanted a full larder for the week managed to guide my handsome hopeless hero home, desperately hoping that I wouldn't bump into anyone who knew us.

Mamai protected us from her own despair, as she managed to make do with what little money she was left with. She would offer it all up to the Virgin Mary in her prayers.

"Why does he do it, Mamai?" I dared to ask, desperately wanting there to be a good reason because I didn't want ever to hate him.

"It's because he is not well in the head. He's sick in the head. He's got an illness – schizophrenia and alcoholism."

"It's a sickness."

Hearing the word from Mamai's mouth was too much confirmation. It was far too true to be a comfort, and I was afraid. Could she not have told me that he was grand and that there was nothing at all wrong with him? I spat out my thoughts that were by now brewing into a soured broth in my mind.

"But I hate it, Mamai, and I hate feeling showed up all of the time, and I hate it that you never know where the next penny is coming from, and that he hasn't got a job so that we could be a normal family. And it's not fair that everybody is talking about us, and that nobody knows about him having that sickness in the head." I couldn't believe that the words came out of my mouth, and I thought that I would be struck down dead right there and then by God in heaven for saying such terrible things about my own father, whom I adored.

Mamai put her arms round my shoulders and looking into my eyes, she studied my face that had misery, humiliation, and fear written all over it. "It's not his fault. I know that you're the apple of his eye; always remember what it is that you love about him. You hold your head high and never be ashamed of him because whatever bother and trouble we have in our house, it's clean trouble and it's not because your father is bad. You might hate him sometimes, God knows that I know how you feel, but never forget how much he loves you and how much you love him. When people are talking about us and our troubles, they're leaving someone else alone."

I managed not to hate him but instead hated friggin' schizophrenia and stinkin' alcohol. He wasn't bad; he was not well in the head. He had flumen schizophrenia – the illness that nobody talked out loud about, and it wasn't because they couldn't pronounce or even spell the friggin' thing, it was because it was such a terrible thing like a mortal sin. Over time, we all got to know the word and it had different meanings to all of us. One night, in fact the only time I remember that Mamai had seemingly walked out on us; she said that she would be back in an hour. But she didn't return. It was getting late, and we were becoming more and more worried. Where the frig had she gone? Earlier on in the evening she had said, "I feel like lifting my coat and not coming back, otherwise I'll be driven to Gransha myself."

I knew that Gransha was a place for mad people, and mothers were often saying that they were going to be "driven to Gransha", "ready for Gransha", "ready for jumping off the bridge", "ready for the Foyle" (the river Foyle) or ready for the hills for some reason or another, mainly because their weans or their men, or the troubles or everything was driving them mad.

Chapter 5 DADAI; MY HOPELESS HERO - OUR CHAMPION

When I watched the riots in the streets and when I heard of the bombings and more riots on the news, I had visions of a steady stream of people heading for the hills, jumping off bridges or getting into cars to end up being driven to Gransha psychiatric hospital where they would be locked up with the people who were 'the wiser in- looking out'. We understood that many of the women in Derry were on 'nerve tablets' because we heard them talk about how they would take 'a wee Valium' to settle their nerves and a Mogadon to help them sleep.

We knew that Gransha was a real place because it was just in front of Stradreagh hospital, an old institution for people who were considered-sub- normal' and 'not the full shilling'. Eileen, my granny Murphy's sister was admitted when she was fifteen years old because someone had decided that she was subnormal, "slow in the head" they said. We were told that the final straw before she was taken away from the family was her jumping into the river to save her young nephew who was drowning even though she herself couldn't swim. It didn't seem to matter that she saved her nephew's life. No, that would be too much of a leap of faith to think that a 'slow' young woman was quick when she needed to be and able to do what she needed to do to save Paddy's life. No not at all – that would be insane. Nevertheless, the whole sorry episode was in fact conclusive evidence that she was not right in the head.

That was one of the reasons that Mamai would tell us that there were "wiser in looking out," meaning that the asylums were full of people who shouldn't be there, whilst the mad were feely just out in the community pretending to be wise. As a very young child, I visited Eileen in that scary place with Mamai and Granny Murphy. Granny always got upset and came away crying, and blowing her nose into her handkerchief, she would say, "Margaret, if anything ever happens to me, promise me that you will look after Eileen because when I'm gone, she'll have nobody."

"Aye, Mamai, I'll look after her if God spares me."

Mamai had no sooner made her promise to Granny whilst at the same time offering to help out my Aunt Francis, Dadai's sister who herself had a house full of weans but she had become ill and so her young infant Gary came to live with us. We adored him and Donna and I regularly fought over who would push him around the streets in his pram.

Mamai loved infant weans. When she picked them up in her arms, she held them close and put her cheek to theirs. Dancing around the room with the baby in arms, my mother sang to their hearts' content. Mamai seemed to take a particular delight in bathing and dressing infants and doing what she could to curl what wee bit of hair they had by sweeping it in the opposite direction of its natural flow. The most satisfying part of the baby washing and dressing seemed to be when the baby was all patted with talcum powder and then tucked safely inside the baby-grow. I got a deep sense of satisfaction myself when watching Mamai, as she popped and pressed all the wee fastenings into place all down the middle of the baby-grow and then down its legs. Relieved and satisfied that the baby was now all held together, clean and secure and in no danger of any limbs falling off, Donna and I were beside ourselves to pick him up and have a cuddle. After the whole baby washing procedure, just before sharing him us, mother would lift the baby up into her arms, hold him close to her face and say, "You're my wee nine pots of jam!"

That must have been Murphy for "You're my sweet wean," and she did have the nine pregnancies, so we were her nine pots of jam! and wee baby Gary was doted on as though he was her very own child. We had him for many months, loving him like he was ours. The day that Aunt Francis and Uncle Harry came to take him home, Donna and I were in convulsions crying and Mamai sniffed her tears up into her head, as she handed him over and tried to console us by saying, "We only had a wee lend of him. He was never ours to keep, and he needs to go home now to his own mother and father where he belongs."

I just didn't want to give him back, as it really did feel like he was ours. He was our wee pot of jam and it was just too hard to let him go.

We knew about people not returning home just like we had known about people being admitted to mad hospitals like Stradreagh Hospital – it wasn't easy to get them back out again and some of them never returned home.

The night that Mamai had gone missing, we were all looking out of the window, scanning the view for a glimpse of her and getting restless, yet unable to confide in each other about our worry because that would have made it too real. There was a sense that if we didn't talk about it then it didn't exist.

"Right that's it. I'm going out to look for her. Liam, you come with me, Caroline and Donna look after the wanes," Tommy tried to say with some sense of calmness.

"I'm coming too," I instantly responded, as though I had been under starter's orders and unable to tolerate it a minute longer. I grabbed at my jellybean plastic sandals and frantically fastened them on to my feet.

"Donna, you watch the weans," I said, as I felt guiltily aware that I was running out on her and her only nine years old.

Donna was pulling me back into the house by my cardigan, crying that I should stay and that she wanted to come too. But I broke free and Donna wisely but fearfully managed not to run after us, knowing that she needed to stay for the three youngsters because she was one of 'the four big' uns'.

I ran after Tommy and Liam, who kept chasing me back home. They weren't going to tell me what to do I thought, and I was big enough at ten years of age to go searching for my own mother. We thought that she might be in the chapel but she wasn't. We went to Granny's – she wasn't there. She wasn't in Mrs. Campbell's house, and she wasn't walking the streets of Creggan. It was getting darker outside, and I was struck by the warm bright lights, which lit up St. Mary's Secondary School. Something was going on in there because the school was never lit up at night. This was going to be my next school, the one that I would be going to the following September, and it held as much promise and anticipation for me, as it did anxiety and worry that I wouldn't be smart enough. As we passed the school, and turned down into Broadway, I could see tears in Tommy's eyes, and my heart banged and thumped in my chest, as his eyes confirmed what I didn't want to think about... that he was afraid, that I too was afraid.

The three of us were now walking quickly, all trying to keep up with each other, and as the panic walked with us, we shared a knowing through what was unspoken. We were on the homeward bound without our mother and no sign of her.

"It's all his fault... he has driven her to this," Tommy finally confessed.

"I hate him!" He dared to add out loud but in a voice no more than a whisper, as if afraid that the words themselves would run back into his mouth and cut the tongue out of him.

"No it's not his fault." Liam fearfully and tentatively tripped over his words and blurted out, "He's sick and the sickness runs in the family and if your father gets it, the sons can get it too, I could get it... even!"

Liam by now was walking as fast, as he had been talking, and I was trying hard to keep up with him.

"Its schizophrenia, that's what he's got," I urgently made a contribution to the conversation. This was the first time that the word had been mentioned between us and the first time it had passed the secrecy of my own lips in public, and my stomach turned in relief and dread.

"How do you know, who told you that?" Liam shouted at me. "You shut up you wee bitch, you're too young to understand."

"Get lost you big brute," I feebly responded, fearful of the conversation because we had never before acknowledged 'it' to one another and a bit shocked too because Liam and I were close friends at the time so how come we were getting into an argument.

Liam then kicked me and pulled my hair, "You shut up and get lost you mad bitch."

By now, I was screaming and crying out. Liam's physical attacks, our joined-up thinking, and the talk of madness seeped into me and it all hurt too much. I was furious that Tommy didn't seem to want to stop Liam or to protect me from the attacks, and I was crying out loud for Mamai. Now scraping in the street, we were outside a house, which had a huge black ribbon on the door and lots of people milling about. A man appeared at the front doorway and shouted at me.

"You wee tinker. Do you not have any respect, crying there like some mad banshee? There's a man lying in here dead and can't even get any peace at his own wake. Get to blazes off home."

"But he's kicking me and calling me names," I pleaded in my defence but the man had no sympathy.

"Catch yourself on you cheeky wee article, you should be ashamed of yourself, get home to blazes!" was his response.

Could that friggin' man not see my predicament? Why was it my entire fault? Why was I getting kicked and then told off into the bargain? Was it because schizophrenia runs in the family? Were Liam and Tommy punishing me because I wasn't a son who could get schizophrenia? Was it their way of emptying themselves of the illness, madness, unfairness, and fury, and then ramming it into me? Now I was full of dread and madness, and I wanted to empty somebody and myself. Now that Liam had dumped his flumen feelings into me, he could friggin' laugh at me rubbing salt into the wound. I was ready to explode!

And who did that man think he was trying to make me feel guilty for a dead man and the stupid 'ejit' was so stupid that he couldn't see that I was already 'effin ashamed of myself, and of being kicked and called names and ashamed that Mamai had walked out, and ashamed that we didn't know where Dadai was, and ashamed that Dadai had schizophrenia and that my five brothers might get it too, and that Donna, Mamai, and I were doomed to suffer the madness forever, and that we too might even get schizophrenia and that the whole world might find out about it.

That wee man was a stupid wee eejit and a pig and 'A get up the back' and 'a big effer' that needed emptying!

We arrived home to find our mother, taking off her scarf and coat. With sorrow and fondness in her tired and swollen eyes, she managed a weary smile when we told her that we had been out looking for her. Donna had done a great job. The weans were sound to the world in bed asleep and Mamai made a big plate of toast and a mug of cocoa for us four big 'uns before we took to our beds, our bellies full of the warm toast of our mother's return.

The warmth and relief was short lived as the events of the next day burned into my mind and branded into my memory forever. I was playing in the street with Sandra Cullen when Mamai urgently called me to come in home and to gather all the weans home for bed. I hated it when our friends teased, "You're wanted, for bed. You have to be in bed for six o clock!"

It was far too early, and only wee tiny youngsters should be in bed at that time but Pauline O'Hara, who couldn't help herself went on in a busy body tone, "Caroline, your mother told me to warn you to get home really, really quick – it's your bedtime!"

All seven of us arrived into the house and were told to go upstairs to our bedrooms. Father Carlin had arrived and there was Uncle Liam just approaching the house with Uncle Mickey, Mamai's brother in law. Seated at the top of the stairs listening to the commotion downstairs, we remained in silence. I sneaked down to see if I could hear anything about what was going on and could just make out through the bevelled glass door that Dadai was on the floor again rocking and shouting about his Dadai and about the 'B specials', and that he was crying on and off. Uncle Liam, the professor of physics and chemistry, six foot, two inches tall and as skinny as a beanpole, was having an obvious calming effect on Dadai, who had always been very fond of Liam and used to say about him, "Liam's got brilliant brains... enough brains to burn!"

Perhaps Uncle Liam with plenty of brains could, by some chemical-professor-type experiment, pass some of his mind into Dadai who was definitely losing his and now crying like a wee wean.

A loud bang at the front door added to the commotion, and my heart now in my throat was nearly choking me to death. I scarpered back up to the top of the stairs. Father Carlin came out and opened the door to a policeman and ambulance men who entered our hallway. They all had a quiet chat with Father Carlin who directs them towards the living room. Us weans were all still waiting and worrying at the top of the stairs frozen and quieter than we had ever been in our entire lives. My heart was practically jumping out of my chest as we heard Dadai screaming and cursing and lots of voices, saying, "Come on Johnnie, It's for your own good! Think of Margaret and your weans. You need the help."

Mamai was asked to sign a form but she didn't want to. "Could you not just give him something, to calm him down. I don't want him to have to go in to that place. I've managed him before and I'll manage him again. He wouldn't want it. He'll never forgive me if I sign him in."

"It's for his own good. He can't go on like this. Think of the weans, Margaret, and it's not good for them either. You have to sign it."

Sniffing back the tears, Mamai signed the form and the doctor told her that she had done the right thing because he would now get the help that he needed.

The commotion spilt out into the hall where the men and the policeman dragged Dadai out. I wanted to shout out, "Leave him alone, don't take him away, he's not bad. He's sick in the head, he's our Dadai."

But I couldn't, as I was dumbstruck with terror. Unable to bear to look, yet I couldn't manage not to look. By now, Dadai was sobbing like a wee infant and kicking out at whoever he could, "I'm not going to that fucking place!"

Floored by the weight of the ambulance men and policeman pinning him down, a big white contraption was put on Dadai, and his arms were all wrapped over him and tied at the back. Mamai was begging them not to hurt him and not to put the white jacket on him. He eventually calmed, and we all watched from the stairs as the fight drained out of him, and he was all tied up and carted out of the house into the ambulance outside. I slowly walked downstairs to the front door, my heart bleeding with pain for him.

Looking out to the street, my eyes sting with the sight of half the street, who had seemingly gathered around looking on. Two nosey parker women who had been standing right beside the ambulance comfortable as you like, as though they had bought tickets for the show, were watching intently and commenting as the events unfolded.

"Och, it's a terrible pity of him. He's away with the fairies."

"Aye that's right and look at them poor weans."

As both women turned and looked towards us in pity, I wanted to die of shame. Mamai stood at the gate at the top of our steps dressed in dignity and courage, and somehow seemed able to bare the humiliation. I wasn't sure if I could ever face the world again.

Gransha, the psychiatric hospital, was away out in the countryside. On Sundays, Mamai piled us all into the bus from Creggan down to the town and we would then set off over the Craigavan Bridge, which was the only way over the River Foyle and to Gransha Hospital on the Waterside, the Protestant side of the city. If Mamai had the money, we would get another bus from the city centre to the Waterside, which would drive us out into the hospital but often we had to walk what felt like endless miles in all kinds of weather.

The first time we went to visit Dadai in Gransha, I couldn't wait to tell him about my May altar that I had made in my bedroom where I was praying for him to the statue of Our Lady. Looking forward to sitting on his knee and him singing Carolina Moon kept me going until the visit. There were lots of houses dotted around the hospital site, which we came to know as the villas Beech, Oak, Larch, and Lime. Dadai was in Lime Villa. Mamai was invited to go in first while we waited in a room with glass windows all around. There was nothing for us to do so we wandered out into the fields to play in the grass.

It seemed to take forever until it was our turn to visit but finally Mamai appeared, looking concerned. She wondered if it might not be a good idea for us to visit because he still wasn't well. I refused to listen to what she was saying because I just had to see him and was feeling desperate by now. Tommy said he didn't want to go in; he would stay and watch the three weans. I pleaded with Mamai to let us go in so Mamai, Donna, Liam, and I were taken by a male nurse, who had a big bunch of keys hanging from his belt, through three sets of locked doors. We saw many strange and scary people making grunting animal noises, walking around with their clothes hanging off them. Some man spotting us came towards me. Saliva dribbling out of his mouth, he stuck his head right into my face. Quick as a flash, Mamai put her arms round my shoulder.

"Two lovely wee girls," the man managed to say, whilst chewing his tongue.

"Aye that's right son," Mamai said respectfully, putting an end to the verbal exchange, as she stood behind us, her arms extended across our shoulders.

"I want to go home now," said Donna, responding quickly to the tension and scary atmosphere but we had arrived at a room where Dadai would come to see us. We waited in silence, all huddled around Mamai and finally the door opened and an oul' man dragging his feet and dangling his arms by his side as though they didn't belong to him came into the room accompanied by a male nurse.

"When's Dadai coming?" I asked Mamai. Even though a part of me recognized this man, I didn't want to know him. He was not our Dadai – our Dadai didn't have white hair, his was black and curly. Our Dadai didn't walk as slow as an oul' man; our Dadai was a champion boxer. The oul' man slowly sat down facing us, his eyes glazed, his face puffed up, and through my tears, I could see my father's own face looking out of this oul' man's body. He slowly reached out his arm toward me and with eyes as dead as a doornail, he slurred my name and asked me what I was doing.

"I've made you a May altar… and… I say a prayer for…" I stopped, couldn't get the words out, and was desperately fighting back my tears. A May altar was doing no good. How was Merciful Mother Mary in heaven able to let our father end up trapped inside some oul' sick man's body? I could never sit on this oul' man's knee, this was not Dadai's knee. I turned back to look at Mamai.

Thank God for Mamai, she was there. She was always there, and Liam and Donna sat silently at either side of her. There was sorrow in Mamai's eyes that I'd never seen before: defeat, disappointment, and despair. The sorry silence was interrupted by a slurred and tongue chewed speech from the oul' man,

"Be… good… for … your Mamai," he said looking towards us, gazing through us, as though he were blind, and his knee shaking and jumping like a pneumatic drill. Whilst I was trying not to notice the bizarre tongue chewing, what I couldn't bear to swallow was that he had no teeth. What under God's heaven happened to his beautiful, straight white, perfect teeth?

He got up off the chair, dragged himself away, his hands now shaking and he's dribbling like the other scary, tongue chewing man, as the nurse who supported his arm slowly helped him out of his chair, and Dadai shuffled his way out of the room.

We sometimes visited during the week too and came to know that Dadai had been having ECT, some kind of electric shocks to his brain, which meant that for some reason, they had to pull out his teeth. As things improved for our father over the following months, I began to recognize him again, and he wasn't so dribbly and mad looking. We could then meet at the hospital canteen where we got lovely big cakes but sometimes we couldn't eat them because we had to put up with the mad people coming up to us, saying weird things, slavering all over us, asking us for our cakes and sticking their hands into our plates. Some woman grabbed Dadai's cigarette right out of his mouth and then rammed it into her own mouth and ate it.

"It's a terrible pity of her," Dadai said. "She's not right in the head!"

Yet it was good to see our parents sitting together talking more normally and laughing together.

Tommy hated going to the hospital and managed whenever he could to get out of it.

During one long hot walk to Gransha, Mamai, Donna, me, and the three weans were running out of steam feeling that the walk was never ending, mother whispered to me, "Your Aunt Joyce has invited us to go over to live with her in England so that we can have a better life away from all of this. What do you think Caroline, should we leave him and pack up and just go?"

Mamai had never before asked me my opinion about anything important, and I was shocked and excited and felt closer to her because of it, and I wanted to repay her confidence in me by giving the answer that I thought she wanted.

"Yes, let's go live in England. We can come back when he's better."

The thought of a better life in England was an injection of hope.

Mamai went on to say that Granny Murphy had told her that she needs to stand by Dadai no matter what happens, that she has to offer it up to the sacred heart and to the angels and saints.

Mamai sighed, "I suppose I've made my bed and I'll have to lie in it."

She shook physically at the thought and feeling of running away, and as we turned into the entrance of Gransha, her determination of standing by her man and his weans seemed to take hold.

Tommy and I started getting into fights with each other, as he assumed the role of 'the dadai' in the house, and although I was glad that he was there and a great help to Mamai being all sensible and all, I wasn't having him ordering me around because I was the eldest girl. So we ended up putting on the big fat red, boxing gloves, and fighting it out, and although he was two years older than me, I gave as good as I took.

Liam was in my corner coaching me and telling me how to swing a left hook and to keep my right hand over my face for protection. Liam and I were twins in my mind, and I could always rely on him to help me out if I got into scrapes in the street with my friends and I became more comfortable around the boys. Liam and I had become close, and he would let me join with his friends and their games of lassoes, trolleys and, Cowboys and Indians. With Liam's coaching, I became a good boxer but Tommy always seemed to become afraid to hit me too hard like the time I ended up with a bloody nose. He nearly broke his neck trying to make up to me by getting cotton wool and making me a piece of bread and jam and being my slave for a wee while in case I told Mamai of his misdemeanour.

We all scrapped with each other on and off but there were also obvious closeness too. We gave each other nicknames that became both a source of irritation and endearment. Tommy was called Tomato Face because he would easily flush red with embarrassment. We tried to name Liam Freckle Face because he was blessed with a healthy splattering of dark freckles but the name didn't stick so he became known as Leaky. My name was Cat Woman, and if anyone called it to me, I felt like ripping their heads off. Donna was called Ducksy, Sean was Festus, Mark was Mo or Horr, and David Dixie. The nicknames were exclusive to our family, and only the boys seemed to have theirs known outside of the family. If anyone came knocking at our door asking for Leaky or Horr, then Mamai would tell them that there was no one here by that name and they weren't to come back to our door until they were able to ask for the person who had been christened with a proper name.

But we four big 'uns had to help out and give Mamai a hand now that Dadai was in Gransha. Donna and I had the job of cleaning and washing up, and we hated cleaning the boys' bedrooms because they were full of comics, which we flushed out from under their beds with a load of smelly socks and sling shots and a very particular 'smell of boys'... not pleasant!

Tommy and Liam had the job of getting the coal and lighting the fire and doing any heavy work. But I wanted to light the fire so after a while, Tommy swapped jobs with me; he would do the washing up if I would light the fire. It was a deal. Tommy confided in me that he had been having nightmares about the fireplace and described his dream ...

"The house is usually deathly quiet but I can hear Liam, Mark, Sean, and David running mad outside in the garden. I have to clean out the fire and set it with newspapers and sticks. I look towards the black hole of the fireplace in the middle of the room and slowly walk towards it, unable to take my eyes off it for a tiny minute. I hate the friggin' job of lighting the fire but it has to be done, and I want to run away from it but something is drawing me towards the black hole. I take a wee slow look into the hearth and have a good look into the grate and thank God everything seems okay, so then I get on with the job and stick my hand into the grate to dig out the ashes when my hand starts shaking like a leaf. Jesus aaaaaaaagh!... a fuckin' oul' woman's hand comes shooting down the chimney. Out of the blackness, grabs me around the wrists and pulls me up the friggin' chimney!"

Tommy explained how he usually woke up at this point and was unable to sleep for the rest of the night. He continued to have the dream on and off for many years, especially disturbed that the hand belonged to an old woman. I tried hard not to be scared about the fire myself but spent many a time trying to work out what the dream was all about and wondered why my big brother, who was so sensible and clever, had suddenly become fearful of lighting the fire. I told him not to worry since I was the eldest girl in the house, I would always give him a hand with the jobs. Soon enough though, lighting the fire and keeping warm wasn't the only thing to be frightened about.

An unfamiliar knock came to our door one day and I was keen to answer it as from our bay window, I'd seen a very well-dressed man and woman arrive and the woman was carrying a real attaché case. I shouted for Mamai who arrived from the kitchen to the hallway fixing at her hair and hurriedly removing her apron. The couple introduced themselves, saying something about Child Welfare and asked if they could speak to my mother in private. I returned to the kitchen where Mamai and me had been preparing a stew for teatime and wondered what it was all about.

Mamai had been in there having a talk for a very long time when the kitchen door opened and I could see that Mamai's eyes were red. The couple had a look round the house and soon disappeared. Not another word was said about it, and I was afraid to ask because Mamai was awfully quiet for the rest of the day and kept blowing her nose into her handkerchief. Many years later, I overheard Mamai telling her friend that someone from our street had reported my mother to the welfare agencies and that the couple who had arrived that day had come to investigate if we were being properly looked after.

Chapter 6
THE COLDEST CHRISTMAS

CHRISTMAS was just around the corner, and I was ten years old. As I watched from my bedroom window, I could see our neighbours getting off the bus and arriving home with big bags of shopping: Christmas trees, Christmas decorations, and lots of parcels. I wondered what Christmas would be like for them and about what went on beyond their private closed front doors. In our street, most of the families' fathers had a job and some of the mothers had jobs too, which meant that they could afford Christmas. I could see them bringing Christmas home in their shopping bags and knew that there was no sign of Christmas arriving in our house. When my dadai had been in work and not away with the fairies, Christmas past had always been one of the happiest and most magical times in our lives. Our parents helped us write the letters well in advance of the big day and then ceremoniously they were posted up the chimney to Santa.

This Christmas was a different matter altogether with the troubles in the streets and the shops in the town centre getting bombed and Dadai losing his mind. I wasn't feeling too confident that we'd be having a good one – or having one at all. The run up to Christmas's past were full of excitement because Mamai had to start planning the previous summer as she tried hard to ensure that we all got what we wanted.

The 'Rickety Wheel' was a wheel of fortune renamed by the community, as the big wobbly and worn wheel made such a klickety klick sound. The Christmas Creggan Parish Fair happened down at the Beachwood Parochial Community Centre and ran in the months leading up to Christmas. What I didn't know then was that it was an initiative organized by the parish priests with the aim of helping the less well off in the community. Toys, food hampers, and clothes could be won in the wheel of fortune rather than given as charity, which would not have been as gratefully received by the kind of salt of the earth people, whose character seemed stitched together by pride when poverty had been ripping at the seams of their family life. Mamai never failed to win a sack full of prizes, which became our presents. For mother, the Rickety Wheel was a godsend and she would come to rely on arriving home with Christmas sacks full of biscuits, hampers, and secreted toys, as well as our Christmas turkey. Dadai, when he was around, hung the bird up in the bathroom where it would be kept cool, but every time we entered the bathroom, I was tempted to squeamishly inspect the dead critter, attempting to pull its feathers off. Mamai was so proud of its weight and announced to friends and neighbours, "Even bigger again this year, sixteen pounds," as though she had just given birth to it. The turkey was often so big and fat that Dadai had to flatten it to make it fit into the oven.

Father Carlin would call round for a cup of tea and a wee bit of something to eat. "Margaret, I hear you had a great win again this year. I hear it was twenty pounds," he would say sucking at his pipe and scrounging around for some freshly baked scones in the kitchen. Mamai would give him a feed of scone bread with a big knob of butter on the top."Well nearly Father. Twenty pounds next year, that's the plan because they are all growing that much. It is beyond feeding 'the five thousand.'"

"Well Margaret, knowing you, they'll never starve. Should you have to beg, steal, or borrow, your weans will never know what it is to not have Christmas."

"Well you're not wrong, Father. As long as I have a tongue in my head, I'll never be afraid to ask, because if ye never ask ye never get."

It was one of her best known sayings often activated out of sheer frustration with any of us when we didn't or couldn't speak up for something. Given that we had tongues in our heads, there should never be anything stopping us speaking up for what we needed, wanted, or for what we thought was right. This however was an idea that didn't seem to apply when challenging our mother, who seemingly was exempt from the rule, and she would warn us that she would cut the tongue out of us if we talked back to her.

I remembered that on the Christmas just before Dadai really lost his mind, we were all practically swinging from the ceiling light shade with excitement. The usual routine was to have our baths on the night before, Dadai polish whatever shoes needed polishing, placing them with any new shoes at the foot of the Christmas tree; all in a row, and each pair was placed beside a pile of new clothes for each of us to wear for

Mass on Christmas morning. In my new Christmas pyjamas, I stared into the flames of the turf fire and sniffed up the comforting smoky smells that were now mixed with aroma of turkey roasting and Dadai's piped condor tobacco, which he always smoked at Christmas. Mamai and Dadai started cooking Christmas Eve, although the Christmas cake, of course, had been on the go for months.

We hung up our own socks and stockings along the mantelpiece, and they were held in place by the heavy brass ornaments that Dadai had taught us to clean to perfection, so they glistened and shone like pieces of gold. Donna and I tried to be clever by hanging our best pair of woolly tights up there on the mantelpiece with the five pairs of boy's socks so that we would get two long legs of goodies. On this Christmas Eve, we watched White Christmas with Bing Crosby on TV and then all up to bed. Together, we knelt down as a family and ended our prayers with,

"Angel of God, my Guardian Dear, to whom God's love commits us here, ever this night, be at my side, to light and guard and rule and guide. Amen."

This prayer helped us all to let go of the day and up to bed. We all got a kiss and a hug and then Mamai and Dadai shouted as we ascended the stairs, "Nightie, Nightie."

And we replied in unison in the Owens ritual, "Pyjama, pyjama!"

This particular Christmas was too much for Donna and I, and we just couldn't sleep. We had been a wee bit unsure about the whole Santa thing. Was he real? We wanted him to be but the facts of his existence and his ability to get around the world's children in one night, stood some questioning. We tried hard not to think ourselves out of the excitement. It must have been about four in the morning, and I heard bells ringing in the sky outside. I leapt up to the window and there with my own two eyes, I saw the sleigh, Santa, reindeers, the lot. I woke Donna and told her to get up to the window quickly to see it.

"Look, look, quick, can you see? Can you hear the bells?"

"I see it! I hear them, he's coming, he's coming," and again, Donna's sighting was confirmation and I knew that Santa was real!

Just then Mamai burst into our bedroom in her nightie, her hair in rollers and hair net, scolding us severely for making so much noise as we might wake the weans.

"Mamai, come on in quick, look out! Santa is in the sky, we saw him, and we heard the bells," I whispered.

Mamai came to the window, "Well there you are. Not many weans get to see the real Santa in the sky on Christmas Eve and you two have because you have been so good. Now you know that he can't come in until you are all fast asleep."

With that, she lay down beside us and sang us to sleep with a verse of "Away in a Manger".

Nearly everything we'd requested from Santa had arrived just placed by our pile of clothes under the tree. We took great delight in eagerly finding out what we all had received.

"What did you get? Look what I got."

Mamai and Dadai's bedroom was invaded in the morning, as we ran in and climbed up onto their bed to show them what we got. Our parents played along and inquired with surprise and disbelief about what Santa had brought.

I got my much wished for Cowgirl outfit, with guns and holster and fabulous cowboy hat, and I thought that I was Doris Day. I also got a wee post office set and the much-longed for 'Touch Tapestry' where I spent many an hour bringing to life a horse's head – I was in heaven! Amongst Donna's presents was a much-anticipated toy grand piano from which we quickly plinked out tunes. The boys, who tried to pretend that they weren't interested in them, cosseted our beautiful magical kaleidoscopes. I got my blonde doll and Donna got her black haired one, and we had enough selection boxes to keep us going through the winter - well at least for the next week. Our stockings were filled with fruit and wee handmade gifts that Mamai and Dadai had individually wrapped. Tommy got a scientist set, and Liam got a magician's set with cloak and wand. The biggest blue and white Teddy bear was for David and was quickly named Raymond who became a part of the family and had to be factored into all domestic arrangements and plans, and was eventually battered and bruised by the bigger boys so much that it's stuffing burst out of its skin. Mamai had to sew a zip on to its back so that she could refill it with old socks and tights when it was looking particularly pummelled.

Well that was Christmas past, and this one was a whole different story as the stuffing was thoroughly knocked out of it because Dadai was away with the fairies. Christmas in our home had never been so grey, cold, or empty. There was no money coming in, and Mamai seemed to spend most of her waking hours down at the benefit and housing offices because the upstairs bedrooms were showing up damp on the walls. We didn't have a telephone so Mamai would have to go down town to the housing office, forever sitting, waiting, and hoping in long queues for emergency payments or to speak to someone about the damp. And at times she would take us all down with her so that they could see how many mouths she had to feed but we were there half the day because it seemed as though the other half of Derry was in there too, waiting for the same thing.

Time was running out, and it was two days before Christmas and no sign of the giro payment from the benefits office. Mamai was going out of her mind with not knowing what to do so she set about salvaging what she could of our old toys, and made new clothes for our dolls and repainted some of the old wooden toys for the boys. New covers and pillowcases were made for our dolls' cradles but I was aware that she was running out of steam, and although she managed to do what she could to get us our Christmas clothes, this year they were mostly from the St. Vincent De Paul Charity Shop where she and I went rifling through the mountains of used clothes until we got something for everyone.

I needed a new coat and shoes but nothing was to be found for me so off we went in the rain and sleet down to Aunt Rose's house. Well she was not really our aunt but had always been a close friend of Dadai's parents and we had always known her as our aunt. Rose was a tiny wee woman who looked like a foreigner with her jet-black hair and swarthy skin, and she lived down town in the Bogside, which was just on the edge of the town centre. Apparently, she only had half a stomach, and spent at least a few days a week in bed throwing up and was right as rain the other days when she was full of life.

Having arrived at Rose's house, she made us some tea and cake, took me into her bedroom opened her wardrobe, and invited me to try on whatever clothes and shoes I fancied. I came away with a red woollen trouser suit and a pair of very ill-fitting shoes, and this was to be my Christmas outfit this year. I tried to be pleased but couldn't help think that everyone would know that I was wearing an old sick woman's clothes, and I began to feel a wee bit sick myself at the thought of my friends Sandra and Kitty seeing me in the outfit and asking me where we had bought it. Perhaps I could get away from the shame if I told a lie that they had been bought from the Freeman's catalogue. That's what I would do, and then I would confess my sin in confession and do my penance, which was a better option than telling the shameful truth.

By now Mamai was frantic because she knew that we would barely have enough money to see us through as bills needed to be paid, weans needed to be fed, and Christmas still needed to be bought. I'd had enough of the whole poor and sorry shenanigans' and stuck my head in what I'd thought was a nice warm Christmas book, 'Little Women' and wrapped myself up in the warm story of the American March family who had become poor at Christmas time as their father had gone off to war. The family of four girls and their mother were left to depend on each other and on their friends and neighbours for support when they had suddenly found themselves poor.

I didn't know who we could depend on except ourselves, and I was sick of being depended upon so I climbed into my book and up into the loft space in my mind to hide away from the fact that we couldn't afford a Christmas. I could only manage brief intervals of my chocolate box Christmas March family story because one way or another, I was called back to the harsh reality of my own family life.

A few days before Christmas, when I was being carried away by the story of Little Women, Mamai told me to put on my anorak as she and I were going down to the town centre to see a priest about a message. I quickly placed my red ribbon between the pages of my book so that I could return easily to the right page. It was raining ice when we stepped out into the street and the grey freezing sleet was burning my face as we hurried down town to the very posh Queen Street where the priest lived. It wasn't until we arrived at the door that I became aware of what we were doing.

In hushed tones, Mamai was explaining that Dadai was in hospital and that the benefits hadn't come through. I wanted to scream my head off with shame. I was affronted. I couldn't bear to hear the words coming out of her mouth and what made it worse was that the priest then asked us to wait there on the step and he closed the door leaving us standing outside. Mamai put her arms around me, and we stood there in the freezing blustery cold not uttering a word. I had no words in me that could say what it meant to witness my mother ask for money. Eventually the priest opened the door with a white blank face that wasn't smiling: the kind of face that looked like nobody was inside, an empty face. He handed Mamai an envelope, and she thanked him gratefully.

When the envelope had been opened on that cold step, I saw by the expression on mother's face that the envelope did contain something but not as much as she had hoped for. I had decided that I would rather have starved than go asking the stupid, empty priest for money. Mamai sighed, held her head high, and off we went out into the rotten weather to buy some bits and pieces to go towards Christmas morning.

Full up with feelings of emptiness, I was weighed down with the hating feeling of being poor and upon our return home that day, I found it almost unbearable to return to my book. That friggin' March family was another universe away from my own. How could I have allowed myself to think that I could escape this stinking Christmas in this bloody town by turning to such a sugary American story? How come the March's could have such a beautiful kind of sweet poverty whilst ours was so bloody bitter and ugly? In desperate frustration, I conjured up thoughts about us winning 'The Pools' or of us receiving some magical windfall.

Donna and I set up a wee shop outside of our garden gate and we tried to sell off our little trinkets and unwanted and old toys. I quietly placed my precious jewellery box that my godmother had bought me beside the rest of our wares and fought with myself about whether I wanted it to fetch a good price or if I just couldn't part with it. When my friend Kitty appeared with her pocket money and offered me a shilling, the decision was made, and I watched as my most precious little box was carried away. Donna and I made about two shillings and six pence but we knew that it was not enough but it was a start. I lay in bed that night torturing myself with thoughts about how we could manage to have a Christmas. I had visions of my mother in tears, an empty larder, no toys, and our house being closed for Christmas, and I could see the March family, where Jo the writer plots to secretly sell her hair to make money for her mother. The red velvet colours of Christmas and the March family were seemingly a sign that I, just like Jo, could sell my hair.

It was the day before Christmas Eve. Mamai was busy downstairs in the kitchen, and I crept into my mother's bedroom and sat in front of her dressing table staring intently without blinking at myself in the mirror until my eyes were dry, and I could see the face of Jo March from Little Woman looking back out at me.

"Christmas won't be Christmas without any presents," she whispered, smiling, as she nodded her head towards me and then towards the scissors.

In a hypnotic trance, I lifted the dressmaking scissors in one hand and in the other, I had bunched my long hair into a long ponytail and mindlessly cut through my hair, which was immediately detached from my head. There it was, a bunch of long thick hair just sitting in a fist in my hand like a bunch of dead daffodils. Gazing back into the mirror expecting to see Jo's reassuring smile, I could only see my own disappointed reflection staring back. There was no Jo, just some wee freckle-faced, nine-year-old girl with a hair do that looked like it belonged to a poor orphan wean. I thought I must have lost my mind, as well as my hair because I was a sorry sight. What would my mother say? She might kill me. I would have to sell this dead bunch of hair as soon as possible. Mamai's blonde wig was sitting on the dressing table and quickly I grabbed it and put it on my head. The improvement in my looks was slight but having no time to ponder what I'd done, I ran downstairs, out the front door, and down to the hairdressers at Beachwood shops where me mamai would go for her shampoo and set. Maureen the hairdresser looked at me and smiled, "Great hairdo, Caroline! Are ye wanting to make an appointment for yer mamai or for yerself?"

"No. How much would ye give me for this?" I said, sticking out my hand towards her and presenting the hair as if it didn't belong to me. I couldn't bear to look at it even though the hairdresser and the women sitting under the dryers were all looking directly at my dead ponytail.

"Dear God, love. Is that yer own hair?"

"Aye, I was wondering if ye wanted to buy it off me."

I could see by her face that she didn't know whether to laugh or cry and that she definitely didn't want to buy my hair.

The two women sitting under the hair dryers rummaged in their bags, dug out their purses, and asked me if I would run a wee message for them and they would pay me a tanner. Trying not to look at the image of myself with the blonde wig in the mirror facing me, I agreed to go the message and waited for the answer about my hair.

"Well, I didn't really need any hair but I could buy it off you if I can afford it. How much were you looking to get for it?"

"Well I don't know, but I was hoping to buy Christmas presents with it."

I couldn't bear to say that it was because there might not be a Christmas in our house if we couldn't bring in some money. The reluctant hairdresser opened her cash register and handed me two shillings. I had also earned one shilling and sixpence from the women for running the message for them so added to the proceeds from our wee sale of trinkets we had raised five shillings. I wasn't sure if it would make much of a difference but I would wrap it up in my lace handkerchief and give it to my mother so that she could buy some things for Christmas.

"Dear God," I soon worried. "How was I going to tell Mamai about my hair?"

I would just wear the wig until the time was right.

We all sat around the kitchen table at teatime and Mamai urged me, "For God's sake, will ye take that wig off, ye look like nobody's child."

How the flumen heck was I going to take it off? I couldn't stand the whole business of sitting at the table with everyone looking at me, and my head now itching like mad and sweating. Mamai had told me again for the third time to remove the wig when Liam reached over and pulled it off my head. Everyone sat looking in shock and silence at first. Mark looked like he was going to cry, and Tommy and Liam screeched with laughter. David and Donna were dumbstruck looking towards me, and then straight back at Mamai, awaiting her reaction. Mamai almost fainted. "What in the mother of God happened to ye, where's yer hair? Sweet God in heaven, spare me this day."

I handed me mamai the handkerchief. This was nothing like how it turned out in the story of 'Little Women'. Mamai went off her head. Having given her something else to worry about, she marched me down to the hairdressers to have it tidied up, and I don't know how much that she paid for that.

Thank God, Mamai had won the biggest turkey ever this year; it must have been at least twenty pounds in weight. It was the size of a small pig, and it was safe in the Parochial House Pantry until Christmas Eve. But there was a funny smell on Christmas morning when the turkey was in our oven. Mamai ran to the oven opened the door and fell to her knees, "Caroline, the turkey is off! Sweet mother of God what are we going to do?"

Back down to the Parochial House we marched and Mamai explained that the turkey that she had collected from her winnings only yesterday was only fit for the bin, and Father Carlin who, seemingly mortified about the whole carry on, exchanged it for a great big cooked duck and our dinner was saved... just.

But I wasn't so sure about who was going to save Ireland because it surely needed saving. The British Army had been stationed in cities and towns across the north of Ireland and serious rioting was seemingly relentless. The Bogside in Derry city featured daily on the news where God only knew who was blowing up the shops and cafes. I recognized something odd within myself about witnessing all of this drama on TV; it was a sense of terror but excitement too and perversely, it became a happy distraction from thinking about family troubles. Whilst Derry City was being slaughtered, I didn't have to dwell on the fear, frustrations, and shame of what was going on in our family life. Our streets were being hacked to pieces, and our city shopping centre looked like a mouth full of decaying teeth, showing intermittent black cavities where there was once a row of shiny shops. The rioting was also heavy now in nearby towns and cities, Dungivan, Dungannon, and Belfast, where it was reported that the British Army had shot dead eight people – the first policeman in the troubles was shot by the UVF and two civilians were shot dead. Bombs exploding here, there, and every friggin' where, and the British Army had been firing CS gas on the rioters and establishing curfews, which meant that we were trapped in our homes at night, just like in the war films. Well if schizophrenia and the shame of not having the price of Christmas would not be the death of us, then the bloody war on the streets surely would.

Chapter 7
THE WORLD HAS GONE MAD

IT was 1970, and the year that Granny Murphy died. I was ten years old and didn't want to look at her in the coffin because I didn't want any more nightmares like the ones I had when Granda Murphy died. Mamai encouraged us that by saying a wee prayer for Granny at the side of the coffin and saying a wee cheerio whilst touching her hand, then she would rest in peace and would not visit us in our dreams.

"It's not the dead ye need to fear – it's the living," she said.

Right enough, I thought because I had been a good bit afraid of Granny when she was alive. She was nearly always stern and strict and fed-up looking. Great at feeding us a Sunday dinner and plates of Derry stew – minced beef rolled up in balls with carrots, onions all stewed together with potatoes and a couple of Oxo cubes – it was so thick and heavy that it could have been used as cement but it was delicious. Despite her ability to make us a good feed though, when she was alive, Granny created a feeling of tension in me. She would often barge, "Hould your whisht!", which apparently meant "be quiet or to stop complaining. " Granny often appeared sad and distant, and I had more fond memories of my grandfather's smiley face when he returned home after a long hard day's work in the gas yard.

Lots of people came to Granny's wake and said nice things about her. Mrs. McCool was blowing her nose into her handkerchief and then sticking the wee frilly handkerchief up her sleeve. "Och, sure she was an angel of mercy. Sure if she couldn't do a good turn, she wouldn't do a turn at all."

"Aye that's right enough, when they made her they broke the mould. There will never be another Cissy Murphy," said Maryanne Kivelehan, folding her arms in under her great big breasts the size of two soldiers helmets, and I found myself scanning all the women's breasts, as I served the sandwiches around, comparing and contrasting the different shapes and sizes of breasts and wondering what size mine were going to be. Hopefully, mine wouldn't be too big because I didn't want everybody looking at them and anyway they would probably just get in the way. Mamai's breasts were just right, medium sized. I wanted mine to be medium not like Granny Murphy's, whose breasts were long and droopy, and I could only dare to think it to myself now that she was dead.

But I should never think ill of the dead, 'cos that's what the women said as they talked of how Cissy Murphy delivered many a neighbour's wean into the world and that she was the one whom they relied upon if there was a death. Apparently, Granny was often called upon when someone in the community had passed away. The women talked of how Granny was amongst the few women in the town who could give the corpse a bath and lay it out clean and fresh from the soils of life in readiness for the holy souls that would come and take the spirit of the dead person away. I hoped to God that I would never have to do such a job.

Mamai wasn't herself for a wee long while after losing her own mother but with the women in the street now turning to her to do the delivering of babies and the boil removals and the dead washing, it was as though she herself had brought Granny back to life... by becoming her! And so, it seemed like my own mother was disappearing and Granny Murphy was never far away.

"You never know what you've got till it's gone," that's what my mother lamented many a time, and she often sang about a mother's love but I couldn't bear to listen because I was reminded of the possibility that I might lose my own mother, and I longed for the relief that would come when she might say again, "There's nothing else for it, we just have to get up and batter on."

Mamai got renewed life and seemed to come back to herself when she made arrangements to have our Great Aunt Eileen discharged from the asylum to come and live with us. Where would we put her given that our house was already bursting at the seams? On account of our visits to Eileen at the asylum, there was no question of us not making room for her in our house because the relief was mighty that she would not be left to rot in that mad place.

Eileen was like a wee child herself and was happy as Larry, as long as she had a few fags in her handbag, a bag of sweets, and a few bob in her purse.

Donna and I were especially happy because Eileen always used to fight to do the washing up and she went berserk if anyone touched her pots and pans or if anyone tried to do her jobs in the house. Sometimes we'd tease her by hiding pans and dishes, and she'd tear the house apart until she found and returned it to the rightful place. We weren't so happy though, that we had to share our double bed with her, as she was awake half the night with her smoker's cough. Mamai was as kind and patient with her as if she was a wee infant, and Donna and I had to help with bathing and dressing her, as she was keen that Eileen learnt how to do the things for herself. Often Eileen arrived downstairs with her clothes outside in, back to front, and some piece of underwear sticking like a big lump out from her dark tan tights.

"Margaret, take a wee look at me. Am I nice?" she'd ask.

"You are beautiful, Eileen but I think you got a wee bit mixed up," said Mamai, trying not to laugh.

Yet we all loved Eileen, and even the neighbours who got to know her brought her bags of sweets and cigarettes. Eileen was a wee doddery woman who tilted from side to side when she walked and even if she was standing, she rocked this way and that way. How she loved her own hair and sometimes she and Mamai went to the hairdressers for a shampoo and set. Eileen told tall tales and some horror stories about what went on in 'the hospital'. She talked of nurses tying people to chairs and locking them in cupboards. We couldn't work out what was fact and what was fiction but guessed that it was a wee bit of both. Anytime my friend Moya called in for me, Eileen would run and call out with excitement that Maude was here. Maude Gurley had been an old friend of Eileen's in the hospital, and Eileen seemed convinced that Moya was her so she used to sit and carry on conversations with Moya as though she was talking to Maude. Moya enjoyed Eileen so much that she just played along. So Moya became renamed by our family and was forever affectionately referred to as Maude.

Dadai's visits home were few and far between until eventually he could come home for weekends and Sundays. I came to understand something about mixed blessings because we loved having him back home but we had to go through the rotten business of saying cheerio and of watching him struggle to leave as though he were going to prison. Being sick in the head meant that nobody seemed to talk about the illness. Nobody ever seemed to say, "Yes Margaret, how are ye keeping, and how's Johnnie's wee touch of schizophrenia, any better?

No, I never ever heard anyone say the sickening word out loud; it was only whispered as though the sickness was a crime. Dadai may as well have set fire to the cathedral and burned all the holy statues to a crisp for all the sense of offence and shame attached to the wretched thing. Yet life at home without him became familiar and in some ways, it was easier because we had a good routine and Mamai wasn't all the time worrying about where Dadai was, or what he was going to do next or if he was going to be carried home in a drunken mess.

When the Family Assistance was sorted and my mother could come to expect her giro to arrive on the same day each week, we could rely on food on the table. Mondays, Wednesdays, and Fridays were baking days. We came home from school to the bread smells like a magnet sucking us from the street into the house and into the kitchen. Along the kitchen counter were big treacle, current, and plain scone loaves resting against the wall and wrapped in tea towels. We fought over who would get the heels (the crusty ends of the loaf), and our mouths watered as big knobs of butter melted into the still warm bread sometimes topped with homemade rhubarb or blackcurrant jam. We were blessed, as we had as much to eat as we could manage.

The house was always immaculate as Mamai prided herself on our bellies being full, the house and weans washed and clean, and contented to have enough money to pay Vinny the rent man, Jimmy the spud man, Harry the milk man, Charlie the bread man, Willie the coal man, the bald headed Provident man (money lender), Teddy the turf man, and the Cavindish man (furniture store), not forgetting the egg woman with no name and, sometimes Mr. Thompson, the Maine man (lemonade man). The fresh herring man always called on a Friday, and Mamai would run out to his van with a plate and have the plate filled with fresh fish... Dadai's favourite. The ragman would come less often but would give us a load of balloons, and Mamai could choose some wee ornament or piece of crockery in exchange for a bag of old clothes. The ragman always came with his horse and trap, and it was a mixed blessing for Tommy and Liam because although they loved the balloons, they weren't too keen on having to follow the ragman around Creggan with a shovel and bucket, collecting the horse dung for Dadai's rose garden.

Mamai was a skilled chancellor of our exchequer as she was brilliant at managing what money she had: child benefit for seven wanes and some incapacity benefit for Dadai didn't go very far. She was able to plan her outgoings in relation to the income and had payments down to every penny, as she became skilled in the art of robbing Peter to pay

Paul. A drawer in the dining room housed the various books in which the collector would make an entry showing payment or non-payment. I was acutely either comforted or irritated by the entries; a tick indicating 'paid' and I was comforted. A forward slash indicating no payment, and I was immediately anxious.

At weekends, a steady stream of money collectors knocked at the door, sometimes greeted by one of us saying, "Me mamai said she isn't in. Could you call back next week, and she'll give you two weeks next week?"

"When will she be home?" we would be asked.

"Mamai, when will you be back home, he wants to know?" Mark would call out to Mamai in temporary hiding in the kitchen.

The collector knowingly would sometimes smile and then walk away, shaking his head in frustration, as though he'd heard it a thousand times before and had been given various versions of this on his travels around Creggan.

There was a sense that if they were giving us the loan or delivering the goods then they were the good fairies but when they came to collect the money, they were the robbers who we had to hide from or face with the bad news of no money this week.

Ordinary anxieties about the week's finances were flattened by bigger worries about a war. I was approaching ten years old and life in our family and in the Creggan Estate was to change forever. The troubles were well underway, and I couldn't for the life of me work out who was fighting whom and who were the goodies and who were the baddies. As a young child, I had thought that God was 'the goodie' and that The Devil was 'the baddie'... it was that simple. Then when I got a wee bit older, Cowboys were goodies and Red Indians were baddies but as I watched Cowboys and Indians on the Sunday film matinees, I was a bit confused because it looked like the Indians were having their land taken away from them and they were considered the baddies because they fought back. I just for the life of me couldn't understand it.

Then as our real life war came wrecking through our streets and banging on our doors, I couldn't figure out who was fighting who and who was who. I thought that the Catholics were the goodies and the Protestants the baddies. The 'B specials' and 'Fenians' were the baddies because both words were usually sandwiched between the words 'Fuckin' and 'Bastard' – "fuckin B Special Bastard" and "Fuckin' Fenian

Bastard." Fenian was I word I never learned at school and it was a real was a puzzle too. Given that I just didn't know the word Fenian, I had heard it as 'Venian' like the venial sin. So in my confusion a 'Fenian bastard' was a 'Venial bastard'. Now, a venial sin was a small sin compared to the much more serious and bigger 'mortal sin'. So I had put two and two together and deduced that the 'Venian bastard' might not be as bad as the 'B Special', which was 'especially' bad because it was the B Specials who started these troubles in 1969 by barging into the home of a Catholic called Sammy Daveny and battering him to death in front of his family. But it was still far too confusing and I would get mixed up and refer to 'Fenian sins' and it took me a good while to realize that the Catholics were the 'Fenian bastards' and although I didn't know then that the name Fenian although having originated from Irish mythology and referred to a band of men who protected Ireland from assault or attack, it became associated with Irish nationalism and was generally used as a sectarian insult about Catholics.

The Orangemen too were the baddies and the civil rights marchers the goodies; the red-white and blue was bad, and the green, white, and gold was good; the Prods were baddies and the Taigs, the goodies. Then the Provos were the goodies and the Stickies were the baddies, and they were the same gang, as the Provisional IRA who were supposed to be the goodies and the Official IRA were worse so Baddies. Then the Derry IRA was good and the Belfast IRA was bad. The UVF – Ulster Volunteer Force, UFF – Ulster Freedom Fighters, the UDA – Ulster Defence Association, which were all Protestant paramilitary organizations, and anything beginning with U generally represented the baddies because it referred to an allegiance to Ulster, and only Protestants talked about or referred to Ulster. But as a young child, it was far too hard to work out and it just became a string of letters like a kind of code that was to do with war. I didn't know who was whom and what was what and who I was supposed to be supporting and who I was supposed to be against and how many gangs of people were fighting us. Then there was the British Army whom I thought were the goodies but then realized that they had for many years tried to take Ireland away from the Irish and that it was something to do with a potato famine in Ireland many moons before.

As young children, we didn't have a clue but we all just had to grow into the stories like a hand me down outfit, which we were forced to wear, and if I had been born into a Protestant family then the goodie/baddie conundrums and script would just be the other way round. So being Irish in Northern Ireland in the 1960s and 70s was hard work and far too confusing for us to make any sense of, so it was easier to throw the complexity out of the window and just settle for a romantic Mother Ireland like in the songs where there were forty shades of green, cottages, freedom, colleens, and parlous where there was a welcome on the mat for everyone, even Protestants.

Mrs. McLaughlin, the lovely and dear elderly woman who lived next door to us, had a vegetable patch in her back garden to rival ours. She regularly presented us with a box filled with rhubarb, lettuce, scallions, and runner beans, and freshly baked apple pies and she was a Protestant so what the hell was wrong with her? Nothing, in fact she was the kindest of souls. The McNallys who lived up the street, Susan and Jennifer, were the same age as us and we often played together. Their mother and our mother shared childcare, which allowed them to work evenings in the Broomhill Hotel. I even remember getting bathed in the same bath as Susan and Jennifer and they didn't look any different to us and they were Protestants.

How the hell were we supposed to work it out? I remember how we would laugh at our Mark who loved to play by the barricades, and he'd proudly announce that he was helping to keep the Fenians out. Another time when he was about six years old, he painted a Catholic neighbour's step red-white and blue. Neither he nor I were easily able to hold on to the notion that we were supposed to be the fuckin' fenian bastards because we were the Roman Catholics, how could we know that we were also Republican Taigs who were supposed to be servants of the Protestants. And where did the Romans come in to it? It only seemed to be Protestants or Paisley, in particular, that referred to us as Roman Catholics.

Our history lessons in school began with the Iron Age progressing to the Tudors but nothing to do with the history of Ireland so we hadn't a clue about what was going on, apart from picking up what we could from the news and from popular folklore from traditional Irish music, which lamented the Irish as the victims of the English; Mother Ireland victimized, oppressed, and undermined at the hands of the British, who tried to take away our land and our rights. The Mother Ireland was both romanticized and idealized and as much as I would turn to such notions in search of some kind of comfort against the obvious upper hand of the seemingly triumphant Protestants, I resented the fact that the popular version of our history was based on oppression. I didn't want to be thought of as the weak Catholic – the one who could be pushed around but there was something entrenched in our identification as victims. Over time, I understood that the war was to do with the Protestants having all the good jobs, housing, and education, and they made up over nighty per cent of the police force and a government, which was highly discriminatory of the Catholic population. So bits of the jigsaw were beginning to make a recognizable picture but it seemed at times that the bits were changing shape and just as soon as I thought I had found the right shape, it would again become a puzzle. Yet a strong sense of something being deeply unfair in the fabric of our heritage and culture was beginning to take shape in my heart and mind and I didn't like it one bit and hoped that the Yanks would soon come and sort it all out.

As well as all of this to contend with, we had the wrath of the Catholic Church, priests, God, and the devil to manage. We were supposed to love our neighbours, turn the other cheek, and show kindness to every colour and creed. The Ten Commandments underpinning my skeletal spiritual bones threw me into further confusion and consolation with the commands, 'Thou Shalt and Thou Shalt Not'. I was supposed to love my neighbour and not kill and not tell lies. So how was I supposed to hate people I didn't even know or even to think of myself as being different from my Protestant neighbours whom I didn't even know that they were Protestants before the troubles began?

Creggan and the Bogside, which was a Catholic residential area on the fringes of Derry city centre, were 'no go areas' to the police, and 'B specials' who were out to get us. We heard stories about how the 'B specials', the special part-time unit within our Protestant police force, again battered and kicked Derry Catholics into oblivion following peaceful Catholic protests. In contrast, the Protestant Orangemen marches were marvellous parades that everyone in the times before the troubles used to look forward to.

I remember being younger and sitting on Dadai's shoulders eating candy floss and watching the parades with the dancing men dressed in orange were throwing their sticks and banging their big drums. But the fun had long since faded and the 'B specials', all of whom were

Protestants and themselves Orangemen, had some kind of authority to mob rule and beat the Catholics into submission. At one time, the real police were not allowed into Creggan and the Creggan men organized themselves into a rota of vigilantes, sometimes congregating down at the Red Walls, keeping an eye on who was coming and going whilst building camaraderie between themselves. Sometimes Dadai would do his stint too, and I remember him saying that some of the men thought that the vigilante activity was 'counterproductive'. I didn't know what it meant but was pleased that my dadai could use such a big word. I don't ever remember anybody else's dadai using a big word like that but then again not many of them had as big muscles as our dadai.

Many ordinary decent Derry men, including priests became vigilantes, and I could feel that they had a sense that they were doing something practical and useful and for quite a few of them, it was a wee change from the pub life.

When the English Army first arrived on our streets in the Creggan Estate, I heard somebody say that it was to prevent a "blood bath." That sounded scary to me, as I imagined all of Derry's Catholics lying in baths of their own blood at the hands of the 'B specials'.

Tanks, saracens, jeeps, and armoured cars came flooding into our street. Broadway, the widest and longest street in Creggan played a leading role in channelling the fighting machines into the adjacent streets.

We looked on in terror, astonishment, excitement, and trepidation, as we could feel the ground shaking under the weight of the British Army's Tanks. When I looked out of the window nothing seemed real, like some kind of American battle movie – it was so utterly unreal that I think that it was as though we were climbing into the television and straight into a Sunday film matinee. It would have been far too scary to contemplate anything other than excitement because some of the tanks had huge long guns protruding outwards and enormous chained tires spanning the wheels. These were just like the tanks that my brothers had got in lucky bags and the ones in the comic cuts but these were real and as big as our houses and they just kept coming, pouring in as though all the war films in the world had sent their tanks and jeeps into our streets.

At first, the soldiers were our friends because they had come to keep the peace between the Protestants and Catholics. The Derry women fed them tea, sandwiches, and Irish stew. The soldiers allowed us to climb on top of the saracens and sometimes hold the guns. I loved to hear the soldiers speak in their foreign English accents.

"Morning Mam!" and "Thank you Mam," they would say to our mothers. Many were young men, some of whom Mamai said were only weans themselves but even so they seemed to bring something solid, protective, and good into our streets, and I felt assured that there couldn't possibly be any blood bath after all.

Somehow though, it all turned bad and terribly confusing. It was not long before we were to consider them as enemies. We were to walk past them in the street and not ever speak to them nor look them in the eye. With blackened faces, camouflaged uniforms, and hard helmets, the soldiers patrolled our streets. Sometimes they frightened the life out of me, as I turned into our house to find half a dozen of them with huge rifles in their arms laying in the garden or at the bottom of the steps that led into our front door. I had to climb over them or ask them to let me pass to get into my own house. The soldiers became a permanent fixture on our streets and gardens, and we grew weirdly used to them. But getting used to them meant eating our fear and worry time and time again but sometimes, it was just too hard to swallow and I would notice myself feeling really afraid.

The blood bath began the afternoon of an otherwise ordinary day in Broadway. Rapid and continuous shooting rang out seemingly coming from all directions. Mamai ran out into the street like a mad woman falling to the floor and rising again, falling to the floor again for cover and getting up again, not returning home until she gathered us all in from the madness in the street. Down the steps of our house, she clambered and threw us into the hallway, and we all lay on the floor until the long and noisy battle ended. Eventually silence eerily settled and after a long quiet while, we could hear the isolated, lonely, desperate, and pitiful cries for help coming from outside. Mamai looked out of the window and told us to stay on the floor and not to move.

"Don't go out Mamai, you'll get yourself killed," Tommy pleaded. But Mamai had already opened the door crawled up to the top of the six steps and ran across the road to a young soldier who had been screaming out for his mother. He was covered in blood and my mother lifted his head and rested what she could of his body on to her lap. A woman came running down the street towards my mother and the injured soldier, and the two women sat with this young soldier wean, prayed with him, and cradled him as he lost consciousness, and critically wounded. Eventually, the street was awash with armoured cars and Saracens that emptied soldiers out into our street, and the young soldier was taken from my mother's arms and carried away.

Mamai returned towards our house and stood at the top of the steps for a few minutes before coming inside. She looked like she was falling apart; like parts of her body were going to fall off and that there was nothing inside of her holding her together. Breathless and tears blinding her, she made her way down our steps and in to the hallway where we were quietly waiting. Her powdery white face now drenched with angry tears appeared demonic and terrifying. It had never before looked like that and it reminded me of an alien 'Dr Who' face. Mamai slowly and intently looked right inside every one of us.

"That was somebody's son. He was only awean. He was just a poor wean. If I ever catch any of you getting involved in these troubles, I will kill you stone dead, so help me God. We have enough trouble inside these four walls without any of you going out and getting yourself killed or killing anybody else. So help me God, as long as there is a breath in my body, I vow I will kill you stone dead. Some poor mother somewhere will have her heart broken this day."

We all knelt down together with our mother in front of the picture of the Sacred Heart of Jesus and prayed for the soldier wean and for an end to the troubles.

The following morning, we woke to find that our house had been blasted with paint bombs in the night. This was some kind of retaliation for Mamai having been disloyal to 'The Cause' by helping the soldier. My mother's face never looked the same again.

I don't know if Mamai in reality did become harder, stricter, and colder after that or if it was more to do with the fact that I was growing up and having to accept that the person whom I loved and depended upon was also the same person whom I could allow myself to oppose and challenge. But I longed to feel the softness of her attention and her carefree spirit, which had become something of a distant memory buried under the rubble of mental illness, the stress of bringing up seven weans on her own, and piled on top of all that, a bloody war that could claim any of her weans at any time.

Mamai made sure that Tommy practiced his violin and that all of our boys became scouts and that they would attend the scout meetings without fail so that they didn't have time to get mixed up in the troubles. They became the best 'Bob a Jobbers' in their group and spent a lot of time away camping. Mamai tried to teach us what she could of the Gaelic language, and she went to the library and got books out about Irish legends that she would read to us at night. She ensured that Donna and I never missed our Irish dancing lessons and encouraged us in Irish verse speaking.

We regularly sang together as a family and Mamai taught us all of the old Irish ballads and explained what she could of the origins of the song.

When we had visitors, the poor unsuspecting souls had to sit through seven weans party pieces.

"No one will ever accuse any of you of not being Irish just because you don't take up a gun. You will all stand proud on your own two feet and know your culture, keep it going because the way things are going in this town there won't be anything or anybody left to fight for and if the rest of us don't keep going, there won't be any friggin' culture to keep going."

The battles nevertheless, continued to rage and there was plenty of talk that things were going to get worse before they got better. Well they did get worse when Mamai came to us in the middle of the night, told us to put our coats on over our pyjamas because she was taking us up to our auntie's house where we would be safe. Dadai was still in hospital, and the shooting had been going on and off all day. The IRA had pounded on our door demanding to come inside to hide. Mamai opened the door, and three men looking like three black spiders dressed in black with Black balaclavas covering their heads and faces with holes cut out for their eyes, tumbled into our house shouting at each other about where to hide. Mamai said that there was a shed out in the back garden where they could go. The shed was our house for playing in; Dadai had even made it lovely by putting wallpaper on the walls and he had made us a table and chairs so that we could spend hours in there playing house. I looked out the back door and into the shed and saw the rifle glistening in the light of the moon. The men were quiet now and one of them picked up my attaché case and placed the rifle inside. Sweet God in heaven – that was my attaché case that had my initials on it... C.O.!

Chapter 7 THE WORLD HAS GONE MAD

All of a sudden, it looked like a rifle coffin with my name on it! One of the IRA men then grabbed a shovel and dug a hole in the garden where he set about burying my case that now had a rifle inside of it! Mamai grabbed me by the arm and stuck a hat on to my head and when she thought that the coast was clear, we were to leave our house quietly. We all held hands. David was carried Mamai's arms, Mark walked in between Donna and me, whose hand I held for dear life. Sean walked in between Tommy and Liam and held their hands, and we all stood in the hall listening carefully to the instructions not to make a sound and to follow Mamai. I was now in the Sound of Music film, escaping the Third Reich Gestapo but without a father to rely upon. Before we set outside of the house, we prayed together the prayer that we had to say every morning before we left the house.

"Angel of God my Guardian Dear
To whom God's love commits us here
Ever this night be at my side
To light and guard and watch and guide, Amen."

Once out into the silence of the dark night we didn't make a sound and followed Mamai's instructions to the letter. Nearly at the top of Broadway and we could see clearly the Creggan Chapel's marbled walls glistening in the night light. An almighty roar of tracer flares lit up the black sky and disturbed the silence, and Mamai heaped us on to the ground, her arms stretched out over us like a swan protecting her signets.

"Don't worry weans, stay down. God's good... we'll be okay."

She told each of us in turn that we were all right and that our guardian angels would keep us safe. Squeezing my hand Mark whispered to me, "Look up, Caroline, see the stars."

Mark, the second youngest, always seemed to have a knack of making things feel better. He would often be found digging in the garden with a spoon lost in a world of his own. Mamai always used to say, "I don't know I have that wean. He's never an ounce of bother, and if he didn't need to be fed and watered, I'd never know I had him!"

If Donna was David's wee mother, I was Mark's, as I loved to look after him and look out for him as though he was my own real life doll. One time when Mark was about three years old and he and I were playing in the street, he had fallen and hurt himself really badly and his knees were cut to ribbons. I picked him up in my arms, attempting to carry him home but he was so heavy that I let him fall and he landed face down on top of a metal hinge and his face was scarred forever. But Mark never lost faith in me and still managed to turn to me when he needed help or to show me his digging. Mark was for ever sitting digging in the soil in the garden with a spoon. He always seemed far away in a world of his own, engrossed, involved and excited to make potions and concoctions, and I loved to watch him making magic out of muck. As he pointed towards the stars that night, which were all the more dramatic a backdrop to the colourful flares yelping and swooping across the night sky, he managed magically to distract me from the impending danger and ease my fear. We smiled to each other, as we beamed ourselves up into the sky as though we had found an escape through a secret passage. Earlier that week, we had both been watching Neil Armstrong on television as he landed on the moon and now laying there on the ground and holding my small brother's hand, I tried to see if I could see Neil Armstrong walking across the sky taking giant leaps for mankind on the Sea of Tranquillity.

I wanted Donna and Sean to look up and see the stars too but couldn't manage to get their attention, as Donna's face was to the ground and Mamai by now was stretched over her and David the youngest. Sean had aproned himself around Mamai's waist, holding on for dear life and at the same time, providing something of a shield for her.

Tommy and Liam lay with their heads slightly raised, looking serious and watchful, assuming a spontaneous military authority over the boundaries of our family heap.

We all lay there for a while in a shared silence that knitted the strands of our different, excited, worried, panicked, petrified, and protective selves together like the complicated pattern of an Arran jumper.

Some man came running out of his house, "For Jesus sake Mrs. Come on in here out of the way before yous are all killed."

He guided us safely into his house where we waited until it was clear that the gunfire had died down, and we set off again on our journey up to our auntie's house and out of harm's way.

We did not to return for a couple of days until the shooting and riots had stopped. On our way back home, we had to pass the Creggan shops where we could see a people in panicked activity and lots of people standing around. I could hear a kind of wailing amongst an eerie and weird silence and I tried to look in its direction.

"Jesus Christ, God of Holy Heaven, don't be looking over there weans," Mamai whispered to us, as she was unable to prevent the tears from welling up in her eyes.

So with that, we all had to look.

At first I couldn't work out what it was but then a gradual picture emerged and the shock of it kicked me in the stomach.

I could just about make out that two young women had been tied to lampposts. They were covered in tar and feathers, which had caked in to their hair and faces and all down their clothes. Their heads were hanging down and I didn't know if they were dead or dying. They had a sign around their necks saying, "Soldier Doll".

I thought that the soldiers must have done it, and I became immediately terrified. What if they found my attaché case with my name on it and the rifle inside? What if I'd be tied to the lamppost and tarred and feathered?

I couldn't sleep that night and for many nights afterwards, I awoke to the sight of me being tied to a lamppost covered in tar, with it running down my face that it now looked like the IRA balaclava 'cos only my eyes could be seen. Loads of people are looking at me, and I am looking down in shame and at my feet is my attaché case with my name on it. The army put a big sign around my neck saying C.O. Soldier Doll!

I later learned that those girls whom we'd seen that day had been found guilty of going off with soldiers, and that they had been warned that if they didn't stop, they would be tarred and feathered. I saw many a tar and feathering after that and watched on as the young girls hair was hacked to bits by someone who had taken a pair of scissors to the tarred head and cut off the clumps of hair. My heart bled for these girls and I could only think that it was a sin, a great mortal sin that they had been tied to lampposts, tortured, and shamed like Joan of Arc. These were just teenagers and although they were older than I was, perhaps they hadn't a clue about the war either. Maybe they were only interested in boys and even soldiers as a way of turning their minds away from the desperate situation that we were in. Perhaps it was their escape.

On the long summer evenings that year, Mamai had a job on to keep the seven of us cooped up in the house so she had no option but to let us stay out and play a bit longer, sometimes until eight o'clock, whilst she maintained sentry at the top of the steps leading down to our house. She'd exchange banter with the neighbours as they passed by but keeping a covert watchful eye over us as we played to our hearts' contents. Her solid determination to be there for us and to watch over us as well as the belief in a Guardian Angel meant that I didn't have to worry or to think too much, if at all, about the stresses and strains that she was having to deal with and that's even before she had time to worry about a bloody war. We were able to get on with playing hopscotch and skipping and we loved it when Mamai and the other mothers joined in too. Queuing up to take their turn to run into the rope we all sang out,

"Mary in the kitchen doing a bit of stitching
In comes the burglar and pushed Mary out
Oh said Mary that's not fair
Oh said the burglar
I don't care, don't care, don't care don't care."
And, "Mother, mother tell me do
Who shall I get married to?
Tinker, tailor, soldier sailor,
Rich man, poor man, beggar man, thief.
Doctor, lawyer or Indian Chief."

Intently I would listen and imagine what it would be like to me married to anyone of them. I knew for definite that it wouldn't be a soldier.

I thought that it would be a good idea if it were a doctor because I couldn't go wrong if I was sick but if anyone ever asked me who I would like to marry when I grew up I would say, "Seeing as I can't marry me dadai, I would like it to be Cassias Clay, Elvis, or Val Doonican." John Wayne was probably too old for me but he was secretly high on my list anyway. When we tired of skipping, we climbed up the street lampposts, and tied the skipping rope high up the post creating a long noose that we climbed into, sat in, and happily swung around. It wasn't without hazard though, especially as I wasn't too proficient at it and received many a bump to the forehead as I spun around and whacked my head into the concrete post. But lampposts lost their attraction and never seemed to have the same excitement after seeing the tar and featherings. So I turned to playing Red Rover and loved it when the mammies and daddies joined in.

There was no shortage of street games collected and invented by boys, and I was far more compelled to play with them than playing house. When they would let me play with them, I joined in games of marbles, corks (tops of cola or beer bottles), conkers, boodles, ice pop sticks, and trollies (soapboxes on wheels) with a lead attached at the front, which steered the nifty makeshift sports car. So our streets were busy and packed with wanes, toys, games, and childhood activity 'cos we were usually out in the streets giving our parents' head peace and only nipping home briefly for bread and jam or a visit to the loo.

One hot summer weekend, Dadai, when on weekend leave from the hospital, was working hard in the garden. While sweeping the pavement outside of our house, he noticed that the streets appeared more than usually littered with ice-pop sticks and matchsticks so he sent us wanes off to collect them and bring them home as he could make use of them. Between the seven of us, we gathered hundreds of sticks, and Mamai was going mad saying that we were bringing germs into the house but she filled the bath, and we soaked the sticks and gave them a good swilling with detergent so that they were nice and clean. Eventually, following many weekends of painstaking work and dedication, Dadai had built a replica of the Derry Cathedral with those sticks. It was a beautiful thing. He had even managed to create the effect of stained glass and put an electric bulb inside the creation so that light would shine out of the windows at night just like our real cathedral. Father Carlin thought that it was powerful, and Dadai gave it to him for the Christmas Chapel Raffle. The tickets were sold out, and some man who lived down the Bogside won it and we never saw it again.

Dadai was then the talk of Creggan for something other than being drunk or sick, as he became known as the man who was great with his hands and the man who built the wee cathedral and so his reputation as a great builder and handyman was revived. People soon came knocking on our door asking if he would make them a wee fence or a wee sink unit or a wee set of wardrobes as if by adding the 'wee' made the job sound more attractive and like it would only take five minutes to make. Dadai took on the jobs depending on what mood he was in, and he usually would only charge for the materials and a few bob on top.

"Jesus Christ, Johnnie, it's no wonder we haven't got the nails to scratch ourselves with if you keep giving stuff away for half nothing."

"Sure they don't have much, Margaret."

"Aye surely that's right Johnnie, and we're sitting here like Rockefellers!"

Chapter 8
EVACUATION

DADAI was discharged from the hospital, and we thought that life would be better because he was better but life just became very different. One night, following another spate of fighting on the streets and the threat of worse atrocities looming because the British army had now turned into the baddies, no longer protecting us from the Protestants but fighting against us, Dadai announced that we were going to be evacuated with lots of other Creggan families. Mamai was determined that our family would not get caught up in what people were saying would be the worst of blood baths and, perhaps worried too that Dadai might easily slip into his old ways and go off with the fairies again or turn to the drink 'cos of the stress. So we set off in a big bus with lots of other families to a Southern Irish army camp to find some respite from the war in the streets and the worry that Dadai's madness might return.

Now, I was confused again: who were the Irish Army? Dadai explained that this was the legitimate Army of Ireland and basically they were goodies and they wanted to help. They were different from the IRA who were beginning to feel like baddies because they were shooting, bombing, and killing soldiers and Protestants right, left and centre. Many families in the Creggan estate refused to leave their homes perhaps feeling disloyal to the cause, perhaps feeling that they might be considered cowards, or they may have had as many good reasons for staying on, as we had for leaving. But we packed a few suitcases for the whole family and were told to travel light. We were refugees and I was bursting with excitement to be setting off on an adventure. Although unable to take many toys, we didn't mind as we felt as though we were going on holiday.

Our convoy of buses arrived initially in Finner Army Camp Co Donegal, but it didn't feel too exciting there, nothing like a holiday camp. A collection of long wooden huts set in a somewhat remote and exposed location appeared stark and unwelcoming. We were shown to a big canteen where we had as many sandwiches and cakes as we could eat. Following the tea and cakes, the adults were having a meeting with the soldiers, and they seemed generally restless, which made it all the more unsettling for us. It was soon announced that we would be moving on and were all herded into army trucks and travelled further down south to Coolmoney Army Camp in Co Wicklow.

Coolmoney Camp was set in what looked like an enchanted forest in so beautiful and peaceful a setting that I felt sure that it had been awaiting our arrival. We were allowed to choose our own huts, which would become our temporary homes, and so we children excitedly sped around the camp like excited puppies running in and out of the huts until we had settled on our favourite and then persuaded our parents to bed down in our new home. Donna and I picked bunk beds where we excitedly made a wee home for ourselves. There was great fervour as more busloads of people arrived from Belfast and a few families were invited to join us in our hut.

Donna and I were delighted to make friends with Ailish Webb, whose family had been evacuated from New Lodge in West Belfast. Ailish was the same age as me but a lot taller and had long black curly hair. We became the best of friends: climbed trees together, went swimming, and followed Cookie the chef all around the camp. Cookie was a jolly chatty and lovely friendly soldier, as well as being a fantastic chef who let us help him peel vegetables and fruit and allowed us to cook our own fruit pies. When we weren't pestering Cookie, we were obsessing about Lee, a young swimming instructor who humoured us but luckily for him, he managed to keep a healthy distance.

The Officer's Mess was often set up for family entertainment and many a party and social activity was laid on. The parents went there at night time for drinks and socialising whilst one or two of the other parents looked after the children in the huts. One Saturday night ,when our parents were out at the Officer's Mess and we children were tucked up in bed, Mamai appeared at my bedside, whispering to me to wake up and come down to the Mess with her as there was a talent contest on and I could sing Danny Boy. I was chuffed to be given the privilege of going out late although a wee bit anxious too. Mamai took the sponge rollers out of my hair and off I went in my nightie to sing Danny Boy. I was no sooner in the Mess up on the stage, sung my song, won a box of chocolates, and was taken back to my bed. I hid the chocolates under my bed and begrudgingly shared them out in the morning to the other weans who found the whole story of me winning a talent contest in the middle of the night hard to believe.

Chapter 8 EVACUATION

Soon our carefree adventures in the camp were interrupted by television footage of fierce fighting in the streets of Derry and Belfast. Things had gotten worse... much worse. We watched the shocking scenes on a news report. A convoy of huge big British Army tanks and Saracens, the ones with the big long guns sticking out of them, rolled up our street in Broadway: the way that was broad, was now the way that was wrecked! The friggin' army tank had only just ploughed straight through our garden fence and right into our garden, and it was nearly as high as our house. We were ushered away from the TV, but it was not before we had been rammed with fear and worry that we might not have a home to go back to. Now eleven years old, I was becoming more aware of the seriousness of the situation and less able to switch off the worry. The children in the camp were all telling stories about terrible things that had happened in their streets and housing estates. I heard about the Shankhill Butchers, who were Belfast Protestant paramilitaries who actually cut people up, whilst they were still alive! We heard about Catholic women and men in Belfast who had just vanished and were nowhere to be found. Terrified, I consoled myself with the thought that the Derry IRA was never as bad as the Belfast IRA because our IRA went to Mass and cared about the Catholic community too much and I knew that because everyone was talking about how the IRA was fighting to save Ireland. All too soon Dadai, Tommy, and Liam had to return to Derry. I worked out from the women talking that the men in the camp were beginning to feel uncomfortable and guilty about being away from Derry when it was being smashed to bits, so many of the men and boys returned home without us. We were not far behind them though, when a few weeks later a bus arrived to take us back home.

Although Mamai seemed to care less about the military cause, she remained determined that we would know that we were good Irish Catholics and that we should have some knowledge of our Irish culture. I began to understand that our mother was a nationalist who fully supported the Socialist Democratic Labour Party (SDLP) and their attempt at negotiating a peaceful resolution to the problems of poor housing, unemployment, and a democratic voting system. She believed strongly that we didn't have to take up the gun to solve the problem of oppression or to convince our friends or anyone else that we were Irish. Like many of Derry's mothers, Mamai was in an impossible bind by the central messages of Catholicism and a belief that we should love our neighbours: thou shalt not kill, turn the other cheek, not condemn someone else's faith, and all the stuff about burning in hell if we fell short of living a good holy life. Yet she was only too aware of the problems of being a pacifist or of being viewed as being disloyal to the Irish cause if we didn't show an active participation in the political struggle. As if there wasn't a friggin' struggle enough to bring up seven weans in the middle of it all. During Sunday morning mass, retreats, and holy days, Catholic spiritual sentiment wafted like a medicinal aromatic perfume in the Irish Derry air and was sucked into our thirsty, poverty stricken, socially and politically disadvantaged bones making Catholic calcium, like a holy tonic that works for everything.

People would say, "There's nothing before prayer."

Whether it be illness, riots in the streets, exam worries, debt worries, marriage difficulties or family problems, prayer was the answer and it would smooth away the surface suffering.

Yet the suffering caused by the bloody war fought in the name of religion, Republicanism, and Catholic Civil Rights drove many Irish mothers mad with frustration as they attempted to manage their own conflicted feelings. Any sweet smelling spirituality emerging from religion turned sour in the heat of politics and stank a vile and sickening stench when weans were being sacrificed on the altar of republicanism. The IRA refusing to swallow anymore political or religious poison, injected a powerful and vile toxin into the body of Irish politics, which caused the system to erupt into a near fatal organism that shook and shuddered and vomited out what couldn't be stomached and killed off both healthy and diseased parts. Supporters of the armed struggle believed that like many a foul tasting medicine, it was for our own good and that the only way to overcome the oppression was to enter into a bloody war; whilst others spat it out in preference to the less severe and slower release drug of moderation, which produced only minimal results over a longer period of time.

Our mothers had a choice: either aggressively treat the political cancer in the hope that oppression would be eradicated or just go on with pain relief and symptom management.

No wonder many of our mothers became hard and harsh. They often didn't know which way to turn nor if they were coming or going so they would have to adopt a hard line position one way or the other because sitting on the fence was too torturous a position to be in. Many of them ended up nervous wrecks doped on prescription drugs.

It was starting to get to all of us now, as the atmosphere of attack and defence seeped under our skin and as violence was in the air that we breathed.

I started to become more worried about my brothers because so many of Derry's youth were being attacked, shot, and killed.

At fourteen and thirteen years old, Tommy and Liam were becoming more rebellious and the temptation to join the IRA was immense.

They started joining in with the rioting and became more verbally challenging of the British Army. One day, Tommy was on a bus with his friends, when an army patrol stopped the bus and came on board, and in their usual antagonistic fashion, they proceeded to ask the passengers for their names and addresses and questioned them about where they were going. When one of the soldiers approached Tommy and asked for the information, Tommy refused to answer and he was 'lifted' and taken to the Army Barracks in the town.

Being 'lifted' was a kind of unofficial arrest, which could happen without any good reason. Even though he was only fourteen years old, Tommy was badly beaten and interrogated by the army on that day.

During the interrogation, one soldier told him to sit down on the chair and not to get up from it. The soldier then left the room and another one came in and slapped Tommy across the face.

"Who told you to sit down? Stand up!"

Then in comes the other soldier again who says,

"Who told you to stand up? Sit down!"

This went on and on, and Tommy was slapped and thumped each time.

He had been in there for most of the day until Mamai managed to get John Hume the leader of the SDLP to go in and have him released.

By now we, like many of our friends, had become hateful about everything that the British Army represented because the feeling of not being able to be free in our own town was hard to stomach. Watching the swarms of soldiers patrol our streets and dictate to us what we could and couldn't do and where we could and couldn't go was just too much to swallow. The barbed wire that ran around the whole town was so much in our faces that where ever we turned, it was there in one way or another and became so familiar that we didn't really see it... it just was. So I wonder if in defence and defiance, we responded with our own barbed wire attitudes that both offered protection and attack at the same time.

I started to recognize my own defiance and rebelliousness in my attitude towards the army and I stopped saying hello to them in response to their provocative daily greetings towards me. So my big act of protest was to walk by them as though they weren't there. I was aware that it was a small act of defiance given what others were prepared to do, but for me, not being civil to someone whoever they might be was a huge personal act of protest.

On the other side of the fence, we had to resist the pressure of the Catholic paramilitary groups and they were even more difficult to oppose because they sniffed out the stench of guilt and shame of those amongst us who were not being actively involved in the cause of fighting for a united Ireland. Mamai became worried sick about us even going to school because the rioting, 'lifting', bombings, and beatings continued relentlessly.

Our uncle Liam had given Mamai his cat and his car before he left to take up a job as a scientist in Canada. The car was my mother's pride and joy and she passed her driving test first time. So she drove us up and down the country to Feis's and scouting events just to get us away out of it all. Following a particularly bad phase of rioting, she decided to drive us all to school one morning so that she could be sure that we got there safely. We were all squeezed into the car on a winter's morning on our way to school when a group of youths wearing balaclavas with two holes cut out for their eyes and brandishing rifles stopped our car. Mamai lifted her umbrella got out of the car and waving it at the gunmen, she demanded to know why she was being asked to stop. The gunman, who was really a gunteenager, told her that her car was needed for a barricade, and he continued to order us to get out of it.

"What's wrong with your head? Do you honestly think I am going to hand over the only car I have ever owned to you? Get to hell's blazes out of my way. In fact, I think that I know who you are and if you don't get out of my way, I will go straight down to your mother and let her know what kind of carry on you're at."

We were shouting out of the car to her to be quiet and not say anymore when the youths stepped aside.

"And another thing, do you know that I have not been able to give these weans as much as a slice of toast this morning or yesterday because you burnt that friggin' bread van that is sitting there in front of me ready for the scrap yard and there's not a stick of bread in any of the shops. Ye need to catch yourselves on because ye don't know who ye are fighting or even why ye're fighting. If our weans starve then there will be no bloody Ireland to fight for because we will all be driven to Gransha or to the Cemetery."

"Sorry Mrs. Owens. Go'n on."

Mamai got back into the car, drove off, and again warned us that she would kill us stone dead if she ever caught us at any of that carry on.

Not long after that, the Western Education and Library Board Initiative managed to organize Holiday Projects for the Families of Derry's Children. The excitement in the city was powerful, as we heard people all over the town and housing estates talking about all of the wonderful experiences and places, and I stood with my tongue hanging out, waving every one of my brothers and my sister off on the big buses. Tommy was sent to Nottingham in England, which he soon hated and couldn't wait to come home. Liam went to Holland and loved it. I nearly hit the roof when Donna was chosen to go to Reykjavik in Iceland and there was no way that I could go. I just had to wait, as my turn would come; Mamai said so. I prayed my heart out that I would be able to go to America. My May altar in my bedroom was a meadow of whatever flower I could pick from anybody's gardens, even the chapel flowerbeds, to adorn the altar, as I lost myself in the fantasy of arriving in the USA into a family like the Walton's, where a big tall Johnboy would be waiting for me and he would be kindness itself.

"Holy Mary Mother of God, if you grant me this intention I'll never say another bad word in my life again and I will be glad for everybody who has more than me and I will never again hope that some terrible thing will happen to them just because they have something that I haven't got. God's good, my turn will come."

Donna returned from Iceland with a lovely furry coat for me and lots of photos of her walking on the hot volcanic springs, and I had to sit on myself not to want to kill her with the jealousy.

Sean got to go to France and came back speaking French like he lived there all his life. David went to England, and then Mark was flying off to New York to an Irish American family whose father was a boxing coach in the police force; it was perfect for Mark who by now was eight years old and a junior boxing champion. Mark stayed in America longer than expected because the family had wanted to keep him; in fact, they had requested to adopt him! Well, when Mamai read of this in a letter, she nearly had a heart attack and demanded that Mark be brought home on the next flight. So that was the end of holiday projects for our family, and my turn never did come. I begged Mamai to get me a place on one of the holidays but she said that if I went away, I might never come back and anyway she needed me at home, that she couldn't do without me, as I was the greatest help to her. Nobody could wash dishes like me nor clean the house like me so for my reward, I got to go to sunny nowhere.

My disappointment ate away at me and I couldn't stand the feeling of how unfair it was. Why was I the only wean in our family who didn't get to go anywhere? Mamai told me that something far better would come my way and that I would have plenty of opportunity when I was bigger to go wherever I wanted. I thought that I would lose my mind completely with the sense of unfairness of it all and the sense that God was punishing me for something because if God was always good then it must be me who is bad and that's why Our Lady is unable to answer my friggin' prayers.

My fury about it all had to be suffered in silence but I vowed to myself that one day I would make it to America if it was the last thing I did, if God spared me and if it killed me stone dead.

Chapter 9
BLOODY SUNDAY

WHEN we returned to Derry after a three-week long summer break in Colmoney Camp, the childhood games of the street where a hazy memory. Our streets were no longer safe to play in. Riots were a daily occurrence and often involved youths getting out of school and straight into a riot with the British army. I was supposed to be a bit more grown up now at eleven years old. I was preparing to start St. Mary's Secondary Intermediate School, and I turned from worry about the streets to worry about my ability to manage in my new school. The Army had often camped around the schools, and we heard stories that they had messed up the toilets and graffied the walls in my new school.

The excitement and anticipation about starting my new high school was not the milestone that it might have been because the riots were getting worse. On the way home from school at the end of my first week at my new school, there was a mighty riot. Buses and cars were burned and used as barricades. The nuns called us back in to the school and asked us to stay in the playground for a while longer until the riots had died down. When it was thought that the coast was clear and things had calmed, we were allowed to go home. Our house in Broadway was only a ten-minute walk from our school. Once at the top of Broadway, at the same place where we had all laid down before on that starry night, shooting erupted yet again. I lay on the ground feeling the hard dusty pavement close to my face and holding on to my schoolbag as though it were a security shield. Strangely, having my face on the ground seemed a familiar and odd comfort.

Lying there, looking at other schoolchildren in their new school uniforms scattered across the ground like sweet wrappers littering the streets, I turned my mind to thoughts of my new start at my new school. Would I make it? Would I be good enough? Would I make the grade? I was thinking that I had made a good start but was a wee bit scared of Sister Agatha, our new form teacher and the tallest, biggest nun I'd ever clapped eyes on, when suddenly a chocking and burning sensation erupted in the back of my throat. The noise of the gunfire had become louder and people were shouting out that we should stay on the ground. The back of my throat was burning like hell, and everyone was coughing and choking. I couldn't see, my eyes were burning holes in my head, and the panic was made all the more intense because I couldn't get up and run for cover. I crawled over to a grassy patch and stuffed my head into the grass and mud where I hoped I could get some relief. When the battle had died down, we were being picked up off the street by adults, who were handing out handkerchiefs and bits of cloth steeped in vinegar. I was told to put the cloth to my mouth and nose and that it would help me breathe until I got home.

Following that battle, the streets were littered with rubber bullets, big broken concrete pavement pieces – used by the rioters as ammunition – and CS gas canisters, which looked like grenades and had become another familiar feature of the war. Rubber bullets and plastic bullets the size and shape of toilet roll inners became trophies and eventually replaced games of marbles, as we excitedly collected them and invented games as we rolled them across the pavements. The big black fat heavy rubber bullets with the pointy tips were shocking to look at because I couldn't think why a bullet need to be so big and heavy, it looked like a toy space rocket. The yellowish, white-coloured, plastic bullets were without a tip and heavy and hard as granite. They were supposed to be a softer option to metal bullets, as they were intended for maiming, not killing but there was no doubting the damage that they could do and they were regularly and indiscriminately fired into crowds of women children and youths, many of whom had been seriously maimed.

I couldn't understand why the Army used the tear gas, because it seeped into all of our homes and attacked everyone not, just the rioters or the IRA. It was as though it didn't matter to the British Army that children, elderly and innocent people would be attacked, and it seems as though in their view we were guilty too, guilty simply of being Irish Catholics. By now, people were regularly being stopped in the streets and being frisked and searched by the Army. Most streets in the city centre were blocked off by Army checkpoints, and I often had to open my coat to be body searched by some woman soldier. The male soldiers were free to search our handbags and were not meant to frisk us but they would make a meal out of searching the contents of a schoolbag as they sometimes used it as an opportunity to chat us up. We could expect to be searched going in and out of our own homes, streets, and our shops. It made me feel like dirt and like my own body didn't belong to me, and I was guilty just for having a body, an Irish Catholic body. Why did I end up feeling guilty every time I saw a checkpoint? I had nothing to hide except my shame that my own body didn't belong to me and could be mauled, shoved, tugged, and grabbed without a word of explanation or apology about it.

I tried my hardest to get used to it all; there was nothing else for it because soldiers were raiding our houses two and three times a week. In the beginning, it was great craic as the women and children would be out in the streets banging bin lids on the ground, warning neighbours that raids were underway. I remember Donna and me giggling and falling into hysterical laughter at the sight of Mamai banging the bin lids, and we would grab the pots and pans from under the sink, take them out into the street, and bang them with our entire mite. The novelty soon wore off though because having up to ten soldiers regularly come into our houses and scrutinize or vandalize our home and private life was hard to bear. They trampled their way through our rooms, opening the drawers in our bedrooms, and pulling out all of our underwear and private things, leaving them strewn on the floor or bed. Sanitary towels and wash bags were ripped apart. Bedcovers were pulled off the beds, which were pulled away from the walls and looked under. The dirty washing in the wash baskets was poked about with rifles. I was mortified and seemingly it sometimes affronted everyone involved because I could tell that some of the soldiers were embarrassed to have to do it. Some of them almost respectfully handled our private and personal things and were good at putting things back and apologizing for the inconvenience; whilst others didn't seem to give a dam and got some sadistic pleasure out of picking up our underwear, offering them up to their comrades for a good laugh. When my mother got wind of it, she always made sure that she accompanied the soldiers into our bedrooms, and her presence seemed to put a stop to the shenanigans when she confidently demanded that they respect our things.

"This is my wee girls' room and I would appreciate you respecting their personal things. I'm sure that you all have mothers and some of you will have sisters, and I would hope that you would extend the same courtesy to me and my youngsters as you would show your own flesh and blood."

Sometimes that was enough for the soldiers to leave the room immediately in shame and embarrassment, but for others it produced a defiant reaction whereby they would completely wreck the room.

Following these times, we just had to pick everything up although I wanted to leave it all there because I knew that the next day or the one after, they would be here again. Yet pride got the better of us, and Donna, Mamai, and I would set about fixing and folding, as we quietly tried to tidy up our feelings of resentment, anger, humiliation, and shame at the same time.

"Some of them are not half reared. For some of them, the Army is the only family they have ever known. Some of them are probably Borstal Boys who have been criminals all their lives and they wouldn't know the meaning of respect!" My mother muttered to herself, as she tried to manage the feelings of disappointment in herself because she was unable to protect us from such humiliation.

"I'm not having any British soldier thinking that we don't keep a clean house. God only knows the state of their own homes but they won't be coming into ours and thinking that we are not civilized."

When the house was spick and span, we stood back in admiration of our hard work as the rooms were immaculately clean and tidy and smelled of Johnson's bees wax furniture polish.

"There ye are, look at that. It's all a wee bit more Protestant looking now, and fit for the Pope and Paisley himself!"

Unfortunately for us though, keeping a clean house involved us having to rise out of bed an hour early every morning in order to clean every room in the house, even at the weekends we couldn't have a lie in. I was getting cheesed off, it was too much hard work, and I was becoming more resentful of being subject to it all. My resentment generalized towards the British Army, the IRA and the UVF, and the Catholic Church... and the Irish Government for not doing enough, and I was even fed up with the Americans for not having arrived to just sort it out.

I tried to get it into my head that there was a higher purpose in all of the fighting and that Irish Freedom would have to be fought for if we were going to have a better future and a better quality of life. But it was at times too hard to hold on to such a notion when our streets were being ripped to shreds and smashed to bits and used for barricades and rioting missiles. Soldiers and snipers overran our houses and gardens, our cars and buses were overturned and set on fire and used as barricades. The streets and pavements that we once played on actually weren't there any more 'cos they were being ripped up by weeboys to use in the riots. It was all a bloody, friggin' mess.

Things were getting worse for everyone, and the residents of Derry planned to have a peaceful march organised by the Northern Irish Civil Rights Association. Hundreds of law abiding men, women, and youth of Creggan and other less troubled parts of Derry attended the march on the 30th January 1972 to show the strength of opinion about the injustices, which were becoming more strongly felt even by the mildest and most moderate Nationalists.

Dadai set off with many of the other men who set out from the top of the Creggan Estate, and I was proud that he was doing his bit for Ireland. Tommy and Liam were warned not to set foot out of the street but they managed to sneak off and join the march tagging on at the end. As I was also warned not to set foot out of the street, I was mindful of looking after our weans but I had a sense that this was to be a really big protest and the atmosphere was serious, even for us weans. As we tried to play in the street, we were filled with a sense of uncertainty and unease. Soon we were distracted from our play, as the helicopters were out in force buzzing and swooping around the air like birds circling their prey. We could see smoke rising up into the air, which was thick with tension. We didn't know what the hell was going on because the marchers had reached the down town centre and the Creggan Estate was built high up in the hills of the city. Some of the weans in our street decided to go up into the cemetery where you could get a good view of the city to get a look at what was going on, but Mamai wouldn't allow us to leave the street and in any case, the tear gas was starting to drift up into our streets, and we were called to come inside.

The sound of shooting banged and rang through the streets, and I sensed that there was something different about this battle. What if it is the blood bath? Rumours that women, men, and young people had been killed reached our street. There really was a war going on down the town. Mamai stood outside at the top of the steps to our house talking to some of the women. Eventually it was clear that people had been killed, and we could see through the smoke and gas that people were being carried home injured and maimed. The panic was worse than anything I had felt before. There were no distractions for me this time, no place in my mind where I would escape, no stars in the sky, and no songs in my head to transport me out of the fear, and I sensed that we were all terrified. Dadai wasn't home yet, and there was no sign of Tommy or Liam. News kept coming in of more people dead. We had been getting used to the bombings riots and shootings but there was something oddly scary about this day.

I stood at the garden gate looking out down towards the Red Walls where there was a lot of commotion, then amongst a crowd of the walking wounded, I could see Dadai being carried home by two men, and surrounded by people holding handkerchiefs to their mouths and noses. By now, I could barely make out what was going on in the street because the CS gas and smoke was so thick. I could see the men drop Dadai, as they were struggling to hold his weight, and I looked on, quietly screaming in my heart, convinced that he was dead. Mamai ran out with the handkerchief around her face and guided the men into the house. Dadai was neither drunk nor dead but overcome by the tear gas. Mamai thought that the gas might have affected him more because of the strong medication that he had been on. One of the men who had stayed with him told her that he had fallen whilst in a crowd who were running for cover from the British paratroopers who had totally lost their minds, shooting at everything in sight, and some man had apparently shouted to him, "Johnnie, just stay down and let on you're dead!"

I couldn't get the words out of my head because lying down and letting on we were dead was so much a part of our childhood games when we played Cowboys and Indians and now it was happening for real with grown-ups, in a real war.

During the time of laying there on the ground, the CS gas had poisoned Dadai. Once inside our house, Mamai seemed to sort Dadai out pretty quickly, then she noticed that neither Tommy nor Liam were accounted for.

"Jesus, sweet mother of Ireland, what have ye done to my weans? Caroline, you stay here with the wee wanes and your father and don't leave the house whatever happens."

Out she ran into the gas-filled streets. I gave the weans some bread and jam and made Dadai a cup of tea and then turned on the TV to scenes on the news of the worst battle in Derry that I'd ever witnessed. It was reported that some of the men killed were only youngsters, and I was terrified for Tommy and Liam when I looked out of the window. My mother was approaching with both boys, barging at them that she would surely kill them for what they had done by following the march. They were sent straight up into the bath and were told to get ready for an early bed.

School was cancelled the next day, and a new and unfamiliar fear, rage, and shock had gripped the people of our town. We learned that British Army soldiers had shot twenty-six unarmed civil rights protesters and bystanders. The dead included thirteen males, seven of whom were teenagers, and another man was critically wounded and later died of his injuries. Two protesters were also injured when army vehicles ran them down. Many of the dead had been shot in the back. It all happened in the Bogside where my Aunt Rose – with only half a stomach – lived, and we were worried sick because she lived alone, and some of the dead and injured had been shot right outside her house in Glenfada Park.

Soon enough we got the news that our twenty-two year old uncle had been one of the seriously wounded. The shot had gone right through one arm and out the other and badly damaged his chest on its way. The shots fired that day by the British Army caused untold damage, devastation, and suffering to the families directly involved, and they would ring out across Ireland and the world. The British Army had altered the course of a generation, as they had shot through the hearts of every man, women, and child in the city, and so we were all surely wounded one way or another, some more seriously than others.

Thirteen dead bodies were laid out on the altar of the Creggan Chapel. I watched at the chapel door as crowds of people had been coming and going through the day. So many people were flocking to look, that it seemed that the whole world had arrived in our town. After a while, when the crowds abated, I managed to take myself up to the chapel alone at a time when there had seemed to be a bit of a lull in the activity.

Walking through the doors, I was not prepared for the absolute shock of what I saw. Within the alter area, thirteen coffins were laid in a row beneath the altar with the huge statue of Our Lady at one side and St. Joseph at the other.

I sat there in the chapel loosing track of time. Anger, sorrow, fear, frustration, and a sense that there would be no end to it all, dripped on to my hands, which were trying to pray but no prayer came... only tears. I just sat there like a big wet lump feeling guilty at the thought that at least my father was not in one of those boxes and my brothers were still alive. Mamai's words were ringing in my head. She had said a long time since that she didn't want any of her wanes sacrificed on the altar of Republicanism, and here were somebody's weans and somebody's fathers and not one of them had been involved in anything other than a peaceful demonstration nor did any of them belong to any paramilitary organization. Were they the sacrifices? Had the IRA hijacked their peaceful demonstration? Why had British Army Paratroopers just opened fire and murdered people, many of whom were trying to run away to safety? What on God's earth was going on?

In the days and weeks that followed, the shock and disbelief came like black clouds gathering over the town. No longer would I feel like a child. Play in the street had almost immediately become a thing of the past, as it was a rare thing to see youngsters playing in the streets from that day onwards. I had a sense that the soft cradle of childhood, which had nursed us through the ups and downs of family life, school life, and all the scrapes and sores of growing up, was a thing of the past because there was the hard reality that no matter how good our parents were, how brave, tolerant and strong our mothers' wills; however, hard my mother and all the other mothers tried to be our guides, nurses, councillors, and therapists, they couldn't always kiss it better. The reality of death and murder had rammed it through to me that I needed to grow up fast.

It was clear that we were now living in the middle of a war zone, and it seemed that everyone was at it, as riots, shootings, and killings by the British Army, the IRA, and the UDA were as common as putting the kettle on. The people of Belfast and Derry had taken the brunt of it all, and it seemed to be closing in on us, seeping into every aspect of our lives. I was desperate to get myself down to the Bogside to see the state of the place with my own eyes because I had been watching a constant stream of reports on the television of the damage caused to the streets. We didn't have a colour television and somehow the images didn't look real. So when I was sent down to my aunt Rose's house to give her some freshly baked scones, I jumped at the chance.

When I arrived at Glenfada Park, I was again stopped in my tracks. The reality was no longer black and white. Pavements and walls all around were saturated in blood and none of the TV reports had prepared me for what I saw – I had known that there was a war going on but I didn't know the real colour of it until that day.

A few months after Bloody Sunday, at around four o'clock one afternoon in May 1972, there was another commotion with British Army helicopters buzzing around overhead, and one, notoriously named "Joe Ninety", the Army helicopter, was spinning around the sky like a vulture about to swoop down on to its prey. There was panic again in the streets when we heard that a young nine-year-old boy had been shot whilst coming home from St. Joseph's School at the bottom of Creggan Estate. Mamai was beside herself with worry, and once all of our boys were safely home from school, she sent Tommy and Liam around the street to invite families to our house that evening to say a Rosary in the hope that the young boy would not die. Mrs. Doherty across the street from us, one of the people who had a phone, came running out into the street with the news that the young boy who had been shot was Richard Moore. He had been shot in the face, and he would either die or be left blind. I was standing at the top of our steps when I heard the news and it was another time in my life when I felt as though I might faint. My head was buzzing as though the friggin' helicopter was right inside it, I couldn't breathe easily and felt sick.

"Caroline, run up to the chapel and light two candles." Mamai ran down the steps into the house, grabbed her purse, and lifted out two new shiny five pence coins.

"Daughter dear, run up to the chapel and under the statue of Our Mother of Perpetual Succor say a prayer for that poor wean and his two eyes. That she will keep him safe and that he will live to see the end of all of this madness! Mother of God in Heaven, the world's gone mad when they are now shooting our weans!"

Mamai couldn't have known that Richard was my boyfriend but the news smashed through my innocent secret, and reality came crashing through me like the tank that had forced its way through our garden fence. I ran in panic. While running with my two feet with my two coins in my two hands looking towards the chapel with my two eyes, the tears ran down my cheeks. For Richard was the boy with the beautiful eyes, the boy who I had chosen because he was different, braver than the other boys, the one who was able to look the girls in the eye when he said 'hello', the boy who seemed more sensible, kind, and mature, the boy who would call me over in 'Red Rover' and who would say, "Yes, Caroline. What about ye?"

Lighting the candles, I looked up at the statue, not a bit of me convinced that she could help and i sat quietly for a while looking into the flames. At other times, the lighting of candles beneath a holy statue and staring into the flames would transport me to a place in my mind where I was safe and secure and able to transcend the problem even if briefly. But now, as I tried to say a prayer for Richard, fear for my brothers, Richard, my family, and myself gripped my cupped hands, which were pressed hard to my nose and mouth. For the first time, I was aware of feeling an absolute surge of hatred, resentment, and a deep sense of anger towards the British Army, the Protestants, the English, and the Mother of Perpetual Succor because neither she nor the other statues in the chapel were of use nor ornament.

As I returned from the chapel, it was getting dark and out of the chapel gates, I looked down towards our house and saw that crowds had gathered outside. On closer view, I could see that people were kneeling, and I stopped at the sight of all of the sparkly, flickering flames. People were holding candles like torches lighting up the dusky sky. I could hear the chanting and sat down on a wall nearby, as I watched the crowd join the impromptu Rosary congregation, which had spilled out on to the streets from our house. I couldn't get my head around it, that religion was the cause of it all, as well as the cure. But I was calmed and comforted by the sight of the candle light, which gave the affect of something bigger or greater that could be called upon, and I thought that it was more to do with the will of the people rather than any Catholic God or Mother Mary.

There was lots of praying in the streets and in people's houses following the shooting, and we were all relieved to know that Richard was alive but came to learn that he had been left blind. After he had been discharged from hospital eventually, I used to walk over to his house and watch him in his garden, safe in the knowledge that he couldn't see me. Walking over to the park one day, I could see Richard walking towards me, jumping from side to side, as he ensured his way was clear. I struck up the courage to say:

"Yes Richard, What about ye?"

I managed to get the words out of my mouth although they were so faint that they could barely be heard inside a paper bag.

"Who is it? Who's there?" Richard asked, with a curious smile on his face.

I wasn't sure what to say as I was shocked that he didn't know who I was. I had never spoken to a blind person before and just expected that he could see even though I knew that he couldn't. I was distracted too because I was trying to get a closer look into his dark glasses to see if I could see his eyes. I could see something of the shape of them but not clearly enough.

"Who is it?" he asked again.

"It's Caroline... Caroline Owens."

"Yes Caroline, what about ye? Where are you heading?"

I told Richard that I was going to the park, and then out of nowhere I asked, "Richard, what about your eyes?"

Richard looked uncomfortable and a wee bit put out.

"What about my eyes?" he questioned, seemingly fed up that I had asked the question.

"Well I was wondering if they're sore," I feebly responded, feeling totally stupid because he might not have any eyes at all, and I might have embarrassed him. At that point, I wished that I had lost my tongue and Richard might have wished that I had too, as somewhat irritated, he started to waft a stick about in readiness to move on, "Well, I'll see you later, Caroline. I'm away up to the chapel."

How stupid could I be? Thank God he couldn't see my red face.

I kept thinking about Richard, saying that he would see me later when in fact he wouldn't be seeing me at all, well not with his eyes anyway. But I knew in that moment that it was important for Richard to be seen as ordinary and not as someone who was blind. In fact, I don't think I ever saw him with a white stick. For a long time after that, I often wished that I'd had a different conversation with him on that day. Perhaps I'd have been better off asking him if he was still able to see in his dreams or about what it was that he could see instead of asking him that stupid question, "Are yer eyes sore?"

Chapter 10
PRIDE BEFORE A FALL

"NOT a sight for sore eyes," Mamai said, about the awful state of the town centre.

"The town is wrecked and there's a terrible lot of activity going on. Joe Ninety is out, and I think we might be in for another night of it as far as I know because Jim Figerty is on the war path," Mamai is telling Dadai, as she took off her coat and scarf and hung them up on the coat hanger in the hall.

'Activity' was reference to rioting, civil unrest, police or army manoeuvres, and or 'terrorist' shenanigans'. 'Joe Ninety' was reference to the army helicopter locally named after the television character because like the character, the helicopter could seemingly see everything and was the army's bird's eye view. 'Jim Figerty' was the name given to a British commanding officer who had one of those impeccably manicured and cartoon style moustaches that curled around both sides of his face, similar to the one donned by the mad Salvador Dalai man in the TV advert for fig rolls, about a search for the man with the funny moustache who stole the fig out of the fig roll. Much of the troubles was talked about in this double speak, and it was an odd kind of comfort that fantasy and humour blended into reality. Just like when mothers chatted and laughed together about some of the less serious stuff, this seemingly was their way of normalizing and detoxifying what they could of the troubles. They had little option because 'the troubles' had become the norm. I suppose we would never have stepped out of the house if we hadn't found ways of making it unreal.

My friend Betty Curran told me about an old woman, Bernie, who lived near her house and who was a generally anxious old soul. One evening, when the activity in the city centre clattered out so loud that it reached the streets of Creggan, the old woman came running into Betty's house panic stricken and breathlessly explained that she had spent half the day hiding under the stairs because she didn't know what was going on. Betty's mother explained to her that there was a terrible lot of activity in the town and that a few bombs had gone off.

"Thank God for that," Bernie said. "I thought it was thunder!"

I later heard that story told many a time and it seemed to become a wee joke. Yet the joke was perhaps an example of how it was sometimes easier to worry about the more ordinary shocks and shakes of life, as the reality of political horror could only be briefly contemplated because we all had to live in a war as though there wasn't a war. I was growing up now, nearly a teenager and often felt affronted by many newspaper and media reports about 'the troubles' or 'war'. I was embarrassed and frustrated that what was being reported was a version that was seemingly putting us down and showing us up, and it just wasn't the whole story. What about the experience of ordinary decent people, parents and youngsters like us who had to live through it? In some of the reporting, particularly in the more official English media, a picture emerged of a pack of uncivilized, peasant Protestants and Catholics alike, who clung on to primitive beliefs about ownership of territory. Within myself, I battled against such a view and had a sense that many versions of what was being reported just weren't fair accounts of what was either motivating and/or perpetuating the war. What did the rest of the world think of us? I was becoming more aware of a sense of injustice, particularly at the feet of the Catholic community. Had I known then that the war would span thirty years, I'm sure that I, like many others, would have lost my mind and been driven straight away to Gransha. So thank our lucky stars that there were the times when our minds were places of creativity, crucial to our survival, and we were not easily going to lose them. Without realizing it, many of us, adults and children, had developed our own psychological strategies, where our minds became havens from the horror, internal bunkers, and shelters where we would direct and produce our big exciting adventures and alternative worlds. Safe in the knowledge that our mothers would do the worry work by turning to each other, the heavens, and humour.

Betty's mother and father, 'Big Betty and Willie', were great ones for doing what they could for the community and keeping youngsters off the streets. More than happy to support us when we decided that we wanted to start up a folk singing group, they entered Moya, Marion Douglas, Betty, and myself into a talent competition, which was about thirty miles away at a wee place named Toome Bridge. We practiced hard in the warmth of Betty's house, stoked by a roaring fire and fed from a pot of Derry soup that was always on the go. Under the tuition of Betty and Willie, we were beginning to sound like we could sing, and we looked the part dressed in outfits made by my mother. The long Crimpelene black skirts with the high waistbands were worn with matching waistcoats. We each bought our own swanky, bright pink, nylon, puffed sleeved, pointy collared blouses from Littlewoods, and we looked great!

Eventually on the night of the competition, Betty and Willy drove us up the road where we sang 'The joy of love' in the best harmonies we could muster. Winning the runner-up prize was a bit of a surprise because we were up against serious folk singers and groups, who seemed a bit put out because our song wasn't even a folk song. But that was the beginning and end of our singing stint. I think we knew that we were just in it for a laugh, and it was something different to do at the time. Yet, our parents, like many of the parents in Creggan whatever their political persuasions, did whatever they could to keep us distracted and emotionally buoyant and helped us turn our minds away from the troubles.

I was now attending my new school, St. Mary's Secondary Intermediate School for girls that sat beside the Creggan Chapel at the top of Broadway. A3 was my new class and Sister Agatha my new form teacher. Her reputation had gone before her, and my aunts who had heard of her had told me that she could be a bad "un but that she got good results for the girls. A huge tower of a nun with rosy red cheeks and a wide mouth, which staged a mass of misshapen, uneven, shiny yellow teeth that seemed to be clinging to the front of her mouth and peering out from a stage like a children's choir, my new form teacher appeared to look at us with a mixture of joyful anticipation and suspicious trepidation. The height of her was equal to the mite of her for she was the tallest nun I'd ever set eyes on. The age of her was old, and the hint of grey hair that peeked out of her veil would sometimes have me wonder about the woman in her who was peeking out from underneath the long black robes. Her white, purple hands were as big as shovels and the great big lumps on her fingers and hands, which I tried not to look at, had a magnetic power over me, pulling my eyes towards them even when it was clear that Sister Agatha had noticed me looking. She would then inspect her hands to check for abnormalities, and her face would flush with the discomfort of it all.

It was as though I needed to know that the lumps were a sign of her vulnerability, depleting her strength, and relieving any worry I had about the possibility that she might or could grab me by the hair. Yet the lumps made me feel sorry for her too, and I was immediately concerned for her health. If she hadn't been a nun, she could have been somebody's granny and would have surely been loved.

Sister Agatha was methodical and meticulous and had high expectations for us girls. We had to sit at our desks with our arms folded and fingers to our lips. She checked our uniforms and hair every morning, as her girls were to be immaculate. My mother had bought my uniform a few sizes too big in order that I could grow into it. The white shirt and blue and orange-striped tie were worn inside a thick blue tweed tunic dress, and mine was particularly heavy as it was meant for someone a foot taller than I was. When Mamai had altered the dress, she decided not to cut anything off the hem, as it was her hope that I would grow into it and it would last me the whole of my high school life. But that heavy tweed dress now had a hem so big as it was turned up and under so far that it was almost up to my waist, making me look like I was wearing a big heavy tweed bell that dangled side to side against my skinny legs that peeped out underneath... I never did grow into that dress.

Sister Agatha had many rules and obsessions. School register was a highly serious daily event, and we were instructed to listen to the names, as she called them out in alphabetical groups and if anyone were missing from any group for that day, someone present in that group would raise a hand and say the name of the person who was absent.

I was so worried about getting it wrong that I listened intently soaking the names into my brain like a sponge and singing the rhythm to myself,

Breslin
Breslin
Cullen
Deeny
Doherty
Douglas
Downey
Doyle
Duffy
Dunlop

Friel
Gallagher
Gallagher
Gill
Harkin
Kyle
Lamberton
Mallet
Melrose
Morrison
Murray

O'Donnell
O'Hagan
Owens
Roddy
Shields

Taylor
Toy
Ward
Wilson
White

Then there was a pregnant pause, where we had to indicate to her if any of the aforementioned were absent, and Sister would then continue to read out 'The 'Mc's', which were saved to the end.

McCann
McCauley
McClintock
McDonnagh
McGavigan
McGrellas

I was not to know then that my school register would remain in my head for the rest of my life I would carry it with me always as every name would bring to mind the image of the girl and I would often wonder about them all and what had become of their lives.

Soon Sister Agatha, although strict, had stimulated further in me a thirst for knowledge and a belief in myself. She managed to reach into the best parts of me that had already been spotted by my mother and then by Miss. Brown at my infant school. She would often invite me to read my compositions aloud to the class and then send me around to Sister Finbar, Head of English, to read my poems to her class. One time, we were working on writing techniques in poetry and we were invited to make a poem out of a word. I had chosen the word 'Ireland' and Sister Agatha was so impressed with my poem that I was instructed to take it to read to Sister Finbar's class and then to the head nun, Sister Aloysius. Even though I had been asked to stand in front of the class for having done something good, it reminded me too much of the public humiliations at my old school and the nervous feeling was sickening. I stood there with my poem in my hand but no words came out, only tears welling up, and I wanted to run far away. Sister Finbar told me to take my time and that she and her girls would wait. I was immediately reminded of Miss. Brown from my junior school, and I could see her smiling towards me in my mind's eye. Nervously, taking a deep breath I began,

"The Irish love Ireland it's our hearth and it's our home
We have fought for it; we've cried for it, imprisoned, maimed and died for it.
I is for the inner strength that our mothers' make for the heal
R is for the rights that we have but to take them from us is to steal
E is for the endless fights, the bombs the shots and the screams
L is for the love that we have stoking the coals of our dreams
A is for the anger shown, our feelings we cannot conceal
N is for the nights that we pray, "Oh God is this all real?!"
D is for the dare to war; to put in our minds and in our hands and when we grow might we know our rights to home in our land?
So you who are not Irish and who judge our hearts mad and bad
Think of your own home; your hearth and your kin, your hopes, and your deserves. Should your rights be denied and cheated by stealth, what kind of sentence would you serve?"

Sister Agatha sent me around the school to read that poem and soon unbeknown to me, I had been entered for various writing competitions; only discovering that I'd been entered when a letter arrived with a commendation or a prize for winning. Our class-writing compositions about chocolate beans and about anything our imaginations could dream up about chocolate were entered for the Cadbury's Creative Writing awards and a great big box filled with tins of chocolate was sent to our class. I took my letters of commendation home.

At twelve years old, Sister Agatha enrolled me for exams outside of the school. She gave me the bus money and an enrolment number and sent me down to the college in the city centre to sit four Royal Society of Art exams in English Literature, English Language, History, and Commerce. I didn't have time to get anxious about the exams because she only told me about it the day before.

"I just want you to go down to the technical college (known as the tech), hand in your number, go in to the big hall, sit down in the chair, which will have your number on it, and try to answer the questions on the sheets." In Sister Agatha's big lumpy hand was a white paper bag containing a couple of coconut marshmallows and an apple, which I was to take along with me encase I got hungry as I'd be missing my lunchtime.

I sat in the examination hall with the many other older children and it slowly dawned on me that I was sitting an exam. I felt terribly excited and a wee bit scared but as no one but Sister Agatha and myself knew that I was taking the exam, no-one needed to know if I didn't do well, and I could pretend that it never happened.

Months later, Sister Agatha's curly finger with the great big lump on it, summoned me up to her desk. Trying to disguise the broadest smile on her face as she handed me an envelope and fumbling in her usual anxious way with her teeth jumping around her mouth like they were dancing in her head with excitement, she said, "Just you open it dear, and read it."

I was already light headed and giddy as she had referred to me as 'dear'!

It seemed to take me forever to open the envelope, as I hadn't a clue what was inside. I didn't think that it would be anything bad because she would not have called me dear and wouldn't be looking so pleased but I couldn't be sure. The paper inside was pink and showed my name and number at the top with the name of the exams;

Royal Society of Arts: Distinction! was written beside my subjects.

I read that word again and again and looking back in disbelief at Sister Agatha, I saw a face bursting with pride. Behind her glasses, her beady eyes glazed over and taking out her big white handkerchief from her pocket, she blew her nose attempting to erase any sign of sentiment as though she had indulged herself enough.

"Now then, aren't you just great? See what you can do? Never forget that you have a good brain in your head and see that you use it!"

With that, she reached into the big cardboard box at the side of her desk and invited me to choose a Kimberly 'spring-sprong' or Mikado coconut marshmallow biscuit to take back to my seat.

I sat reading the letter over and over again. I couldn't understand how it happened. How come I was the class dunce whilst at St. Eugene's but was now getting these kinds of results? I wanted to run down to Saint Eugene's and tell Miss. Dunne and show the pink slip to the whole world but was contented to bring it home to show Mamai.

"You're your mother's daughter," my mother said in response, and although I wasn't quite sure what that meant, I took it as a compliment anyway. From then on, I couldn't wait to do my homework and hand it in. I loved my school and couldn't wait for my science lessons with Miss. McMillan who was like no other teacher I'd ever known because in her class, I believed that there was nothing too difficult. This was because if we didn't understand, she would explain and re-explain finding a different port of entry in to the part of us that would finally manage it.

The day that we were cutting up bulls' eyes I was so intently slicing into the iris that I pierced through the pupil and the black inky fluid shot straight into my eyes, and I ran round the class screaming as I thought I'd been blinded. I could hardly wait to hand in my homework, and I'd wait in desperation to receive my marks and comments that I would read over and over again. At the end of each term, Sister Agatha made us all stand around the classroom as she called out the marks of the various subjects. Whoever got the highest mark when all the individual marks had been added together for the various subjects was instructed to stand at the beginning of the line and eventually we would all be standing in order of achievement.

I was so proud to be either first, second, or third in the overall line of achievement. I was nearly always in competition with Moya McCann who was to become my best friend, or Fionnuala Breslin whom I resented and had became highly envious of as she joined our class later in the year, having come over from Australia. I hated Fionnuala's ability to attract friends like a magnet, and I resented her for stealing my friend

Sandra Cullen away from me. Then into the bargain, she knocked me off first position in the class at the end of the year, and I just had to live with it. There was me getting all competitive about not being first in the class yet I didn't feel good about the others at the end of the line. I knew something of what it must have felt for them because as much as the exercise was a physical anchor for those of us who had done well, it may have served to weigh down the esteem of my class mates who were at the end of the line and somehow it just didn't feel right. But I felt so good about myself that I could have sprouted wings and flown around the classroom, and I practically had to sit on myself so that my big head would not make the others at the end of the line look small.

The highs in school were often pulled back down to earth by the knocks of adolescent angst that showed itself in shenanigans to do with friendships, fights over boyfriends – those of whom were lucky enough to have one – and where jealousies and rivalries erupted and spilled out into proper fights. We spent endless hours in the playground as a result of bomb scares in the school. Moya and I were often trying to solve some friendship problem or other, like the time she tried in vain to raise me from the ruin that I was reduced to following the impromptu Class Beauty Contest dreamt up by one of the 'class tough shots' who managed to intimidate the life out of many of us who were small and timid and who never seemed to grow into our uniforms. We had the name of being 'Peuks'. I think that it was to do with us enjoying working as hard as we did and it made people sick and 'peuk' up.

The contest organizers forced us into writing the name of the girl who we thought was the ugliest in the class. I refused to join in and protested that it was a wrong thing to do even though it might have been more to do with my terror that I would be chosen.

As the nominations were being opened, I could see the instigators looking down towards me and whispering. I whispered to Moya, "Dear God, Moya, it's me. I know it is."

I breathed in the humiliation, which sunk in through every pore of my skin.

"No, Caroline it is not going to be you. You're not the worst in the class. Anyway it's a stupid contest, don't take them on."

Moya had nothing to worry about herself as she would have been likely to have won if the contest had been for the most beautiful girl, as she had huge big brown eyes, beautiful straight white teeth, a swarthy completion, and long brown curly hair.

The announcement was finally made, "The winner is ... Caroline Owens!"

You could have heard the grass grow, as an embarrassed and uncomfortable silence blasted into the classroom and through any semblance of protective membrane in my skin.

I wanted to be swallowed up in that moment and never be seen again. I couldn't stop the tears welling up in my eyes and the weight of the humiliation dragged my head down, and I was unable to look at faces of my classmates who might pity and mock me.

Moya who had become known as 'squeak' because she had the tiniest voice, stood up and tried to shout out as loud as she could in protest, "That's not fair! How would any of yous like it?"

Mary McGavigan announced that she would have a second count of the votes as she was sure that they had got it wrong. She quickly shouted out that there had been a mistake, and following a whispered confab with the organizers, Mary announced, "These votes aren't for the ugliest girl but the most beautiful, so Caroline Owens is the winner!"

Moya and Mary continued to try to console me, "Look Caroline, don't let the cheeky bitches grind you down. Do you think that they are any oil paintings themselves?"

Moya reminded me that my freckles were a sign of beauty. I tried to smile at her gestures and sentiments but could not be consoled, the damage had already been done, and my feelings of humiliation hung around inside of me like a bad rash of teenage acne that had erupted deep inside my self-esteem. I was officially the ugliest girl in the class and totally mortified into the bargain. How was I going to survive this adolescent business and still live to tell the tale?

Yet I had to 'batter on'. The local school drama festival was another highlight of school life. I was chosen to be Marilla Cuthbert, the mother character in 'Anne of Green Gables'. Anne Roddy, the bravest and most outrageous girl in our class had been cast as Anne and she played the part superbly. Anne was a highly gifted, spontaneous, and oppositional girl who gave the nuns and teachers a run for their money. She often refused the punishment of having her hands slapped with a tea square when the rest of us would just stretch out our hands and close our eyes as the tea square whacked down on to the palms of our hands.

Anne was a loveable rogue whom many felt intimidated by, yet I became especially fond of her. Although very bright herself, she would ask me to do her homework in exchange for a 'Jackie' magazine or an Elvis poster or Donny Osmond and Marie Osmond poster. Anne always seemed to have plenty of money about her, and was one of the few girls who didn't live in the Creggan Estate; she was from down in the town centre. Anne was as tough and rebellious as I was timid and compliant, and we developed a fondness and mutual respect for each other.

In the school play, Moya had been chosen as the child with the croup and Sandra Cullen was chosen as Matthew Cuthbert. Fionnuala Breslin, my nemesis, was cast as the stationmaster.

The little group of us were a merry band of thespians indeed but Sister Agatha's production and direction techniques at times knocked any delusions of stardom out of us, as she drummed our lines into us so forcefully as though our lives depended on this play being right.

Opening Scene:

Matthew Cuthbert – (Sandra, speaks to station master)

"Is the five thirty kind of late tonight?"

Station Master – (Fionnuala Breslin)

"The five thirty? It's been and gone a half an hour ago."

Then Matthew informs the stationmaster that he had been expecting a boy from the train and is informed that only a girl has arrived. Anne, overhearing the conversation, introduces herself to Matthew, who eventually takes her home in the pony and trap to meet Marilla (me) in the hope of persuading her to take the utterly incorrigible Anne instead of a boy. (Donna White has the job of making the trotting noises as she knocks together empty coconuts shells, behind the curtains.)

During rehearsals, Sister Agatha is a woman on a mission and made us do it over and over again until she was satisfied with the subtle variations and intonations as we delivered our lines.

Child with croup – (Moya McCann)

"Ahhh, mwhaaa" – cries and moans

Moya tries to cry but Sister Agatha is not happy with the quality of her crying so she grabs Moya, who is lying in a bed and splashes water on her head and face to give the impression of sweat, fever, and tears. Sister Agatha's big hands repeatedly dig into Moya's shoulder. "Cry,

cry! You're supposed to be sick and in pain and suffering... that's not a difficult part to play. Cry, cry, I tell you!"

Her frustration gets the better of her and she anxiously loses her temper as Moya begins to cry for real, given that her shoulder has just been pulverized.

"Oh for goodness sake! You're useless, if you can't manage to pretend to cry, just get up and give the part to someone else..."

Moya is hauled up from her makeshift bed whilst Sister Agatha continues to mutter to herself; her teeth jumping up and down in her mouth hitting her bottom lips, which by now were working up a froth. The rest of us were unable to sympathize with poor Moya, as we couldn't help but be reduced to sporadic seizures of uncontrollable laughter and giddiness at the sight of Sister Agatha loosing it.

"Right, that's it, you're on curtains," she mutters, as she drags Moya by the scruff of the neck, her tie and shirt now all twisted, and Moya is deposited at the side of the stage, where she is sniffing up her tears and unable to see the funny side of it. Yet she seems clearly relieved to take her place on curtains but terrified in case she might not manage her new role.

For about two months of the year, 'The Play' became the most important endeavour of school life for A3. But the rehearsals themselves were a daily pantomime as we were knocked and moulded into shape. As soon as we got our key lessons over with in the mornings, the desks were put to the back of the class and we took our places on stage ready for action.

Sandra Cullen had become a very close friend of mine as she lived in the street beside Broadway and we knew each other well before we started St. Mary's. I remember running to Sandra's house as soon as I could to tell her that my mother had just told me about periods, and although I was unable to work it all out, especially the bit about the visitor coming every month, Sandra and I spent many private times talking and thinking about the puzzle and excitement of our changing bodies.

But I had to tolerate Sandra's popularity in St. Mary's, as she was another one who had a magnetic quality about her, and she seemed naturally and effortlessly able to attract friendships. I thought that it wasn't fair because she was my oldest friend and should stay loyal to me. I tried various tactics to retain my position as her best friend and seized any opportunity to remind her of the fact that we'd been friends since we were tiny. I used to tell Sandra my dreams, as I was enormously interested in my own dreams and often woke up to vivid pictures and powerful feelings emerging from them, and so I became intensely interested in the phenomena of dreams, regularly quizzing and interrogating my friends about theirs. I seemed to gain something of a reputation around the school, as children would come to me and ask what I thought their dreams meant. I would often invite them to a private place in the playground at lunchtime and listen with great curiosity to the dream, and try to link it to what might be going on in their lives. Queuing up at the canteen one lunch time, I was at the top of the queue and Sandra who was quite a bit far down the line, shouted up to me, "Hey Caroline. I had a dream about you and me last night, and we were having a fight. What do you think it means?"

Having to think on my feet quickly, I responded at the top of my voice, "Well, that's a case of 'opposites', Sandra. Your dream is telling you that you want to be my best friend and that you would fight for our friendship." As soon as the words, that seemed to come from nowhere and out of my mouth, I actually believed myself and thought that I was right.

"Dear God, Caroline, you're a liar. Is that right enough?" Sandra replied, with excitement and curiosity.

"Aye, definitely, Sandra. When you dream about somebody like that, it's definitely because you deep down want to be their friend... it's about opposites!"

"Do you see her?" Sandra turned to the others in the queue, as if she had just been told the secret of life itself. "I think that she is right. She really and truly knows what she is talking about! Caroline, will you meet me in the playground after lunch and tell me more?" Sandra made a public appointment for all to hear, and I was in that moment appointed to the role of 'School dream reader!'

Sandra and I seemed to have reconnected after that, and I was relieved that she now considered me her best friend but we still hung around with Majella and Moya as well and seemed to manage to appreciate each other's differences without too much rivalry. It was all going swimmingly until a few days before the opening night of the local drama festival, which was to open with A3's Anne of Green Gables, and I had sensed that Sandra was hanging around in and outside of school with the other girls and seemingly avoiding me. Majella had become her new best friend and I just had to put up with it because I didn't want to lose Sandra's friendship but the dynamics of four was tricky to negotiate and our relationships became seriously strained in the lead up to the big night.

I had become aware of new whisperings in the class with heads looking my way. I knew that something was being said about me. Again, I turned to Moya, "Moya, I get the feeling that people are talking about me."

"No, Caroline. You only think it."

But I kept thinking it, "Moya, could you try to find out for me what's going on?"

Moya, in her usual sensitive and compassionate way and in response to my continued feelings of paranoia and persecution, sensitively turned to me with a face that attempted to prepare me for bad news, "Look Caroline, don't take them on. They just don't know what they are talking about."

"Moya, for God's sake. What are they talking about?"

"Caroline, I don't think you want to know,"

"Aye I do Moya, go'ne tell me."

Moya was right, I really didn't want to know but I had to know because I was going mad with not knowing and couldn't stand it a minute longer.

"Look Caroline, don't take them on, but they are saying that your dadai is mad and is in Gransha."

I wanted to kill every one of them stone dead, why did they need to bring my dadai into it. School was the place where I didn't have to worry about Dadai and didn't have to think about the struggles at home but now my safe place had been invaded, and I was affronted. No matter how hard I tried to get on and rise above the troubles all around me, it seemed that there would always be another thing to hit me up the face; some other kind of mortification and public humiliation would emerge. Life was beginning to feel too hard and although I had never missed a day at school, I wondered if it would just be easier to go away and hide because I wouldn't have to show my ugly face nor look at the sneering and pitying faces.

Yet I loved my new school. I loved being there and I loved my dadai too and no-one was going to spoil my school for me nor talk about my father.

As soon as Anne Roddy became aware that I had found out about the rumour, she approached me with a confidence and strength, which I immediately copied.

"Caroline, is it true that your dadai is back in the asylum? Is your dadai in Gransha?"

"Aye it is true. Me dadai is sick, and Gransha is a hospital where he is getting better, he's not mad, he's sick. He's got schizophrenia."

"What kind of magazines does he like?" Anne asked.

"Well anything to do with boxing or music, opera or anything classical."

"I'll bring you in some to give to him."

As soon as I said the words to her, I seemed to grow in confidence. For the first time, I had mentioned the word and the fact in public. The word 'schizophrenia' was suddenly not so scary. I loved my father, and I was going to stand up for him.

Anne didn't seem to feel the need to ask me any more questions, perhaps recognizing that enough had been said.

And although I felt somewhat relieved that I no longer had to keep a guilty secret, the anger remained as I knew that people would be talking about my father and making him out to be pathetic or mad, and I just didn't want all of that business brought into my school, my sanctuary. It was true that my father had been in and out of the psychiatric hospital throughout my childhood and youth; discharged then readmitted, then weekends home, and eventually discharged again. Just a part of our family life that I tried to keep tucked away behind closed doors. I thanked God for my school, which became my most important, sane, and safe place, and I just loved it. I secretly nurtured a seed within me that I would one day go to university like my uncle Liam.

Majella had got the blame for spreading the rumour, and I could no longer speak to her and kept away from her and Sandra. I just locked myself away at home in the evenings and got on with my homework and practiced my lines for The Play. One evening Sandra came to my house and I was delighted that she was once again calling in for me. I was just about to get my coat on to go outside when she said, "Caroline, Majella Friel is down the back lane and I'll ask her for a fight with you if you want."

I was sick to my stomach with fear. I didn't want to fight Majella nor anyone else. I never had a physical fight with anyone in my life. Although I had been sparring partner for my boxing brothers, I had never considered myself to be in a fight. But there was an audience of onlookers from our class standing at our gate at the end of the garden and waiting for my response.

I whispered to Sandra, "No, it doesn't matter. It's over and done with now. I just want to forget about it."

"But if you don't fight her everybody will think that you are a coward. If it was me, I wouldn't let anyone speak about my father like that. Caroline, you're going to have to ask her for a fight. She'll probably say no anyway."

My legs were like jelly and my insides were turning over with fear and confusion. I desperately didn't want to have a fight. I was terrified of being hurt. I didn't know what to do but I couldn't bear another public humiliation.

"Okay, ask her," I said, with my heart hammering at my chest.

Sandra was no sooner gone than she had arrived back at my door. Majella had agreed to the fight, and I was informed that it was to happen down behind the Creggan shops that very evening in a small secluded piece of waste land. I had to be there straight away but Sandra would go off and make sure that Majella would be there.

I was left sitting at the bottom of the stairs in our hallway in a mush of terror, bewilderment, and rage at being asked to have a fight. But then the anger that I had about my father's illness came rushing through my body and settled in my jaw, which was clenched tight, and I tried to feel ready for a fight. I wished that I had asked that we use boxing gloves because I knew that I could manage a fight with them but they definitely would have thought me mad too if I had suggested such a thing.

On my arrival at the back of the shops, I was met with a circle of up to ten girls, some from our class and others from the streets who had gathered to look on.

I couldn't back out and any envy, jealousy, and anger that I may have previously felt towards Majella came sparing into my mind and into my hands as we were literally thrown together in battle because neither of us would agree to throw the first blow. Without speaking a word, we scratched and kicked, scraped and grabbed each other's faces. I wanted to give up as soon as I had started but as I was being kicked, I gained a perverse kind of strength and will to fight as though I was fighting my father's corner but the real fight seemed to be about saving face and not letting myself down. The onlookers kept asking, "Do you give up?"

And neither Majella nor I would lessen our grip. We both tore and pulled at each other's long hair for all our worth, banging each other's heads repeatedly on the pavement. I was so tired, I longed for Majella to give up but I couldn't allow myself to and although every inch of my body was hurting and my head pounding with the pain, I couldn't give in and refused to cry.

Mercifully, just about the time when I couldn't stand it any longer, a woman came running out of the back of the fish and chip shop and broke up the fight. The others scarpered away as quick as she looked at them.

"Jesus Mary and St. Joseph, look at the state of the two of you. Where did ye girls learn to fight like that? It's a disgrace."

I immediately recognized the face of the woman and became terrified that she would tell Mamai.

I couldn't stand up. I tried to straighten but was bent over like an old woman as we had been locked into a stooping and crouching position for such a long time. After all that, there were no winners. Just like the friggin' war on our streets, nobody was giving up or giving in.

I don't know how I managed to get myself home but like a wounded animal I found my way home, dragged myself straight into the bathroom, and locked the door. I looked into the mirror and didn't recognize my face. Running a hot bath and barely able to lift my leg I climbed in, lay down, and the tears silently rolled down and seeped into my swollen face. What had I done? I had overstepped some sacred threshold inside of myself and I could never be the same person again. Sad for my father and sad for myself, I cried and cried quietly to myself, as my long hair floated all around me in the surface of the bath. I soon realized that my hair was falling out in clumps. My head would not stay upright. It flopped and fell from side to side and from back to front, I thought it was going to fall off and that I would lose my head. I managed to go to bed straight after the bath without Mamai noticing. All she knew was that I didn't feel too well.

The next morning my head was no better, and I could barely keep it held upright.

Mamai screamed in horror when she saw my swollen face and that my hair had fallen out, leaving bald patches all over.

"Dear God in heaven, did you wash your hair with that Esoderme Shampoo last night?"

"Aye, I did Mamai."

"Holy God, your hair has fallen out all over your head. Sweet Mother of God you have had a desperate allergic reaction because your face and eyes are swollen too. I only got that shampoo yesterday from the chemist and it must be far too severe. I don't think you can go to school... you're not well."

"No Mamai, I'm grand, I'll be okay. I feel okay. I need to go to school. The play is coming up and I have to be there."

The thought of not turning up to school was too much, and I had to go in and show my face bad as it was. Even though I could barely walk, nor hold my head still for a matter of seconds, I couldn't not go to school. Everyone would know that Majella had beaten me and she would be considered the winner. In any case, I had never missed a day at school and I wasn't going to miss one now.

I managed to persuade my mother to let me go to school and she already had the shampoo back in a bag to return it to the chemist with a complaint.

Neither Majella nor Sandra arrived in school for the next few days.

No one seemed to talk about the fight. After two days, I couldn't bear the guilt any longer, and went up to Majella's house and knocked at the door. I hoped that Majella would answer so that I could say sorry and make friends. The door opened to Majella's mother Minnie who had always been a wee friendly woman who thoroughly enjoyed the company of youngsters.

"Is Majella coming out?" I asked trying to smile, as though this was an ordinary question.

"Yes Caroline, what about ye? Majella isn't well she has been sick in bed this last two days and I'm thinking of getting the doctor. Her hair is falling out and her head keeps flopping from side to side, and she has a desperate pain in the neck but she doesn't want me to get the doctor. If it doesn't clear up by the morning, I'll have to send for the doctor."

Minnie invited me up to see Majella in her bedroom, and immediately Minnie had left the room, we apologized to each other. Majella said that she had never intended to spread the rumour and she didn't want to have a fight with me but she didn't feel that she could back down. She had just mentioned 'it' to someone and before she knew it, 'it' was around the class. She told me that she was fond of my father and would never want to show him up. Minnie brought us up some tea and toast and we never again talked about 'it' except to laugh that we seemed to have exactly the same injuries, which gave us a special bond.

The fact that Majella and I became good friends after that was the strangest thing.

But neither of us ever wanted to go through anything like it again.

Somehow it didn't matter so much afterwards that everybody knew that my father had been in a psychiatric hospital, as long as no one ever referred to him or me as being 'mad' then I could live with it and hold my head up high. As Mamai would say,

"Whatever bother we have in this house, its clean bother," so I'd be sure to walk tall.

We managed to get our act together for the drama festival, and I couldn't help feeling envious of Anne Roddy who won the best actress of the year in our category, but the blow was softened, as the proud Sister Agatha gave us a party in class with orange juice, crisps, sweets, and marshmallow biscuits to celebrate our hard work and that we had won best play in our year.

High school would never be the same again for me when we had moved on from Sister Agatha's class and up to the second year. That next year our class was due to play Oliver Twist in the drama festival and I was cast as Oliver partly because I was so small and had a boyish look to me. The role involved me laying in a wooden coffin, which produced many a wakeful sleep and some terrible nightmares but I desperately wanted to play the part, so every time I had stepped inside that coffin, I prayed that I would not wake in the night thinking about my granddad Murphy and me laying in the coffin together. I did dream though that the door of my bedroom was me granda's coffin and that he was lying there looking out at me winking and asking me for liquorice. I tried with all my might to scream but no sound came out of my mouth, and I woke wet with sweat of fear. I wanted to run into Mamai's bedroom but I couldn't because I'd have to pass my bedroom door, which had turned into a friggin' coffin. This dream recurred over and over again, and me being trapped in my bedroom was too terrifying to tell anyone about it. Talking about it might make it more real so unable to get a decent night sleep for weeks, I turned up at school looking just like Oliver, pale and sickly with black rings around my eyes.

And after all that, we were informed that our class was to have our entry to the drama festival withdrawn because some people in the class had been misbehaving so badly. No amount of begging made our new teacher change her mind and even though we were convinced that she would change her mind at the last minute, she was determined to teach us a lesson. And that she did. So, all the friggin' nightmares were for nothing.

We longed for Sister Agatha's return even though she was harsh at times and used the T square on us many a time. Her response to misbehaviour was quick: a sharp slap on the hand with the T square, a stand to face the wall, or a visit down to the head sister Aloysius. Strangely, these were easier to forgive than having our entry withdrawn. That was just shockin' and not fair, and we felt it deeply. I don't even remember what the flumin' hell we had done to deserve it.

All hope of ever winning best actress had eluded me when in the following year at the age of fourteen, our class was to enter the competition again with the Sean O'Casey play, 'Juno and the Paycock' set in Dublin in the 1920s about the Irish rebellion and the fight for Irish freedom. When we read the O'Casey plays, 'Shadow of a Gunman' and 'Juno', you would have thought that they were about life in Derry now in the mid 1970s. I couldn't believe that O'Casey had captured so brilliantly the conundrums, paradoxes, and ironies of the conflict between religion and politics within the Irish context because as far as I was concerned these were stories that we all recognized as being our stories of here and now. I was developing something of a deeper knowledge about Irish politics and had become more aware of the political struggle, so O'Casey's plays provided me with a sense of validation and vindication for my own conflicted views and ruminations. When I weighed it all up in my mind though, I was left with the shocking probability that things hadn't changed since the 1920s and were unlikely to change; perhaps Ireland would always be at war.

I was surprised that the nuns allowed us to perform such a play, as we were not formally taught Irish history and it was not on the syllabus. But there was a new breed of teacher coming through into our school; we even had one male teacher who had the life tortured out of him. I don't know how he stood it, surrounded by a school full of rebellious, prepubertal, and pubertal girls, a nunnery, and staff-room full of women.

The roles for the play were called out in class, and I was deeply disappointed to be cast as Mrs. Tancred who didn't feature much in the play at all, and so I resigned myself to the fact that I was not destined to become an actress.

Mrs. Tancred's son, who had been considered a diehard Republican, had been riddled down and martyred to the cause of Irish freedom. Mrs. Tancred was distraught and inconsolable, and she laments the pains that she had suffered bringing her son into the world and carrying him to his cradle and now she is suffering again, carrying him out of the world and to his grave.

Act Two (towards end of scene)

Mrs. Tancred (me), "Me home is gone now, he was me only child, Mother of God, Mother of God and Blessed Virgin Mary where were you when me darling son was riddled with bullets, when me darling son was riddled with bullets… Sacred Heart of the Crucified Jesus, take away our hearts of stone... and give us hearts of flesh!... Take away this burden of hate and give us his own eternal love."

Well that was about the height of it and I didn't have much more than that to say apart from inconsolable crying and sobbing.

Well I wasn't going to win best actress of the year with a banshee part the size of a sixpence so I wasn't really bothered about the play until the day of the festival when I looked out from behind the curtains to see a packed house, including boys form St. Joseph's School.

Mamai, Dadai and Mamai's sister, Aunt Bridie were in the audience waving up at me.

Three judges sat high above the audience on chairs mounted on top of plinths in the middle of the assembly hall. The adrenalin kicked in, and I knew that I would give it my all in my best Southern Irish accent, which I had picked up in Cork all those years ago. I would not let the class or myself down.

When it was my entrance, I came running on to the stage with my black shall around my head, wearing Sister Agatha's big long black nuns skirt, wailing like a banshee and delivering my lines in the best southern Irish accent I could muster. I believed every bit of what I was saying and really became upset as though my son had just been killed stone dead.

There was a silence at first then a wave of laughter in the audience, and all of a sudden, I felt sick. Had I totally got it wrong, was it meant to be funny all along and I hadn't realized it, or was I just a desperate, crazy, useless actress? It was becoming difficult for my lines to be heard above the laughter and an adjudicator rang her bell, stood up, and scolded the audience, explaining that they needed to understand the subtlety of the play and that this was a serious part.

That was that and I vowed that I would never act again because even having had a part the size of a tanner, I still managed to show myself up.

Two weeks later at the awards ceremony, I didn't take too much notice of what was happening and had taken myself off to the back of the packed assembly hall, climbed up the monkey bars where I could get a good view of the winners, and joined in on the clapping every time a winner had been announced.

The hall was heaving with pupils and teachers from our school, as well as the other schools in the competition. The atmosphere was full of excitement and noisy anticipation, and it was difficult to hear what was going on. There was something of a commotion up the front near the stage and then the biggest cheer ever so I just joined in cheering as loud as I could when gradually quiet descended, and I could hear Miss. Wilson ask through the microphone, "Does anyone know if she is here today?"

I asked some other wee girl if she knew who she was talking about and she said, "She's looking for Caroline Owens, who's won Best Actress of the Year."

I was about seven feet up the back wall of the assembly hall hanging on to the monkey bars and the shock made me lose my grip. and I fell off down into the crowd below who cushioned my fall but I nearly broke my leg as I carved my way through the packed hall. I limped as fast as I could, taking no notice of the pain in my leg for fear that my prize would be given to someone else. I managed to work my way through the chanting, "Caroline! Caroline! Caroline!" Over and over again, I drank the tears of joy and shock, which wetted my red face and seeped into my mouth, as I reached the stage and was hoisted up on to it by a group of sixth formers. I stood there in complete shock and pleasure beyond anything I had ever known; giggling and crying at the same time and looking out into the sea of cheering chanters.

Miss. Wilson made a speech about how well I had interpreted the role and the character, and of how well I was able to speak in a Southern Irish accent. She made the point that having a small part in a play didn't mean having an insignificant part, and that I had played my part so well that I was the star of the show. I would never have dreamt it in a month of Sundays.

I was presented with a box of chocolates, a book voucher, and a trophy, and I drank in through every pore of my body the sound of the applause.

How I loved my school and couldn't wait for every day to start as I had aspired to doing really well and going to university. I wasn't sure what I wanted to do but it would be something to do with English, perhaps I would be a teacher. So I would work really hard so that I would get into the O- level class.

All pupils who reached the standard would be put into the O-level class. There was only one O-level class in the school and it was the gateway to A-levels, which was the direct pathway to university. Moya and I couldn't wait to have our names called out, knowing that our academic achievement was up there with the best of them from all the other classes in our year.

The names were called out. Moya's name was called early on, and we smiled to each other, as we waited for my name. We waited and eventually the class was full, and Sister Assumpta went on to call out the names of the CSE class, which was a lower level exam class that did not provide an automatic entry to A-levels.

I seemed to have blanked out of my mind the immediate feelings surrounding it all. This was the biggest disappointment in my school life. I simply couldn't bear it, Why the 'f..k' was I not in the 'f..k'in' O-level Class, even after having got 99% on my science exam this year and having averaged at 85% overall my exams? I screamed to myself inside, as I watched the door to the O-level class close with Moya and Fionnula securely taking their seats inside and all the others who didn't do as well as me now taking ourselves to one of the CSE classes. Just like the time that I didn't pass my Eleven Plus and didn't manage to go with Roma to the Grammar School, I watched my friend Moya walk towards success and I was left feeling like a reject and a failure.

I just didn't give a dam anymore and a part of me didn't want to know the reason why I hadn't been chosen because I couldn't bear to hear that I wasn't good enough. A few weeks later, however, I told Sandra that I would find Sister Assumpta and ask her why I hadn't been put into the O-level class. If my mother was able to go down and knock on a priest's door and ask for money and if she could challenge a nun then I could go and knock on her office door. I had something to say and I was going to say it.

Sandra came with me, and I tapped on the door as quiet as a mouse.

"Caroline, she won't hear that under a wet newspaper. I think she is a wee bit deaf," said Sandra who then battered on the door.

"Come in." We could hear Sister Assumpta's tiny whispery voice. In we went and I stood there now unsure of what was going to come out of my mouth.

"Well, girls sit down. What can I do for you?"

"Caroline has something she wants to ask you, Sister," said Sandra.

Sister Assumpta turned to me, her kind eyes were all I needed to help me blurt it out.

I breathed as much air into my lungs as I could in order to get the words out of my mouth, "Excuse me Sister Assumpta, I was wondering if …." As soon as I opened my mouth, the tears came welling up in my eyes.

Sister Assumpta's concerned face scanned mine as she bent down, "Oh dear Caroline. What's the matter?"

Well, I gasped, "I was just wondering … Well … Why I've not been chosen to go into the O-level class?"

"Me too Sister. Why am I not in the O-level class?" asked Sandra.

Sister whispered to Sandra that she should hurry back to class and that she needed to have a wee chat to me alone.

Well that was it. It was out of my mouth and into the world and that my disappointment was so heartfelt, I couldn't disguise to myself or to her. Sister Assumpta put her hand on my shoulder and softly whispered into my ear that I would do very well in D4 class and would likely be at the top of the class.

"But Sister, I have got better grades than many of the others who are in that O-level class, and I was just wondering why I'm not in it?"

Sister went on even more quietly, "Well Caroline. Your mamai needs you at home and with your dadai not being well, your mamai will be relying on you to go out and get a job as soon as you can when you leave school."

I couldn't hear anything else, my ears had gone deaf, and I hadn't got the strength to put up a fight for myself because not only would I never contradict a teacher but also there was a sense that this kindly and holy nun's word was gospel. Sister Agatha would never have let it happen but she had retired the previous year. Maybe I could go down to the Convent and tell her the whole story, and she would definitely sort it out. She would shoot straight up to the school like a big black rubber bullet. And with her red face and her long black floaty skirt wafting behind her and her black veil blowing against the wind, she would be spitting froth from her chattering teeth and she would drag me straight out of the CSE class and plonk me into a chair right at the front of the O-level class and not another word would be said about it. I didn't think that Sister Assumpta would be too pleased about that though, and she was such a wee timid and quiet and kind nun that I didn't want to cause ructions in the Convent.

I would have gone home to ask Mamai to go down to the school and sort it out but I wondered if she had been the one who had told them not to put me into the class. Was this where she came to the night she had gone missing when Tommy, Liam, and I went looking for her? The lights in the school were on that night, and I figured that she must have told them about our home troubles but I couldn't let myself believe that my own mother, who told us always to take our chances would purposefully spoil my chances at school. My mother had known full well how much I loved school and how hard I worked and that I had good brains. I knew that because she told me herself.

I didn't give a hoot anymore about school and although I never missed a day the whole five years at that school, that day was the day that I had lost all interest. I couldn't be bothered to study and just did the minimum, and I became one of the silly girls who were only interested in boys and in being difficult for the teachers.

On the last day of high school, there was a big prize giving festival, and I had received a certificate for being one of three outstanding pupils in the school for achievement over the five years and I got an extra award for having had 100% attendance; I had never missed a day in that whole five years. The head nun Sister Aloysius even made a speech about me, which included how I was a great help to Mamai.

I didn't give too much of a hoot about any of it because if I was so outstanding, "Why the frig was I not in the flumen O-level class!"

Chapter 11
ADOLESCENT ANGST

ONE of my mother's biggest regrets was that we left the house in Broadway because it was damp. She had complained to the housing trust time and time again that the repairs needed to be done because we were all getting too many colds that she reckoned was to do with the dampness, it fell on deaf ears, and the Housing Executive refused to do the necessary work. So we were allocated a brand new house just by the reservoir. We were only there a week when crashing noises in the kitchen woke us, and my mother came into our bedroom screaming that rats had been crawling around in the pots and pans under the sink in the kitchen. Mamai was terrified of cats and had been known to faint if she had put her hand on anything furry. The sight of rats was too much and the very next day, we packed our bags and left to go live temporarily in our aunt's house until another house could be found for us.

We soon had our own house in Rinmore, and none of us liked it because it was half the size of our beloved number 11 Creggan, Broadway and you couldn't swing a cat in it. But even though Mamai deeply regretted her decision to leave Broadway, she couldn't allow herself to dwell on it and was grateful that we were now up in Rinmore with her old neighbours and across the street from what used to be her own mother's house.

So here we were, now in Rinmore Drive, Creggan Estate, living next door to the Kivlehan's, twelve of them all living in a three-bedroom house. The bedrooms housed little more space than that needed for the beds, and I couldn't work out where all of the Kivlehans slept because there was barely enough room for the ten of us. Mr. and Mrs Kivlehan insisted that we call them by their Christian names, Maryanne and Mickey. Maryanne was to become Mamai's best friend and to me, she was a rare treasure of a woman, whom I came to depend upon as much as my mamai did.

Maryanne was a big-breasted woman with swarthy skin with an Italian look about her. She always had her hair done in that 'salon newly done' look and had long painted fingernails. She was a heavy smoker and always seemed to carry a packet of fags in her hand, somehow still managing to look glamorous. I looked on in fascination, as she would ceremoniously open the cellophane wrapper of her fresh packet of fags, scrunch the wrapper into a ball, open the flap of the box, take out the gold or silver foil blanket covering the tips of the fags, and proceed to slide the new fag out of the box. She would then place the cigarette between her two fingers with nails dressed in shiny pink varnish, and the cig was then raised up into her mouth, where she would suck and then blow out lovely rings of smoke.

Maryanne came round every day for a cup of tea and a bun and to hear 'the bars', a Derry woman's way of asking to hear the news. The expression apparently came from the shirt factories, which were the biggest industry in Derry and provided work for women in the main. The story goes that following the weekends in the 1950s, the women would return to their jobs on Monday morning. If they had a good story to tell about the weekend, perhaps meeting up with Yankee soldiers from the Yankee Army Base or sailors who had docked down by the banks of the River Foyle, they would rattle their scissors on the metal bars, which ran above the sewing machines to get the attention of other women so that the story could be told. So now it was just normal parlance for Derry women to ask each other, "What's the bars" whilst the Derry men would ask "What's the craic". I didn't know where that one came from but I had thought that it might have been to do with how they told stories to each other about who they managed to have a fight with or gave a crack to. But I later learned that it was 'craic' meaning good fun or 'good value', and Maryanne was definitely both.

She was the mother of the street and managed her money so well that she was often called upon to lend a few pound to somebody or other. If anyone ran out of sugar, powered milk, or needed a tin of something or other, they could knock at Maryanne's door, place their order, and add that they would replace it the next day or when they got their benefit payments. The order was likely to be delivered after Maryanne sent one of her weans upstairs to the bedroom to the 'hole in the wall'; a great big cupboard that stored all kinds of tinned foods, cereals, flour, toilet rolls, and non perishable foodstuffs. Everybody loved Maryanne, and her friendship seemed to help keep Mamai sane whilst we lived in Rinmore Drive.

One of the good things about moving there was that it was nearer to Moya McCann's house and Moya became my best friend. Moya and

I dressed in the same clothes when we could and walked the streets of Creggan looking for 'talent'... boys. Our usual haunt was the Creggan Community Centre, where we'd go to sometimes in the week but definitely to the Friday and Saturday night discos, which we lived for. We were always out looking for a boyfriend, and Moya had a string of admirers and a string of talent whom she had spotted, but I only had eyes for her cousin... Frank McCann.

Frank was a big six-foot, lanky blond-haired lad with beautiful blue eyes, and every time I set eyes on him, I thought that I could faint with the very look of him. So the best place to go look for him was in 'The Centre'. The only trouble was that most of the other girls our age in Creggan were out to do the same and given that there were four females to every male in Derry's population, the pickings were slim, and it wasn't easy to get off with somebody.

Frank hung around with John Clarke, who was a bit shorter than Frank and wore glasses; they had the look of Laurel and Hardy and lived up to the image, as their way of attracting the talent was through telling jokes and acting the clown. I had hoped that Moya would fancy John and that I would get off with Frank and that we'd be two couples together. We did everything we could to attract the boys but we really needed to get ourselves some new clothes, and as neither of our parents could afford to buy us what we wanted, we set about the work of building up a wardrobe of style. Moya and I loved 'the style', and so we had to go out to work and buy our own. Our first real job was as care assistants for the sick and elderly at a Convent Home named Termonbacca.

Moya and I were thrilled to get the job at age fourteen and so got up at five o'clock in the thick black of winters morning and together walked down the long road from the top of Creggan to the Coach road. I was terrified because we had been told that in the olden days, there had been ghosts and banshees who lived in this spooky, remote, and steep valley. We walked that long walk to Termonbacca all happed up with scarves gloves and hats with only our eyes peeping out, and we linked our arms together as tight as we could as though we were joined at the hip. Many a morning, we shivered with cold and fear and the more we tried not to think about the banshees, the more we couldn't get them out of our minds. Every wee sound made us quicken our steps faster and faster and by the time we reached the Convent, we were knackered, breathless, and in need of a lie down.

Chapter 11 ADOLESCENT ANGST

The first job on my first day was to mop out the smelly rooms, which stank with the stench of pungent urine and 'old body' odour combined with a breakfast smell of food. The sickly combination ran up my nostrils and dived immediately into my belly... I felt sick. The heat of the place cooked the smells together inside my stomach, and I could feel myself feeling faint but I took deep breaths as I ran into each room and moped what I could, before running out to the corridor to the bucket of water where I would breathe again. I ran into my third room with my mop, bending down under the bed to mop the floor to find that some poor oul soul had shat the bed and the sight and smell of it sent me into a dizzy spin. The next I knew of it, I was sitting in the chapel surrounded by nuns and old people and as I opened my eyes to see the face of a nun right in front of me, I passed out for the second time.

It was all too much: with the stories of banshees and ghosts; smells of shit, urine, and old people's bodies; the stifling heat, and the shocking face of nuns. I thought that I was in some kind of horror movie and it was all the more odd that I had to beg the nuns to keep me on because I needed the money. They wanted to let me go as I wasn't up to the job and I had wasted half the morning recovering in the chapel. But they reluctantly agreed to give me a second chance, and I was able to keep my job for the best part of a year. I earned seven pounds for a twelve-hour day but had to hand it in to my mother. She gave me three pounds back to spend on myself.

Over time, Moya and me got ourselves other weekend jobs in order to fund our fashion and our discos. We were chuffed to get a job in Austin's, which was supposed to be Ireland's first or leading department store. We both worked there in the café and really enjoyed ourselves, even though it meant working hard.

I almost got the sack again when one day when the owner, Larry Hasson, a wee tiny man about as tall as me, was chatting to this really posh, well-to-do woman who had a wee ugly dog with her. Larry, who had been admiring the dog, summoned me quickly by clicking his fingers towards me and told me to go get a pan and brush and clean up the dog poop, which was freshly steaming right in between them. I was affronted and sick at the thought of touching it or smelling it and returned to Harry handed him the pan and brush and walked off.

"Excuse me. I want you to clean up this mess," he ordered.

"I'm sorry Mr. Hasson but I'm not 'a shit shoveler'. In any case, I'll be sick if I even attempt it."

Mr. Hasson proceeded to clean up the mess himself, and Moya and I watched, as it looked like he was about to throw up but he tried to disguise his disgust and anger. I just couldn't bring myself to do it, as it also made me feel like I was some kind of second-class citizen in front of this posh woman, who should have cleaned up the mess herself. I think that in a different situation, I would have had a go at cleaning it up but couldn't stoop so low in front of her.

The next day, Mr. Hasson Jr called me to the office, and I knew that I was just about to be fired and was prepared to tell him about how insulted I was, when he asked, "So you like working in the café do you?"

"Yes."

"What do you like about it?"

"Well, I love meeting the customers."

"But I understand that you don't like the messy jobs, do you?"

"Well, it depends."

"Maybe café work is not for you then because it involves a lot of mess and sometimes unexpected mess."

That's it, I thought. That's the end of my style and my discos.

"So how would you like a job in the store's crockery department?"

"Thanks very much, Mr. Hasson but I would rather stay in the café if that's all right because I would like to stay with my friend, Moya."

Mr. Hasson looked surprised and a bit put out that I was turning down a kind of sideways promotion but he just sat back in his chair and looked again like he was going to sack me when he smiled and told me to get back to work.

Moya and me would lift our wages, which was fifteen pounds, and go out and buy exactly the same clothes so that we were kitted out for the community centre disco on the Saturday night. Bringing in the money was a constant source of tension because I always had to hand my money into my mother first, and she would then hand half of it back to me.

I began to resent home life, and my mother and I found that I was nearly always at odds with her, and I was caring less about my family.

Chapter 12
FALLING ON GUNS

WITH our new parallel trousers, cream Dexter coats, and shiny brogue shoes, Moya thought that we looked gorgeous, and so we paraded ourselves at the disco in front of Frank, and Jeed – her new crush. Thank God for the Creggan Community Centre, as this was our den and our safe place away from the troubles on the streets, which were relentless, and from the worries about the war, which by now had been going on for eight years practically demolishing our town. Many of the Creggan teenagers flocked to 'The Centre', where we'd dance and lament to our adolescent crushes. It was 1976, and Queen's Bohemian Rhapsody had been at the top of the music charts for nearly a year, and as we all sang along, we whipped ourselves into a frenzied jumping, sweaty mass of hormones, which were just looking for some place to be let loose.

"Is this the real life, or is this just fantasy? The song was about a poor boy from a poor family who was telling his "Mama" that he'd killed a man and that he'd put a gun against his head and pulled the trigger and then he was dead, He told his Mama that his life had just begun but now he was throwing it all away.

It was scarily and hysterically close to the bone to contemplate the lyrics, especially given that a fair few of the youth at 'The Centre' would have been actively involved in one or other of the IRA factions and may have, in fact, killed somebody or had put a gun against someone's head. Our enjoyment of the song was sharply interrupted the night that me and Moya were dancing around our handbags, when in came two hard women from the woman's faction of the IRA on a recruitment drive.

Dressed in black Crombie coats, white parallel trousers, and heavy, black, highly polished brogues, one much taller than the other who was even smaller than I was; the two toughs approached us in the middle of our dance. We continued to dance, and I knew by the look on their face that they were not about to ask if they could join in. My nerves got the better of me, and I smiled at them, hoping that it would somehow alter the look on their face and perhaps dilute the atmosphere of tension.

"Yes, what about ye?" I smiled nervously

Moya and I continued to dance frantically around the bags.

"We're having a joining up at the back of the centre tonight at ten o'clock. We need more women in the IRA. Can we expect to see you there?"

Still dancing but now completely out of step with the music, my thoughts and body movements speeded up in pace with my heartbeat, which I thought would beat its way out of my chest.

I looked at Moya and briefly speechless, we danced on top of the handbags and on to their feet.

"Dear God. I'm sorry about that. Did I hurt your toes?"

"Look, what's your answer. We haven't got all night?"

"Well I couldn't," I looked, as regretful as I could. "Me mamai would kill me stone dead."

The two young women, who were in fact no older than us, stood back, looked at each other, and then looked back at me with an expression of deep contempt for my pathetic response. Their look said it all. Clearly somebody like me would be neither use nor ornament to them. They sighed and turned to Moya, "What about you?"

"Well I couldn't, you seee, with our Hugh being inside and everything me mamai would go mad."

"Okay, right. You don't know who we are, and we have never had this conversation."

"Aye that's Gran. Thanks anyway for asking," I said with the biggest relief of my life.

We wanted to go straight to the toilet afterwards but couldn't move for fear that they would follow us or that we might draw attention to ourselves, so we carried on dancing nearly crying but bursting out into spurts of hysterical laughter.

Another night at the centre ended unsuccessfully as neither one of us got off with either Frank McCann or Jeed McDevitt, and so reluctantly and somewhat manically we set off home. We talked about how pathetic we had been but how relieved we were at the lucky escape. What if they come looking for us again? Well, we would just have to stand up for ourselves. Moya knew that there was little glory in becoming actively involved with the IRA because her eldest brother Hugh had been lifted, charged with possession of explosives, and sentenced to ten years. Moya showed me his letters from prison. Well they were not really letters but wee tiny notes written on pieces of that old hard shiny toilet paper. The writing was so tiny and could only be read with a magnifying glass. The prisoners in H Block were refused rights, and so the letters were folded into the tiniest wee packages, wrapped in cling film, and smuggled out of the prison.

Moya's mother's heart had been broken, as she had to try hard to bear the pain of her first born being taken away for something he didn't do and ending up in H Block on the dirty protest, where the inmates spread their own excrement around the walls of their cells in protest of their lack of human rights and that they were not being treated as political prisoners. We heard the prisoners faced all kinds of horrors and that some of them lost their minds, so Moya and I were hardly in need of a reminder that we would not become involved. But not to be involved or actively in support of the armed struggle brought it its own conflict in our hearts and minds because there were so many injustices against the Catholic population that doing nothing made it hard sometimes to walk tall in the streets for fear of being thought of as a coward or as someone who was disloyal to the cause.

As we walked home towards Moya's house, where we always wound up at the end of the night for a feed of tea, toast, and cake, we looked forward to Moya's mother who would be waiting for us with the kettle at the ready, wanting to hear 'all the bars' about the evenings activity at the community centre. Moya's mother, Anne often worked late into the night embroidering Irish dancing dresses and having earned something of a reputation for her skill, she always had a backlog of orders. But she was happy to await our return and allow herself a break.

Nearly at Moya's house and looking forward to getting inside to the heat, we ran in to the army patrols that were as usual out and about after the community centre had closed for the night. With blackened faces, they scoured the streets, brandishing their rifles in patrols of about six to eight soldiers at a time. We met about three patrols on this particular night in a short space of time so we knew that some activity was going on. As we turned into the bottom of Moya's street, we were giddily fantasizing about when and how we would get off with our fellas and about the madness of being asked to join the IRA. We sat down on a garden wall to plan our next move on Frank and Jeed. Laughing so much at the ridiculous suggestions about what we were going to do and not do to catch our men, I fell back and into the garden onto something so hard that I screamed out.

"Are you alright, Caroline," Moya said, looking worried, as she could see that I was in pain.

"Dear God, Moya. I have fallen on something." I scrambled about in the dark to identify what it was and nearly fainted, as I lifted up a gun to the light.

I had never held a real gun before, and it was heavy. This was no toy. I was standing holding a gun, and Moya stood looking at me as though she had just been shot. We just froze for a while until Moya urgently whispered, "Dear God, Caroline. It's a gun!"

"Dear God, Moya. I know it is!"

"Dear God, Caroline. What are we going to do?"

"Dear God, Moya. I don't know!"

Scared silence…

"Are there any more in there?" Moya asked, as we jumped back into the garden and found another one.

Now Moya had one in her hand, and we sat there pointing them at each other.

"Dear God, Caroline. We just can't leave them here because if this house gets raided the night, then that family will all be lifted, and they already have had one of their sons in Long Kesh."

I was still holding my gun and Moya hers and we didn't know whether to laugh or cry or wet ourselves.

Moya suggested that we take the guns straight away to the Sinn Fein Centre out of harm's way so we stuffed them up our coats and started walking back towards the Sinn Fein office. Off we went, trying to tell ourselves that we were not so pathetic now because we were probably saving somebody from being lifted. For a second, I wished that the two IRA women could see us now, as we were not so pathetic after all.

"What if the Sinn Fein Office is closed Moya... it's eleven o'clock? What if nobody is there, what will we do?"

Just at that, we turned a corner into Central Drive, and I walked straight into a soldier on patrol. I screamed out in terror and nearly dropped the gun from inside my coat.

"Sorry miss, I didn't mean to frighten you," he said, as he walked on.

Moya and I, now unable to look at one another, were in the middle of an army patrol and thankfully, there did not seem to be any woman soldiers amongst them because they always demanded to search us on the spot just for the imposition of it.

We walked past the soldiers and were just about to sigh in relief that we had managed to get away with it, when the last soldier stopped on front of us.

"Evening ladies. Can I just take a few details? What are your names? Where are you going? And where have you been?"

Moya explained that we had just been to the community centre but we had forgotten our purse so we were heading back there. I couldn't speak and was terrified.

The soldier asked our addresses and then advised us to get off home as soon as possible, as it might not be safe to be out tonight. "Goodnight ladies," he ended.

Moya and I walked as fast as we could with sweat of fear running down our faces.

We didn't speak another word until we arrived at the Sinn Fein office and checking that the coast was clear, we began banging on the wire mesh that covered the windows. Panicking now that there did not appear to be anyone in and that we could hear a helicopter in the distance, we ran around the back of the building, frantically banging on the door, when a hand firmly grabbed my shoulder, and the shock and fear of it made me lose my grip on the gun, which fell to the ground.

I couldn't turn around and thought about Mamai and that this would definitely be the end of me one way or another. A man, whose face we couldn't see, asked us calmly what we were doing here and we told him that we had found some guns.

"Jesus Christ weegirls. Are you off your heads, walking around with two guns?"

He took the guns off us and told us to get home as quick as we could because this was not going to be a good night.

"Oh my God. I don't believe it. What did we just do Moya? We're not right in the head... we must be mad. If we'd been caught, we'd have been lifted definitely, and we would not have been able to explain it. What were we thinking of."

I went to bed that night and prayed in thanks to God that we hadn't been lifted, and I promised God that if this doesn't come back on us, I would never think badly of Mamai ever again. But the feeling of terror didn't leave me, as I tossed and turned and sweated my way to an exhausted sleep.

Bang! Bang! Thud! We were awoken at about four o'clock in the morning by a patrol of soldiers banging our door down. Mamai ran in to wake Tommy and Liam out of bed, and Dadai went downstairs with only his trousers on. Mamai in her nightdress told us to get up and dressed before she would let the soldiers into our room. This was no ordinary raid. This was it... I would be taken off to Piggery Ridge, the army camp at the top of Creggan, where I would be tortured and humiliated. I had known women and girls who, even when they had their periods, had been searched up into their vaginas and been made to stand naked for hours in front of male and female soldiers who would laugh at them. If this were going to happen to me, I would rather die now straight away because I couldn't bare the humiliation. The soldiers were more aggressive than ever before, turning over furniture, pulling out clothes, and all of us were body searched. Each of us were asked about our whereabouts that night, and when it came to my turn to answer, I thought that I was going to wet myself with fear. The house was being ransacked, and Mamai was telling us to stay calm. Just as I was about to answer, the soldier was distracted by Dadai who had stepped in, "Look at these weans. They are all good weans. They have never been involved in the troubles, and they have all been sleeping sound all night."

The soldier, pushing Dadai aside, responded,

"Who asked you, you Irish scum. You're good for nothing but breeding like rabbits."

Dadai's face turned grey with rage, and he shifted his position, as though he was about to flatten the soldier, when I ran in between the two of them.

"Leave him alone!" I shouted, the tears of terror flying out of my eyes. "I only went to the community centre with Moya, and we were coming home together when …"

With that, the soldier was ordered to follow his squad leader up the ladder at the top of the stairs into our attic where they had found all of Tommy and Liam's camping equipment and their instructions for their scouting missions. The soldiers thought that they had hit the jackpot not believing that the only patrol that our Tommy and Liam had ever been involved in was Panther Patrol a la boy scouts. The attic ceiling decorated by Tommy and Liam had been adorned with Che Guevara posters and the Irish tricolour trimmed by shamrocks. We heard lots of commotion and army radio discussions, as the soldiers came downstairs and dragged Tommy and Liam out into the street. Dadai grabbed one of the soldiers who had been pushing my brothers around and he told them that if another finger were laid on them, he would break his neck. The soldier rammed his rifle into Dadai's stomach and shoved him into the back of the jeep with Tommy and Liam. Mamai ran out and shouted into the jeep, which was speeding off that she would go to John Hume who would have them released as soon as possible.

"Don't worry weans. You have nothing to hide. Just tell the truth, and trust in yourselves and in god. God's good!" she shouted.

How the hell could they trust in God? God didn't seem to be doing much for our family. Yet Mamai's words and the conviction with which she delivered them strangely held us together in the moment.

Our street was now crawling with soldiers and overrun with jeeps and armoured cars, and people were being pulled out of their beds and houses and into the streets, where they were then rammed into the jeeps. We could see lights on in all the houses in the square, and wee Mrs. Havard, who was about my size and height, had been lifted. They didn't lift her husband or sons or daughters but as she was shouting abuse at the soldiers, they proceeded to carry her into the jeep like she was a bag of spuds.

The guilt at seeing her so badly treated was too much, and I was convinced that they were looking for me, but I kept quiet and held my whisht.

The next day I found out that Moya's house had been raided too that same night. In fact, it seemed that a dawn raid had been carried out in hundreds of houses in Creggan and over fifty people had been lifted.

In the morning, Mamai made her way down Beechwood to John Hume's house again, and he accompanied her with a priest up to the Piggery Ridge Army Camp.

Dadai and my brothers had been detained all night and all the next day, interrogated and abused throughout.

At midnight the following day, Mamai arrived home with Tommy, Liam, and Dadai.

We learned that they had been beaten and interrogated. They had been taken individually into different rooms where they had been subjected to different degrees of punishment and interrogation. Dadai returned a man defeated, he slumped into the fireside chair, put his head into his hands, and cried, "Jesus Margaret! I couldn't do anything to stop them... the bastards are torturing our youngsters!"

"Sweet mother of God," said Mamai, taking a seat at the dining table. Tommy and Liam told us that they only had been questioned. But Tommy later told me that they had done the stand up/sit down routine again, and as he had experienced it before, he knew what was coming. He knew that he could do nothing to affect the outcome because the ritual was what is was, and the interrogators were not interested in hearing their answers because they were looking for information and assumed that our boys and Dadai were lying.

Tommy said that it was harder this time because he didn't just have himself to worry about but given that he was the eldest in our family, he worried about what they were doing to Liam. He knew that Liam was strong because Liam was a good scout and a great wee boxer, but his worry was more about Dadai, who might lose the rattle with the soldiers and be subject to a terrible beating. He couldn't bear the thought that the soldiers would make fun of the fact that our father had been in Gransha; that he would be strip searched, degraded, and humiliated. With tears in his eyes, Tommy explained the terrible predicament that even though he had been terrified for himself, he had a sense that he could bear whatever they were doing to him, but the thought of what was or what might be happening to Dadai and Liam was too much for him. It was almost enough for him to admit to something that he didn't do.

Thank God that Dadai had taken a notion that he would go to Germany to work on the building sites. He had heard that he would be earning up to five hundred pounds per week. I wondered though if it was more to do with the fact that as he was becoming more frustrated with how the army was treating our boys, and that God only knew what other pressures he was trying to manage with his illness and worry that our boys might get involved with the IRA. So perhaps it was his running way or being pushed by Mamai, as a kind of insurance against him doing something that he would regret. I think too that Mamai had encouraged him to go because she feared that he would lose the rattle with the army and end up either getting killed or sent to prison, because although he was easy going, he could lose it easily at the drop of a hat if he thought that his family were being insulted or assaulted and would take any man on.

The troubles were getting worse, and we were in the thick of it. The gable wall directly facing our house was sprayed with the huge slogan,

Chapter 12 FALLING ON GUNS

"If fighting makes you happy, if fighting makes you gay,
Then come and fight for freedom and join the IRA."

We looked at this each time we stepped outside of our door, and it was as though it had been purposefully put outside our house, directly in front of our windows to persuade our five boys to sign up. It was beginning to look a wee bit suspicious that even though there were five boys in our house, none of them was involved in the IRA.

The soldiers were suspicious because they assumed that there must be at least one 'terrorist' among the five boys in our house in the heartland of the Republican Creggan Estate. And the IRA would have had the feelers out to find out what was going on in our house seeing that we didn't have any of our boys signed up.

Not surprisingly, our boys became a bit paranoid because they didn't know who they were talking to. Some of the lads in our streets were known IRA members and openly proud of it. Others seemed to flirt with the idea of joining up... all talk and no action. Some it was hard to know about and others we had to be suspicious about because you didn't know who the informers were.

It seemed as though everyone was under suspicion from all quarters. I was finding it more and more difficult to know where to turn for escape from it all. We were all growing up in what was a desperate and depressed city, and for me at least, I had become less able to think of home as my safe return. It seemed that there was no resting place free from the chaos, drama, and attack. Although I was aware that I had increasingly turned to myself, my treehouse place had seemingly been wrecked too. I could no longer imagine a bright future at university or anywhere else and wondered if I had a future at all; there was no one and nowhere to turn for help.

Growing up in the streets of Derry in the 1970s was hard for all of us, and God only knows what was going on behind the closed doors of people's homes. As if Catholic guilt and the notion that we were all sinners anyway wasn't enough to contend with, the feeling of being under suspicion for becoming an adolescent, with all the shame and sense of secret guilt that goes with living in a body that was now sprouting breasts and body hair, I also had to contend with being looked upon as some kind of whore, just because I was growing up, like the day that our Liam asked me what I thought I was doing wearing lipstick at sixteen years. I could have punched his lights out. What qualified him to have an opinion all of a sudden? So with our Liam suddenly thinking that he was my father, and as my mother was never off my back about what I could and couldn't wear, where I could and couldn't go, who I could and couldn't hang around with, I was in deep despair and wondered if I'd be better off dead.

A young lad, Raymond Gilmore, started hanging around our house and seemingly wanted to be friends with Liam and Sean but he always ended up hanging around with me and Moya, 'cos our boys couldn't be bothered with him, and we felt sorry for him. We used to lie on top of our coal shed in the back garden and discuss who was going out with whom and who fancied who. Raymond fancied Marion Douglas who was another friend of mine but Marion didn't fancy him – she was going out with Rooster McNutt, although it was always on and off, and Rooster was crazy about her. Any time Marion and Rooster fell out, Rooster would come and cry on my shoulders. Marion was becoming popular with the fellas, and we got used to them hanging around with us so that they could have a chance with her. So I wondered if Raymond Gilmore was hanging around with us so that he too might have more chance in getting off with Marion. Mamai thought that there was something a wee bit strange about Raymond and that he had no sense but as he seemed harmless enough, she allowed him to call to our house. Frank told me that he didn't get a good vibe from Gilmore and thought that he might be up to no good and possibly involved in something with 'the boys' – the local term for the IRA. Moya and I laughed at the thought of it because he was 'just Raymond' and hardly tough enough to be 'one of the boys'. Sometimes though he was like a sticking plaster and we couldn't shake him off. We would hide when we saw him coming, especially if we were planning to go out and impress the talent, as he would surely cramp our style.

But the streets were feeling less safe, and I sensed that we all had to show some kind of active support for 'The Cause' as the pressure was becoming more difficult to avoid. By now, Tommy and Liam were big shots in the scouts and Tommy, who was patrol leader of Panther Patrol, seemed to be having an even more difficult time because when he wasn't being harassed by the army, he was being harassed by the IRA.

There were regular fights after the disco had finished at the community centre youth clubs, where the IRA supporters and activists were pressurizing the non-activists to become more active. I had to be home by eleven otherwise Mamai would be on the streets looking for me. And she could never sleep until we were all safely home.

"Tommy, is that you? Are you in?

"Where is Liam?"

"Is everybody in?" she would ensure before she could settle to sleep.

Tommy and Liam seemed to make a rule of checking out where they would be and arrange to get home around the same time so that they could lock the front door safely in the knowledge that we were all inside. I couldn't go to bed until they were in because it was becoming more usual that Tommy was coming home covered in blood, as he was getting into fights following accusations from IRA gangs that he must be a coward otherwise he would have joined up. His denim jacket and jeans were sometimes saturated with blood from his nose and mouth, and as quickly as I could, I would take his clothes into the downstairs bathroom and wash them out by hand in the bath because putting the washing machine on would definitely wake Mamai, and we knew that she couldn't bear any more stress.

I never got used to it, and each time it happened, I worried that it might be the last time and that something terrible was going to happen. One night, the worry got the better of me, and as I was washing out his clothes in the bath, it struck me that the blood from his clothes, now on my hands and turning pinkish in the bath water, was a sign that things were worsening and that my brothers were in real danger. I sat on the floor looking into the bath of blood. I thought of all the times that I'd heard people say that there was going to be a blood bath and here it was in our bathroom in the middle of the night with my hands right in it. It was my brother's blood and God only knows who else's.

Tommy came in to see how I was getting on and sat down beside be on the cold bathroom floor, where we sat together looking into the pinky red water. Tommy told me that he wasn't going to take it anymore. He knew that if he stayed in Derry, he would end up joining the IRA and although hating the British Army, he had little sympathy for the IRA's tactics. There was seemingly no sense in the killings and beatings, and our support for 'The Cause' of a free Ireland was waning because we were out there in the streets living a nightmare. That night, Tommy talked of how he had been joining in on the riots like many of his friends, and that the army had lifted him many times and beaten him badly. A lot had happened to him and his friends, which he couldn't tell me about for fear that if Mamai found out, she would lose her mind too. Yet it was becoming clear to us both that he might not be able to take much more of it and that he might be persuaded to join the IRA... and that would surely be the end of him... and of Mamai.

"Caroline, I don't know who the fuck to support any more. Some days I'm ready to run with the rest of 'the boys'; the next, I'm disgusted and want no part of it. Why the fuck does the British fuckin' Army get away with murder time and time again? It's enough to make me want to join up straight away but that would kill me ma. I don't know how much more she can take."

I couldn't look at Tommy's face. This was the first time we'd ever had a conversation about what was going on in our streets, and it felt very grown up and scary.

"Tommy, you can't take any more yourself can you? Please don't join 'the boys'. Don't Tommy! Ye can't. I don't want you to end up 'inside' like Hugh McCann or shot dead by a British soldier or chopped to bits by the UDA!"

Here we were again, the two eldest, at another point of crisis, where frustration and fear tortured us, and we were trying to fathom the unfathomable to come up with a solution. Unable to turn to our parents or to anyone else in that moment, we shared something of the strain of it all whilst we sat on the floor in silence, trying to work it out for ourselves. At last, Tommy spoke again,

"Caroline ... the only option I have is to enlist in the Irish Army and then no one can call me a coward. At least I can earn some money to send home. Mamai won't like it but I won't tell her 'till it's all signed and sealed."

I knew that he had no option because it was becoming impossible for him to have a life in this town. Together we got up from the floor, reached into the bath, pulled out the heavy jeans and jacket, and wrung out what we could of the bloody water. We carried the washed and weighty clothes out into the back garden, as though we were carrying a heavy dead body out into the night to hang it up on the line to dry.

Dadai had gone to Germany and now Tommy was leaving. What would happen to the rest of my brothers? Who would I turn to now that Mamai and me were becoming locked in battle, and as we were fighting for our lives in the streets too, there seemed no escape from the misery. Loss just kept on coming, and before Tommy even got his head round the thought of enlisting in the Irish army, Liam had already enlisted. Now I was the eldest wean left in the family. My mother was broken hearted but tried not to show it and instead became even harder and stricter with me. She had such a close eye on me that I thought I'd suffocate, and her reliance upon me was driving me out the door and far away from any soft, safe remembered place by her side.

Thoughts of life at home were long since gone, of warm baked bread and scones or cosy turf fires and the sound of music. Now it was a very different life, and my home was filled with the sound of missing family members and the smell of emptiness: empty hearts, empty larders, and empty dreams. It was no different in the streets and town; much had been lost that would never be regained. Many lives had been lost and the grief, anger, and despair from bereaved families spilled out into the Derry air and we all sniffed it in.

I think that Mamai was never the same again, and although she knew that the boys needed to get away from it all, it had never been her dream for them that they would join an army...any army. Even though they had become soldiers in the legitimate Irish Army, these were her sons and this was their home. Her high hopes for Tommy were dashed, and it looked to me like she was becoming depressed, as she was on a short fuse. Through that miserable period in our lives, I could never have known the weight of worry on her shoulders. For she did all she could to manage the troubles in the streets, as well as the troubles brewing and boiling in the hearts and minds of her weans, who were all now in the adolescent melting pot, where teenage emotions stank the house out. The shape of our family and our family relationships were changing fast, and Donna, Mamai, and me moved into spiky conflict with each other – like the barbed wire that ran through the walls and barricades of our city, separating, threatening, and provoking one another. It seemed that Donna and I had become too far out of reach for our mother, who kept reaching towards us but whose heart would be wounded, scratched, and torn by our retreat from her. I marked my retreat and my newfound elevation, as the eldest wean in the family by deciding that I would no longer refer to 'Mamai'; it was far too baby-ish. I couldn't refer to her as 'me ma' 'cos that would be too common and she wouldn't allow it. 'Mother' was too English so I came up with 'Mi'ami'... that would be my mother's new name, and it seemed to feel right enough.

Chapter 12 FALLING ON GUNS

Letting go of Mi'ami's old name was no worse for her than letting go of her weans to dead end futures and it was draining the life out of her but she had no alternative other than to keep managing... to keep on keeping on.

Chapter 13
FALLING FOR FRANK

DADAI arrived back from Germany prematurely. It hadn't worked out, and he came home with no money and no tools, as he had given them away to some "poor fella who had nothing." We managed the disappointment and were glad to see him safely home even though it crossed my mind that the "poor fella who had nothing" might have been a fella standing behind a bar serving whisky and getting a bag of tools for payment.

Thankfully, I had my mind on something far more crucial and was able to not think about family problems and 'The Troubles'. I was sixteen years old when I finally got off with Frank McCann. I was nearly ready for the second faint in my whole life when he asked to walk me home from the community centre disco.

I was wearing my new cream calf length Dexter raincoat, which was pulled in tightly to my twenty-two inch waist, and I nearly couldn't breathe when Frank kept playfully and purposefully bumping into me. I was gasping with excitement and the fact that my belt was so tight. Frank chased me into a lane behind the houses at the bottom of our street and when he managed to catch up with me, he held my face, leaned over, and planted a kiss on my lips. I thought that I had died and gone to heaven.

We stood there together with the moon shining down on us and as he cradled me in his arms, the utter delight of it all brought tears of pleasure and relief that I could now be like all the other girls as I had had my first kiss. The brief moments of complete and utter joy were cut short by the sound of my mother, who was in the street dressed in her nightdress with her hair in rollers and hair net. She was shouting my name into the empty street. In panic and sheer embarrassment, I broke away from Frank and in case she would find us together, I started out towards home when Frank grabbed my arm and asked, "Can I meet you again tomorrow at the centre?" He then found a place to hide from my mother's voice, which by now was coming closer.

I managed to come out of the lane before Mi'ami could see that I had been in the lane, and she scolded me up the street, complaining that I was late and asking where I had been and what was I doing.

At last, I had a boyfriend. The feeling of being chosen by the guy that I had drooled over for so long was beyond pleasure. Suddenly everything changed, and my life had new meaning. I was in heaven, on cloud nine, and over the moon with the cat that had got the cream. Nothing so far in my life yet compared to the feeling of rapture that I had about having Frank as a boyfriend – my first real boyfriend. I did try to have a boyfriend before that but it never quite worked out.

One fella who lived near Moya had asked her if he could 'get off' with me and I reluctantly but hopefully agreed because by now I was getting desperate to be like the other girls. The night of the date, he and I met in the doorway of some flats. I stood next to him in the dark, noticing how his acne caught the light of the moon and trying hard not to notice the sheen of his hair because it hadn't been washed in a month of Sundays, and he leant towards me, awkwardly putting his arms around me. The fifteen-year-old boy smell of him overpowered me, and I ran off feeling nauseous, telling myself that I could surely do better than this but fearing that this might be my lot, I reconsidered the option of becoming a nun. I fancied other boys but they fancied my classmates, and I had mistaken their friendliness towards me for interest in me. I nearly got off with another good-looking lad, Harry; Moya got off with his brother Joe, and I was just on the verge of landing a date with Harry when Frank stepped in.

Frank was everything I could have wished for. He was great craic, always joking and messing about but most exciting of all was that he was so intelligent: a straight A student. I was riveted, as he told me about the internal workings of a fridge and that the quickest distance from one point to another was straight, and that the longest word he knew was 'presdidigitatation', which was something to do with the quickness of movement of the fingers. He could talk about politics and poetry and knew that he would go to university. I loved the bones of him.

Me having a boyfriend turned my mother into some kind of KGB spy, as she seemed to have tabs on my every movement. If it hadn't been for Maryanne Kivlehan next door, I would never even have had a sniff at a boy. Maryanne persuaded Mi'ami that it was going to happen anyway so she may as well get used to the idea and that she should get to meet this young fella. Maryanne had a house full of daughters whose steady boyfriends graduated from courting on the street to the steps of their staircase, and when their front door opened, an elevation of courting couples could be seen sitting on the stairs. It was Maryanne's way of keeping her eye on things and ensuring that her girls' weren't going off somewhere to end up doing something that would get them into trouble.

On Valentine's Day 1976, I received a great big card from Frank for the entire world to see. It had a wonderfully romantic hand-written inscription inside, and my mother did not waste a minute in telling me to invite him over for a cup of tea.

"What McCann are you?" Dadai asked, with a friendly acceptance and quiet confidence in me that I was been dating a good boy.

Frank went on to say that he was Moya's cousin and George's son.

"For God's sake, I know him well. Me and George used to box together. Your father's a good man and comes from a good family. Tell your da I was asking for him."

"Aye, and your mother is a good woman, one of the best in the town, and she was a vision when she was wee... and still is," said Mi'ami, who seemed to be trying not to want to be in the conversation but couldn't help seizing a chance to speak up for another woman.

I was thrilled to bits that things seemed to be going so well when at this point, Mi'ami leans over and inspects my face. "Have you been plucking those eyebrows?"

I nearly died of embarrassment. Of course, I wanted Frank to think that this thin, so heavily plucked, nearly bald look was my own natural look.

Frank stirred his tea trying to give the impression that he hadn't heard the question and providing the deadly silence with the welcome sound of a spoon roaming around his cup.

"If I catch you plucking those eyebrows anymore, I will pluck the eyes out of your head."

Well she may as well have done it there and then because I couldn't look up at Frank's face nor did I think that I could ever look at him again or see him looking at my eyebrows.

Me dadai jumped in to save the day by telling Frank a story about the old days and of the boxing, and went on to ask about Frank's uncles, whom he knew well and asked how they were doing.

But I was still reeling from the embarrassment, and that night I couldn't sleep, for the whole experience kept turning over and over in my head. What was Mi'ami thinking of? How could she show me up like that. I really didn't know her anymore. She was definitely not the mother I wanted and in that moment, I thought she was a witch. How could she come to be so unkind towards me? This change in her seemed a lot to do with the fact that I was a proper teenager and it was as though I suddenly had become guilty of some terrible shameful sin – I may as well have joined the friggin' IRA for the way that she was treating me and inspecting my every move.

I longed for the softness of her. I needed my Mi'ami. I needed her because I was growing up but she was not there. I remembered how she used to be, like the day that I came home from school and told her that I had gotten my period. She was so wonderful and concerned. She sent Donna off to Irish dancing by herself and told her to tell the dancing teacher that I was not feeling well. I was sent to bed and Mi'ami prepared a hot water bottle for me even though it was the height of summer. She called Tommy and wrote a message on a slip of paper that was not much bigger than a postage stamp and folded into a tiny wee message, which he was not to open or read.

"This is a special message. Just hand it to the chemist. You don't have to say anything. Watch yourself son and don't be there until you're back, and if ye fall, run on."

Tommy arrived back with a brown paper package fortified with reams off sellotape, and a bottle of lucozade, which we only had when someone in the family was ill. Mi'ami sat down on the bed beside me and explained in a somewhat embarrassed muffled tone,

"Well, now that you have 'your visitor' (period), it's a sign that you are becoming a woman. You'll have your visitor every month and you might not feel very well. Just let me know, and I'll get one of the boys to go to the chemist for STs (sanitary towels). You know now that you must stay away from boys and keep yourself clean. You might know some girls who use tampons but you must never, never use them because when you want to get married, the man will think that you have been with someone else."

Proceeding to open the brown paper packet, she produced some thick white cotton pads and then pulled out some kind of pink strap with little clips on the end.

I hadn't got a clue about what to do with it and tried to fasten it around my breasts, then around my legs and around my waist, but I couldn't work it out. Mi'ami did tell me what to do with it but I was so mortified about the whole thing that I couldn't take in what she was saying. And what the heck did she mean about a man thinking that I had been with another man? And would I really be ill once a month until I was old? The whole bloody event was mortifying, and I pleaded with myself for strength to face it all again every month. It was years before I was able to go and buy my own sanitary towels because it was as though I would somehow be corrupted by the very fact of going into a shop and asking for them... as though I was confessing to the world that I was a woman and a sexual animal into the bargain.

All our boys had the honour of going to the chemist once a month for a brown package. One day Sean, who was the eldest of the three wanes, was next in line to be enlisted for courier service. Sean John Fitzgerald Kennedy Owens, named after the President of the United States, was not a pushover. The only one of the seven of us to go to grammar school, he was destined for great things. What else could he be with a name like that? Even within our own family, I think that we had a sense of him being gifted somehow. Like a lot of Irish families, our homes were decorated and adorned with iconic images; for example, the alcoves of our living room hosted, pride of place and in reverence, one large framed picture of Mother of the Perpetual Succor, whilst the other was adorned by the Sacred Heart of Jesus and a framed picture of JFK and Jackie Kennedy. I always had a sense that if the going got tough and if Jesus couldn't answer our prayers then JFK would charge over to Ireland on a posse with John Wane and his cavalry and they would sort everything out. The Americans surely would come to our rescue; they wouldn't put up with all of this carry on, and if they knew the half of it, they would send their own Yankee army over to give us a hand. Thank God for JFK and Thank God for America – I don't know what we would have done in our house without them. So in my mind, my brother, Sean John Fitzgerald Kennedy Owens, was bestowed with some magical qualities of independence and leadership. Not surprising then that he protested about having to go on a secret mission to buy STs.

"Mamai, what exactly is in the packet anyway?"

"Never you mind. It's a wee special message. You just hand in the wee note and say nothing. All you need to know is that you are going on a very special wee message."

Sean however was not to be fobbed off and being more headstrong than the rest of us, bought the packet on that day, found a quiet place sat down, ripped through the selotape and opened the package. 'Sanitary Towels' he read on the packet. "What the hell is a sanitary towel?" he asked himself? If it wasn't something edible or readable then it was no good to Sean and he would lose interest so he carefully repackaged the parcel and delivered it to Mi'ami, who then slipped it into the bathroom. Sean was on a mission and wasn't to rest until he found out what was so special about 'STs'. So he asked every one he could at school and was utterly mortified to know that all this time he had been going to the chemist shop for 'women's things'.

The next time he was asked to go for the special message, he quizzed Mi'ami about what was in the parcel. Her reluctance to get into any explanation with him meant that he was off the courier list, and so she called out,

"Mark! Come here! You need to go to the chemist for a special wee message and don't open this wee note ..."

So the mantle was handed down to Mark.

There was no getting away from the embarrassment of growing up – even my school was not a safe place for a growing girl because Majella and Moya and I were being teased on a regular basis about not having any breasts. PE was the worst because everyone would inspect everyone else's, and if you were still wearing a vest and not a bra then you were in for a right old ribbing. I was still wearing a vest at thirteen and couldn't bear it any longer so I asked Mi'ami if I could have a bra. She told me that there would be plenty of time to get a bra, that there was no need for one now. I used to go into her room, try on her very full-cupped bras, and imagine what it was like to wear one. In fact, I remember the shock of the first time I saw my mother without her bra on and was horrified that her big full breasts were so round and droopy because I thought that breasts were pointy and 'sticky out' the way they looked when women were dressed. Well I was desperate for a bra so I decided to save up and go to Littlewoods on my own for one.

Whilst desperately trying hard not to attract attention to myself, I hovered around the underwear department my heart racing in case I would be recognized. I thought that everyone who looked at me would be thinking that I was some kind of prostitute if I even put my hand on the things. I really liked the little navy polka dot one and as I couldn't work out the sizes I just tried to guess and I bought the smallest one I could. It cost me 99p and I hid it in my room until I plucked up the courage to wear it.

At school, girls would run up to us and nip our breasts, telling us that they needed squeezing otherwise they would never grow. So I always thought that a girl in our class who had very oversized breasts was someone who must be letting boys squeeze them so I didn't think much of her even though I would try to squeeze my own in the hope that they would grow.

Given all of the shenanigans involved in my body changing shape, it really was a miracle that my mother even let Frank McCann look at me, never mind let him into our house. Frank always tried to say something nice about Mi'ami, as he knew that my resentment towards her was growing. He was helpful, respectful, and kind toward her, and she soon allowed herself to enjoy him and was happy in the knowledge that he was a good boy.

John Clarke, his best mate, was an apprentice painter and decorator, and they decorated the downstairs rooms for me mi'ami, who soon regarded Frank as a member of our family.

Frank was the second eldest of eight children and worked at Doherty's Butchers with his father, mainly cleaning the equipment like the sausage machines, and scrubbing and disinfecting the place at the end of the day's work. After school, early in the mornings, and at weekends, Frank worked hard, as well as managing to keep up to his studies, and as far as I could see, when he had bought himself some new clothes with his earnings, the rest of his earnings was spent on his mother and me.

The whole time I knew Frank, he was saving to buy a washing for his mother. Frank's mother was an angel who welcomed everyone into her house and laughed and giggled with us all, as though she was one of us youngsters.

"Yes Caroline, what's the bars?" she would ask, greeting me with a welcoming smile. I never remember her without a smile, and she was well loved in the community because of her sunny and kind nature.

Frank was a lot like his mother in nature. On Sundays, he used to take me on the bus to Buncrana, the nearest seaside town, fourteen miles away, where we would run in our bare feet in the sand, stop off at the amusements, and then go to a little seaside café, where I would have chicken Maryland and he would have a mixed grill.

The excitement nearly killed me when he took me into a jeweller's shop and bought me a gold signet ring with a black onyx centre. I showed it to the world, and I was convinced that this was the man for me.

"Dear God, Caroline. Are you engaged" asked Marty Kivlehan.

"Well not really," but I secretly hoped that this was a pre engagement ring and a true sign of Frank's love for me.

Having a real boyfriend gave me a kind of confidence that was even better than all of the good marks or prefect badges at school and seemed to give me a newfound status.

I was now one of the 'in girls', just like one of the girls in my class, Valerie Carey who was an official beauty queen having won many a beauty contest. Valerie had the rare combination of looking beautiful with the bluest of blue eyes and lashes that were so long that they used to pull her eyebrows down when she blinked, and she had a lively magnetic personality that attracted the girls and the boys. Even though Valerie was one of the better-off girls in the class and lived down beside Roma Downey, she still threw herself in to the craic at school and she wasn't a snob.

I remember one day we went on a school excursion to Magilligan Strand, a beach beside the prisoner of war camp where the interned prisoners were caged without charge. A highlight of the trip was a visit to the prison shop, which sold furniture, ornaments jewellery, and art work, all made by the prisoners. Although I was desperate to go on the trip, I opted out because I didn't have any spending money or even enough money for the bus fare.

Valerie came running into the classroom, announcing in public that she had been talking to Frank. My heart sank to my feet, feeling immediately threatened because Valerie looked like Olivia Newton John and she was sure to put a spell on Frank, and I was sure that Frank would fancy her and prefer her and that would be the end of romance.

"Caroline, he sent you this," she excitedly and breathlessly announced. "I told him that you weren't going on the excursion and he gave me this to give to you."

Valerie handed me a wee white paper bag, which I opened and inside found a ten-pound note and a little message saying, "Have a good time in Magilligan. Love Frank. x."

I was as proud as could be, and the classroom was filled with gasps of disbelief and excitement as though Frank's gesture was confirmation to all of the girls that boyfriends really were a good thing. On that day he may as well have rode up on a white horse, swept me off my feet, and rode off with me to happy-ever-after land because the feeling was so publicly validating, and I felt truly cherished.

Chapter 14
GETTING A PROPER JOB

EVEN though I had left school at sixteen and was now working full time in Rocola, a shirt factory, as a 'collar and cuffer', I never had as much money to spend as Frank. I earned around forty pounds a week and had to hand my wage packet unopened to my mother. She gave me back fifteen pounds to spend on myself and that included my clothes, discos, and toiletries. I really wanted to make a proper contribution to the upkeep of the house but I resented having to hand in my earnings unopened.

I hated the shirt factory and was terrified of the women there. Although I did meet one really quiet and kind girl there, who incidentally was Maryanne's niece but she couldn't protect me form the hell. I found myself being afraid and terribly shy, which seemed to be in sharp contrast to many of the women there who cursed and swore at the drop of a hat and were much, much, tougher than many of the lads. There was something about swearing, and women swearing in particular, which my guts just protested about. Even though I had grown up hearing swearing on the streets of Derry, as it was just part of the lingo, it made me immediately fearful, as though the words themselves would cut right through me and cut my insides to ribbons, leaving me feeling weak and pathetic.

Shirt factory life was not for me because I was afraid most of the time, useless at the job of sewing collars and cuffs, and easily reduced to tears of frustration and the thought that this would be my lot in life.

I wanted to leave but Mi'ami wouldn't let me unless I had another job to go to.

Eventually the manager called me into his office and told me that he would have to let me go because I was not up to the job and because he thought that I wasn't fitting in. I cried my heart out in his office and begged him to keep me on otherwise Mi'ami would kill me. He told me that he knew my mother and asked me to tell her to come in to see him. Mi'mai marched down straight away to the factory, and the manager explained that I was not cut out for the job.

"She's not tough enough, Margaret. She would be far better off doing something totally different." He explained that it would be better if he sacked me because then I could at least claim benefit but if I left of my own accord then I would be 'wiped' on the 'brew' (no unemployment benefit!)

"No wean of mine is getting sacked and she's not leaving unless she finds something else." Mi'mai left the office having negotiated that I would be put on to a different – easier – section in the factory (hems), and she was sure that I would manage to grow into it.

I hated her again. I had just received another prison sentence now with no Tommy or Liam to turn to and a mother who seemed far too reliant upon me to bring in the extra cash. How I hated the feeling of being so straight jacketed it was driving me mad.

"It's not fair," I pleaded with her on my way home.

"No it's not fair and neither is a black man's moustache," she said brushing my pleas aside. I hated it when she said this; she always said it when we complained of something not being fair. So I tried again, "Mamai, some of the women in there are cheeky bitches and curse and swear all day long."

I continued crying in the hope that she wouldn't have me sitting making shirts in a puddle of obscenity amongst those women who could eat me for breakfast.

"Well, you're not chocolate, you won't melt, and I know for a fact that there are many a good women working in there who are just trying to earn a decent living. God only knows what they make of you. You're just going to have to toughen up, there's nothing else for it."

So there was no persuading her... I just had to eat it! But there was no way that I was going to stay there for two minutes longer than I had to, so I spent most of my free time looking for another job. Given that the troubles where still raging and half the city centre had been blown up, the hotel, shops, and cafes had been raised to the ground, and there was very little by way of work, I wasn't getting very far. So I set my sights a wee bit higher and decided that I would become a nurse. After my sixth application to become an auxiliary nurse, I was offered an interview.

The job involved basic cleaning of the hospital wards, making beds, and toileting patients. I didn't get the job, and they suggested that it was because they thought that with me having five CSEs at grade two, I would probably not be content to stay in the job.

So having five poxy CSEs was the supposed reason why I couldn't get a job that I would have loved. I believed, as did most Catholics who were turned down for jobs in the public sector in Derry, that it was more to do with my address, as it clearly revealed that I was from the Creggan Estate and so I was a Catholic. Catholics were not being offered these kinds of jobs. The hospital was over in the Waterside, which was the Protestant side of the city, and I had no hope. I was gutted but I was determined to get myself a better job than the shirt factory and soon I landed a lovely job in the BSC (British Shoe Company) where I was taught three different skills, and the workers there were much more civilized and a lot more fun than in the shirt factory. I really enjoyed going to work and came out with one-hundred pounds per week, which was a lot of money, so I didn't mind so much that Mi'mai took half.

After about a year though, I wanted something else. I needed to make something more of myself so I enrolled on an adult literacy course as a volunteer and was given a grant to work on a part-time basis helping adults to read and write. I loved the job and worked with a wide range of people – a very successful businessman, a mother over in the Waterside – and I came across more well-off people than I had ever met, and I found it hard to fathom how come they couldn't read or write. Soon I managed to have two jobs at once, as I landed a job in McCafferty's Chemist, where I earned twenty-three pounds a week, and Mi'mai hit the roof because I had given up a perfectly good job in the shoe factory to earn a pittance. Working in the chemist was just the thing for me, and I loved it. I met lots of interesting and unusual people, and Mr. McCafferty, the chemist showed me how to read the prescriptions. Soon I was able to make up some of them by myself under the supervision of Harry, the chemist assistant/manager. He knew Dadai well, was himself an alcoholic, and often went missing from the shop having nipped out for a drink across the road to the pub. Left alone in the shop one day, I was faced with an irate customer who said that she was not prepared to wait for her prescription and that if it was not ready when she came back in five minutes, she would make a complaint to the Health Council, so I just made the prescription up myself.

The woman came in collected her package, and stormed off only to return later on that afternoon furious, demanding to see Mr. McCafferty. She had gone to the doctors complaining of sore feet and had received a bottle of glycerin laxative with the instructions that stated that she must bathe her feet in it three times per day – so she bathed her feet in it before realizing that the sticky solution was a laxative! I had mixed the prescription up with someone else's who thankfully returned his package, which had instructed him to take two spoonfuls of metholated spirits TTD (three times daily!) I seemed to have put the labels on the wrong packages, and although the woman threatened to sue Mr. McCafferty, we never heard any more about it.

The guilt about bringing in less money to the house was never far from my mind but I felt that in my heart of hearts that the drop in income justified what might be a more long-term investment. I knew that it was somehow my destiny to work with people because I enjoyed the human contact, getting to know about people's ailments and worries; worries that they talked over the counter whilst awaiting their prescriptions. I began analyzing and wondering about all the regular hypochondriacs and about their personalities and characters and about what might be going on in their lives. This didn't feel like work to me, and it gave me far more pleasure than the big wage packet, which was in any case, a tiny wage packet by the time it got to me.

Chapter 15
SITTING ON THE FENCE WITH ROOSTER

THANK God for Frank because I could depend on him always. I had been going out with him for two years, and we were totally devoted to each other. He helped me fill in job application after job application and encouraged me all the way. By now, he had received his A-level results and got As in all eight subjects. We celebrated by going out for a meal but I could sense that Frank seemed distant.

I couldn't bear to acknowledge it because I was terrified that I might hear that he might want to finish with me. But there was no way around it, we had to talk about him going to university, and it was as real as the freckles on my face and my bumpy Murphy nose. I simply couldn't avoid looking at it.

We managed to have 'the serious talks', and we imagined a future when he would return from university and we would get married.

So in September of 1977, when we were eighteen years old, I waved Frank off on his journey to Queens University where he was to study Social Policy and Administration. With a mixture of pride and penetrating pain, which pierced what was left of my now-stretched-to-the-limits skin, I began what turned out to be a long torturous process of letting Frank go.

Whilst Frank was away, I tried to reconnect with my old pals. Moya who remained my best friend was now busy with Jeed, and they had become engaged. Moya had landed a brilliant job in the insurance office and was looking out for a wee job for me. Majella was going out with Jamesy, and Sandra was going out with the best-looking fella in the town, Raymond McNutt. Raymond was one of the nicest fellas you could meet and always dressed immaculately with his Crombie coat, bright blue parallel trousers, braces and neck scarf, and he was even better looking than the lead singer of the Bay City Rollers. Half the town wanted to go out with Raymond but he only had eyes for Sandra, whose popularity knew no bounds and she was even able, seemingly without trying and perhaps precisely because she didn't try, to attract a loyal band of admirers and friends.

So since my close pals were otherwise engaged, I became friendlier with Marion Douglas who had been a friend all the way through high school. Marion was a talent magnet because she had a milky white, shiny porcelain complexion, hazel green almond shaped eyes set within a rim of the most perfectly curled and long eyelashes I'd ever clapped eyes on. Her hair was naturally spirally curly, and she was pretty as a picture. At any one time, Marion had about five or six boys chasing her, including our Liam at one point, but he only had a brief encounter with her just before he went off to join the army.

So it was a bit of a conflict for me because although I became very fond of Marion, I was constantly in competition for her time, and seemingly forever having to accept that the boys were hanging around me because they wanted to get off with her.

Rooster McNutt was totally besotted with Marion and as he lived just at the back of our house, he became a close friend of mine. Rooster was Raymond McNutt's brother and being a friend to Rooster meant that I got to hang out with Raymond. Although I never for one minute even considered that he would fancy me, he was just out of my league. It never entered my head that he might fancy me and in any case, he was off limits because he was Sandra's fella. You wouldn't have even guessed that Raymond and Rooster were brothers, as Rooster had the reddest hair, brown eyes, and his face was splattered with big thick freckles mixed with a splash of adolescent acne and he was beginning to sprout a gingery hairy stubble on his chin; whilst his one-year-younger brother Raymond would not have looked out of place in the centre pages of the Jackie magazine. Rooster was going out with Marion one minute and in the next, she had finished with him. Marion's predicament was that she had too much to choose from by way of admirers.

But I came to love Rooster, and we turned to each other in the late of the night, as we had so much disappointment in common and in particular that we weren't with the one of our dreams. Frank had been coming home from university in the holidays and full of talk about his new world and new friends. He started to hang around with other girls in Creggan and eventually he finished with me. My heart was ripped out of me, and I hated the world and everything in it and started to think that life wasn't worth living.

Chapter 15 SITTING ON THE FENCE WITH ROOSTER

At the end of the evening or on late Saturday mornings, Rooster would call in for me. We would sit on the hard concrete fence at the bottom of our garden and chat about the troubles, what was going on in the town, who had been shot, who had been killed, who had been raided, who had been lifted, who was going out with who and who had finished with who. Together, we dragged each other down to some kind of depths of despair, as we tried to work out what the heck this life was all about and what was the point of it. If the IRA were fighting for Irish freedom then why were we not free to speak our minds, and why were we not free not to support the violence and bombings without being made feel guilty or being made to feel like a coward? Didn't freedom mean that we should be able to decide for ourselves how we would respond to the bloody troubles without feeling that we would have to answer to some more powerful authority? Was there any room anywhere for finding and declaring a different non-religious non-sectarian personal authority? And as for the Protestants, couldn't they just see how bloody selfish they were and just give the Catholics their right to a democratic place at the friggin political table before we were all killed stone dead?

Rooster could see no way out of the black hole that we were all in. The British government seemed far too concerned with keeping the Protestants happy and there was no sign of the Yanks, and we didn't know what the frig was going to happen and if anyone would be coming around the mountains to save us all. Rooster laughed at me thinking that the Yanks would come around the corner and save the day and told me that those kinds of dreams would never come true.

"Aye right, Caroline. If they come for ye, make sure ye call in for me. I wouldn't mind galloping around Creggan in your posse behind John Wayne."

But me and Rooster did have each other to turn to and when we couldn't sort out the troubles. We helped each other out. I would lend him what money I could for the community centre disco and at times, he would just spontaneously bring me a box of chocolate orange matchmakers or the Jackie magazine that he would have specially bought for me.

We met at the bottom of our front garden most nights and sat on the uncomfortable concrete fence for hours until our backsides had become numb.

I was surprised that Mi'ami allowed it but she was fond of Rooster and kept a look out of the curtains, as she would regularly lift the venetian blinds to check that I was still there and that there was no hanky panky.

History, however, began to repeat itself, as Rooster would arrive at our fence covered in blood and tell me about getting involved in fights because he was being accused of being a coward for not joining up. Sometimes I would try again to wash the stains out of his clothes before he went home because his mother would go out of her mind if she knew. Rooster's father had died when he was younger, and his mother had thirteen weans to look after. Our Mark and Sean palled around with his younger brothers, and they were all in the scouts together. Their mother really had her hands full. Just like all the mothers in Creggan, she had to manage worries of no money, no jobs, no prospects, a house full of weans, and a life sentence of watching, waiting, and worrying whether something would turn up, and if some miracle would put an end to the troubles before any of their wanes were killed and or got pregnant.

Like Tommy and Liam, Rooster decided to join the Irish Army and he was gone. And so my world shrank, shrank, and shrank. I tried to fill the gap by going over to Frank's house where I would spend the odd hour here and there chatting to his mother.

As much as I loved Francis, it was becoming too painful to hear about Frank's new girlfriend Aggie and to be in his house with all the reminders of the future I wouldn't have.

So I stopped going out and put on weight. My weight gain was so rapid that people would remark on it, and I would tell them that I had an illness. Not thinking that it would get back to Mi'ami who quizzed and interrogated me about what the hell I was telling people and so we had something else to fight and argue about.

But I suppose I did have an illness, I didn't want to argue any more, just eat and sleep and try to keep myself to myself.

One day, a knock came to the door, and our David shouted to me, "Caroline, there's somebody here for ye."

"Just ask them what they want," I called out, not feeling bothered about seeing anyone.

"Well, you're wanted at the door now, and you need to get out here," David shouted.

Chapter 15 SITTING ON THE FENCE WITH ROOSTER

I reluctantly made my way to the front door and when I arrived, there was no one there. I was ready to eat the face of David when out from the wee porch jumped Rooster in his Irish Army uniform.

"Yes Caroline. What about ye?"

Rooster looked the picture of health and so handsome in his green uniform.

"Rooster, what are you doing here, and you're not supposed to be wearing an army uniform, you'll get yourself shot." I knew from Tommy and Liam that wearing their uniforms in the North of Ireland was not allowed because they could be mistaken for paramilitary soldiers.

"Are you coming out to the centre tonight?" he asked.

"Well no, Rooster. I have no money and I'm a state, look at me."

Well I really didn't want him to look at me because I looked like the rear end of an Antrim goat.

Rooster put his hand in his pocket and pulled out a wade of notes, "Look, I have plenty of doe."

He pushed a five-pound note into my hand and told me that he would meet me at the centre.

Rooster and I managed to catch up that night at the bottom of our fence, and as he told me tales of army life, it was clear that he was not settling in. He thought he might try to get dismissed, and he knew that if he didn't go back on time for duty that he would be in trouble. I told him about how nothing had changed and that Mi'ami and me were at loggerheads and about how she was driving me mad with her tight rein on me.

"Don't give her a hard time, Caroline. Just think about it, what would you do if you were her. She only wants what's right for you and it's the only way she knows how. She doesn't want you ending up pregnant to some good for nothing waister."

What the heck had they done to Rooster in the Irish Army, coming back all sensible and mature?

But somehow Rooster had no sooner joined up in the army than he was out of it again. He had a new sense of conviction that he would get off with Marion Douglas for good and was going to try to get a job.

Raymond Gilmore started hanging around with him because he was a bit of a spare part and had no real friends, and as he just lived a few houses away from Rooster, it was inevitable that they would hook up with each other.

Chapter 15 SITTING ON THE FENCE WITH ROOSTER

Our meetings at the fence became few and far between, and Rooster seemed distracted, hyper and always on edge.

"Caroline, what's it all about? What is anything about: the troubles, no money, no job, no prospects, no girlfriend, no nothing. What's the point in anything? I feel like ending it all 'cos if I don't kill myself, somebody will kill me or worse still I will end up killing somebody else."

He told me that he thought he was "losing it" and that he was paranoid that he was being watched all of the time by the Brits or by the IRA.

It was as though he was drowning in despair and me, who couldn't swim, had jumped in to rescue him, only to drag him down further into the swamp of misery. So it came about that although we would regularly bump into each other through the day and at weekends when we would have a quick chat, our late night soul searchings and talks of fears and hopes for the future became a rare occurrence.

Perhaps like me, Rooster could no longer take refuge in the contents of his mind. It was becoming harder to hold on to fantasies of a brighter future because inside our teenage hearts and minds, we were in fierce battle. War was raging between the parts of us that wanted to grow up and be independent and the parts of us that were terrified that being grown up meant making grown up decisions like joining the IRA or leaving home and getting a job or having sex, if ye were lucky enough to have a boyfriend. Decisions seemed to be about freedom, one way or another: freedom for Mother Ireland or freedom from our mothers and Ireland; freedom from the worries; freedom to have the right to have our own battles and not to run with the gang; freedom that was to do with escape, escaping the British army and the paramilitaries, escaping the tight confines of our family histories and relationships that had been battering through the walls of our hearts and minds, and escape from the thought that life wasn't worth living. The ordinary adolescent task of separation and independence became so tangled up with 'the troubles' and Catholicism, like a spiky and dangerous barbed wire barricading us into positions of fight or flight. Rooster, like me and every other teenager, had a job to do to separate from our parents and our families and to figure out our own personal and political histories and if not physically, then it needed to happen in our minds. But when I tried to take refuge within the walls of my mind, I was often ambushed, caught by a sniper firing a bullet of shocking reality right into my face that there was no escape. Soon there was nowhere to run and nowhere to hide... no more going home to lick our wounds and no safe mind place. My mind place had become a lookout post that housed an unofficial police force who had a persecuting eye on my every move. If I stepped out of line in any way, either in my thoughts or deeds, then I would be battered by guilt and shame like the heavy arm of the B Specials ramming their truncheons deep into my psyche and plunging me into depression.

Chapter 16
FALLING, GETTING UP AND FALLING HARDER

DRAGGING myself by the scruff of whatever was still emotionally and psychologically intact in me, I managed to rear my head out of the black hole of depression and limp half heartedly into performing in the pantomimes and the festivals in the city, where the sense of new possibilities began to feature again in my mind, showing me that I could find a way out of it all and that I would make something of my life.

Things changed too with Mi'ami, who started to respect my opinion and seemed to treat me more like a grown up now that my eighteenth birthday was coming up.

I had been saving ten pounds a week for nearly a year now in Maryanne's Club. It was one of these arrangements that if twenty people were in the club, they all paid in their money and each week, someone would have their turn to have the two hundred pounds. It was a kind of street cooperative savings. I often wondered if Mi'ami's change in attitude towards me was due to her fear that I would take the money and run as soon as I got the chance and that her worst fear that I would leave home would be realized. With a new sense of direction and a new leap of faith in my religion, I took to going to chapel again and spending a lot of time sitting there in the quiet, trying to link to something bigger and better than my life. I would search within myself and within the quiet walls of the chapel for a higher authority. Whilst I was kneeling there, lost in this leap of faith and absorbing the profoundly emotional experience, it seemed that God and Mother Mary sent me some new spiritual and meditative comfort, which filled me with the possibilities that things could be different and that life could change for the better and that the future could be something to believe in. The future was a possibility because here I was alone in the Creggan Chapel caught up in the moment, and my heart could have burst with the joy that enveloped me. It was the purest kind of joy and appreciation of being alive, and I wept with a sense of acceptance of life being just as it was.

Chapter 16 FALLING, GETTING UP AND FALLING HARDER

I met my new friend, Cara whilst lighting a candle in the chapel. Cara was one of two children, and her younger brother Fergal was an altar boy with my younger brothers, Mark and Sean. Her family had moved from Belfast to Derry because her father was on the run from the British Army, and her mother had to manage by working in a doctor's surgery as a receptionist as she tried to rear her two weans alone. Father O'Hanlon, a priest from the Shantallow parish, was always in Cara's house and was a great help to the family. Cara thought the world of him especially as he was a wonderful musician and was helping her learn to play the guitar, as she herself dreamed of becoming a musician.. I couldn't understand why she wasn't interested in this beautiful fella, Ricky who was besotted with her. As per usual, Ricky came running after me. He arranged to meet me one night to go for a walk, so that I would pass messages to Cara from him, and he thought that hanging around me would bring him closer to her. I knew this position very well, and one night ended up taking advantage of the situation and his desperation to get close to her... we somehow ended up snogging. I was seemingly caught up in some kind of love triangle as I secretly fancied him but the snogging was a sure fire way of getting him off my back because it was not really his intended outcome.

When I returned home later on from my sneaking, snogging session, our David told me that Rooster had been looking for me and wanted to know if I would be going to the community centre on Monday night. He said that he needed to talk to me, and he would look out for me but I was not to worry because he wouldn't be far away. I wasn't planning to go to the centre but I would because Rooster must need to catch up with me. Maybe he finally got either over or off with Marion.

In the meantime, Cara took me down to the apartment where Father O'Hanlon lived and showed me the room where he helped her with her homework. I had to confess to her what had happened between me and her old boyfriend Ricky and was surprised and curious that she didn't seem the least wee bit bothered, in fact she was more pleased and relieved. So with my sin forgiven, we giggled about the whole thing.

"I have something to tell you too, Caroline."

"Go on, tell me, Cara."

Cara took me into the priest's bedroom and showed me his bed.

"This is where we sleep together. He looks after me and holds me until we both go to sleep."

"You're a liar Cara. No way!"

"Aye. Look, I have something else to show you."

Cara produced a little square black velvet box, opened it, and inside was a most delicate and exquisite gold bracelet decorated with pearls.

"These are real pearls," she whispered, as her beautiful blue eyes shone through her shyness and she smiled with sheer delight. Well in that moment, I was totally and absolutely envious.

"You must never tell anyone, Caroline." So with that we were sworn to secrecy.

But the thought of it niggled and niggled away at me, and my envy gave way to a thick fog of confusion when during one of my daily chapel meditations the fog lifted, and I allowed myself to know that Cara and Father O'Hanlon were sleeping together, .But what did that mean? What was that about?

Shocked, and deeply, deeply confused I got up off my praying knees, and there I was sitting in this place of holiness and sanctuary with a troubling thought in my holy head that a priest was sleeping with my new best friend. I could never tell a soul. I sat there thinking about this whole religion thing and of all the years on and off that I thought I might become a nun. Then I remembered the time when I went to confession during the retreat when I confessed my sins to the visiting Fathers of the Franciscan Order. I was about twelve years old at the time and delivered a recital of my usual sins,

"Bless me Father for I have sinned, It has been one week since my last confession. I have told lies, disobeyed my parents and fought with my sister, said bad words, had bad thoughts about Paisley and the British Army."

"Anything else, my dear?"

"No Father."

"What about bad thoughts... can you say more?"

"Well I did have bad thoughts about Paisley when he was shouting about the Constitution and No Surrender, and I see him gasping for breath, he collapses, and dies of a heart attack. And I have bad thoughts about the British Army being bad animals."

"What about touching yourself. Do you ever touch yourself in your private parts?"

I didn't know what to say because I did scratch my front and back bum but I didn't know that it was a sin.

That was the day that I learned about masturbation because when I came out of the confession box, I asked my friends if they had been asked the same thing, and after some further investigation, we worked out what he was getting at... the dirty article!

Following my meandering meditations, I dragged myself out of the chapel and looked up to the sky. It was a lovely sunny morning and the fluffy candyfloss clouds in a blue sky provided me with the blanket of freshness that I desperately needed. I didn't need to hold on to anything that I previously thought was true and all of a sudden I felt strangely relieved. I didn't have to believe in any religion. I would have to start believing in myself and depending on myself. That dirty wee priest did me a great big favour because now when I thought about him and Father O'Hanlon, I knew that it was all a big farce and in that moment, I dropped a half-ton of guilt.

Joe Ninety was flying low in the sky, and I wondered what was going on, but didn't dwell on it too much, as my head was full of the notion that the only person I could really depend on was myself, and I would not have to keep feeling guilty for stuff that I was not guilty of, like original sin. A new spring in my step almost sprung me the whole way up Chapel Lane, as I bounced my way home flighty with thoughts that nothing could hold me back from making something of my life.

When I got home, Mi'ami was waiting at the door and all the curtains were closed. In fact, I had noticed that many of the houses in the street had the curtains drawn and this only happened when there was a wake or if someone had just died. I couldn't see a black bow on any of the doors so if somebody had died, it wasn't anybody who lived in our street. The last time I came home to such a scene was when our cat, Jesus, died. Uncle Liam gave the Persian cat to us before he went to Canada and we promised him that we would look after it. It was called Jesus because Mi'ami was terrified of cats and every time it came near her, she would, in shock, shout out, "Jesus, get off!"

Today though, the drawn curtains and the look on my mother's face meant that it was worse than the death of a cat. Somebody had died or been killed... I knew it.

Like a ghost from our past, her face was softer and more compassionate than I had known it for a long time. There was something strangely comforting about the look on her face but it was a face with bad news written all over it. "Caroline, come in and sit down."

"Dear God, Mamai, g'on tell me what's the matter? Who is it? Who's dead?"

"I'm so sorry, love."

The tears welled up in her eyes and she choked out the name. By now, I was crying. I couldn't remember the last time she called me love and her saying it blocked out my hearing of the rest of what she was trying to say.

"What Mamai, who is it?"

"Colm, it's Colm."

"Colm who? Who's Colm?"

"Rooster love. It's Rooster… the SAS gunned him down. He was shot three times in the back."

"But he's not dead Mamai, no he's not. I'm meeting him at the centre the night, he wants a chat."

I looked into her eyes, begging her to tell me that he wasn't dead, but I read the story on her face and it told of the same pain of the day that the soldier had died in her arms all those years ago. The day when the softness of her seemed to die too, and it occurred to me in that moment that for many years, I had struggled to really look into her face because it told too terrible a tale, a tale of too much pain, worry, disappointment, and fear. The kind of story written on many of the faces of Derry's mothers, the kind of face that was hard to look at, the kind of face that was far too sad. What other kind of face would it be because our mothers had become human shields, and they had spent the best years of their lives trying to keep it all together, protecting us from the troubles and from the dangers on the streets?

I collapsed into her arms, too tired to cry but my bones were shrieking and crying through every inch of my body, and I rocked myself into her breasts, where I allowed myself to dissolve into an exhausted sorrow for Rooster, my dear friend, and for everything, including the years of estrangement from my own mother. I thought of Rooster's advice to be good to Mi'ami and to forgive her because she was probably doing her best given everything that she had on her plate.

Mi'ami cradled me for the longest time, and her tears dripped down onto my face, as she bent down to kiss my head. This was not only a cease-fire between me and my mother but I couldn't know that it was the beginning of some kind of peace process for us.

"They say that Rooster was on a mission for the IRA but whatever he did, he didn't deserve that. His poor mother will be out of her mind. She's buried her man and now her son. How will she ever get up from this? There are so many bad animals out there… it's like we're living in a bloody jungle. Sweet God in heaven, how are we to get up and run on? But if we don't try to rise above it, we may as well all be six feet under," said Mi'ami.

I refused to go to the wake at Rooster's house. I was too angry with him and couldn't bear to listen to the talk about him and about how the SAS had jumped out of an unmarked police car and riddled him down, shooting him in the back of the head. He died instantly. I had no idea that he had become involved with the Irish Nationalist Liberation Army (INLA), another bloody faction of the IRA. He had never told me that he had joined up, and I had never allowed myself to read the signs.

Mi'ami persuaded me to go up to the wake and she would go with me. Up we went and stood in line in the queue with swarms of mourners. When we neared the coffin, Mi'ami put her arm around my shoulder and held my hand. Rooster's mother was sitting in her own house as though nothing of what was happening and of what she was sitting in the middle of was hers. She didn't know that Rooster had joined the INLA, and it was as though she was sitting in the middle of somebody else's story. It was not the story that she had written for her red-headed son Colm or for any of her sons. Everyone who had a cause or a need to mourn for something had hijacked the wake, and the poor woman sat quietly staring, looking at all the people who were now in her home. She remained quiet and still with an expression of emptiness on her face, a kind of face that I had never before seen. This was a whole different story from Mrs. Tancred whose son had been riddled with bullets in Sean O'Casey's play. Mrs. McNutt was not wailing like a banshee but sat there, a complete wreck of a woman whose heart had just been ripped out of her.

I barely recognized Rooster in the coffin, as the back of his head had to be reconstructed and was stuffed with some kind of filler. I stayed there looking at him for some time, trying to get in touch with the reality of it all but it was not real, and my emotions were nowhere to be found within me. But just before I turned to walk away, I felt the need to touch him. I kissed my hand and put it in to the coffin on top of Rooster's hand and whispered to myself,

"Bye, Bye Rooster. Thanks for everything. I know you won't be far away."

Chapter 17
MY MOTHER'S DAUGHTER

DURING the weeks that followed, I didn't know what to do with myself. I spent a lot of time on my own in my bedroom listening to the radio and looking up into the night time skies. One night, the number one hit song, Abba's 'Fernando', was blaring out,

"Can you hear the drums Fernando?...

This was a song about Fernando being young and full of life and not prepared to die and he was not afraid to say that the roar of guns and cannons almost made him cry.

...The stars were shining there for Fernando and me and for liberty.

Before now, this song, which had been played constantly on the radio and had become a bit of an anthem, usually washed over me and the words hardly registered but now, for the first time, I understood it. It had meant something real for the first time. Lying there listening and looking up at the stars, I grasped its intended meaning, and I understood something more about Rooster. Smiling to myself, I thought of how he made his decision not to sit on the fence any longer because we could only sit on it for so long before it became a pain in the arse. He had to do something different so he joined the INLA. Even if his decision was based on having very little choice, it was his choice, and he was doing something that he thought was better than sitting on his backside, doing nothing. If he had stayed with the war in his head, he may have ended up killing himself or someone else so he took a risk.

Later we had learned that Rooster had been set up by Raymond Gilmore, the young fella who had spent all of those hours lying on top of our coal shed, the one whom we all felt sorry for, and the one whom we thought was a wee bit pathetic. But didn't realize just how pathetic he would turn out to be, not least because he had delivered a life sentence to every member of his own family who never recovered from the shame of it all and who were all driven mad and to their graves one tragic way or another because of him. Raymond was the most notorious informer of the troubles and was responsible for informing on over thirty members of the IRA whilst working undercover for the British Army. It would have been just like Rooster to take Gilmore under his wing because Rooster was a big softie who easily trusted and cared about people and would have cared about Gilmore and trusted him too.

The troubles in Belfast and Derry were at volcanic temperatures, as killings and bombings were erupting all over the place. The Women's Peace Movement had become established, and many mothers across Northern Ireland were marching for peace. It was a brave and risky thing to do if you were bringing up your weans in the heartland of republicanism.

One day, shortly after Rooster's death, Mi'ami and Maryanne threw on their coats, rounded a squad of their teenage daughters; I grabbed Moya who came too, and off we went down the town to march for peace so that there would be an end to the killing of youngsters...whatever side of the political divide they came from. Plenty of women from Creggan rallied, and I hoped that the strength of feeling would make a big impact and that we would at least have a rest from it all so that we could take time to heal from the last ten years of it all. Well at least we were doing something but it seemed that the more that the idea of peace was gathering momentum, the more that the conflict raised in defiance, a bit like some kind of chemical reaction seeking balance.

The cease-fire between Mi'ami and me was also short lived, as she soon became more fearful that I would 'end up in trouble'. It really seemed as though she truly feared me getting pregnant as much as she feared any of her wanes getting caught up in the troubles. I had no intention of getting pregnant and how could I? I didn't even have a boyfriend.

After Rooster's death, I gravitated again back to Frank's house where I would await his return from university.

One night, we walked the streets together until one o'clock in the morning, and I hung on to threads of hope that we might get back together. I was late home, and Mi'ami was waiting up for me. She went in and out through me with her threats that if I stayed out late again, she would kill me stone dead. I just couldn't talk to her about my turmoil; I didn't think she would take me seriously or even care about how much I was hurting because she had so much on her plate.

So the next night I went to Midnight Mass in need of somewhere to turn, even if it was just to sit in the warm chapel in front of the statues imagining some kind of fantasy world where there was no turmoil and it could all be made better.

When the mass had finished, I was invited with some others in the congregation to have tea and sandwiches with the priests. I suddenly realised that it was getting late - almost one-thirty in the morning, one of the priests drove me home with some other friends from the neighbourhood. I was dropped off first and Father told me that they would wait in their car until I was safely in the house. I went to open the door and a hand shot out, pulling me in side where Mi'ami started shaking the life out of me.

"Where have you been? Where have you been, you bad article? You're breaking my heart and you'll be the death of me?"

She looked like she had lost her mind, and I was crying out in protest and shock and trying to tell her that I had been to Mass but she couldn't hear me. Dadai came running down the stairs and started to pull her off me, whilst Sean and Mark joined in because me mi'ami who couldn't stop shaking me had worked herself up into a screaming crying wailing banshee, and she was banging my head against the wall.

"Stop it, Mamai stop, stop it! Let her go," they pleaded. The front door opened, and the priest who had given me the lift home came in and explained that I had been to Mass.

My mother was crying her eyes out, and the priest calmed her. She managed to explain that I had stayed out late the previous night and that she was worried sick. Dadai made us all a cup of tea and Mi'ami went to bed, unable to look at me, and I couldn't feel anything towards her.

There was nothing else for it, I had to find a way of getting away from it all.

The next day, I went round to Moya's house and told her that I couldn't live at home any longer. I was eighteen years old and my mother could not stop me from leaving, so for the first time in my life, I made an adult decision that I couldn't and wouldn't go back home. Moya went round to our house and told me dadai that I was going to stay for a few weeks at the youth leader's house where I used to baby sit so that my parents would know that I was safe.

I couldn't imagine living at home again and started to plan what I would do with my life. I stayed in bed for the best part of that week, feeling sick and trying to imagine my future. Moya called for me, and we went into town, where I bumped into my aunt, who told me that I should be ashamed of myself and get home because I was making my mother sick with worry and that the doctor had been to see me mother and that he suspected that she had had a heart attack. So my auntie's prediction came true because when I was a wee girl, she would often tell my mother that she would have bother with me when I would grow up.

Well maybe she was right, and I didn't want to break my mother's heart so I got home as quick as I could.

I arrived home to find that the house was a mess and that Mi'ami was in bed. I didn't want to go upstairs to see her and I just started tidying up and cleaning. I mopped and hovered, and polished and I shined even though I don't think that I had an ounce of energy in my bones but I couldn't just sit looking at the mess and couldn't sit thinking of my mother's broken heart.

Dadai was smoking his pipe, asking me how I was doing. I told him that I hated what she had done to me and that I couldn't put up with her controlling me any longer. Dadai agreed that she had been very hard on me over recent years, and he remembered how close we used to be when I was younger. He thought that she only wanted the best for me and didn't want me to get into trouble.

I brought Mi'ami's tea up to her on a tray that night. She asked me if I was home for good, and I told her that I was home for a wee while until I worked out what I would do with my life.

I returned to my room and thought of how I'd broken my mother's heart. I thought of how she was the very heartbeat of our family and that if anything had happened to her then that would be the end of our family. I was crying inside but no tears came out of me.

What's the point in crying if there is no one there to mop your tears? Being a teenager was hard but being a Catholic Northern Irish teenager living in Derry in the middle of a war when your father was in and out of the psychiatric hospital; and you had been voted the ugliest girl in the class;, and your mother could just about manage to feed you and your brothers and sister; and the British Army was in your face day and night and shooting your family, friends, and neighbours; and your brothers were being pressurized to sign up for the IRA; and you were squeezed in to a house that was too small to swing a cat; and your mother was treating you with suspicious contempt as though you were about to leap on every man on the earth because you had now reached the age of consent; and one of your closest friends had been shot dead; and the love of your life had finished with you; and you had not been chosen for the O-level class; and your older brothers had left home; and the Protestants had all the decent jobs and looked down their noses at the Catholics like me who were scratching around for a decent life; and your friends were taking up arms because they were fed up scratching around for the crumbs of a decent life. Well it was all too much, and I wanted to die.

Tommy's old friend Brendan Henderson who had floated in and out of our family life over the years reappeared when I was wallowing in my sorrows and trying to work out what I would do with myself. He always arrived late on a Saturday night after he had been out drinking and would go straight to the kitchen looking for a bowl of Mi'ami's Sunday Soup, which she always made on the Saturday night as it was our starter to the Sunday dinner. We all loved to see Brendan coming as though he was a prodigal son. Brendan was doing well in his piano shop and was driving an MG sports car. He wondered if I fancied driving down to Mullingar with him to see Tommy and Liam.

We went the following weekend and had a great time. I was very fond of Brendan, my sixth brother but without all the complications. We met with Tommy and his girlfriend Helen and even though she was a year younger than I was, she had a Sophie Lauren body and cheekbones to die for... I couldn't understand how anyone aged seventeen could look like that. Tommy was happy and enjoying his new life away from the madness, and he was keen to show me around the barracks. We ended up at a nightclub where a nice farmer asked me to dance. He was lovely with rosy cheeks and manners that any mother would boast off. He was the kind of young fella that your mother would love you to bring home. We spent the late evening talking and finding out about each other. I lost track of the time and the fact that Brendan had said that he would wait outside in the car for me. When I went to the car, it was about one o'clock in the morning, and Brendan was fast asleep and drunk out of his head in the locked car. Although I beat and battered at the windows and roof of the car, I was unable to raise him awake. Brendan and I were meant to sleep at Helen's house but Brendan who wouldn't leave without me, was fast to the world and didn't budge through my frantic rapping on the car window. It was freezing and I had no idea how to get to Helen's house and didn't even know the address, so the wee farmer offered me to come home to his house and that he would take me back to Brendan's car in the early morning.

It was a wee cabin house on the edge of his family farm, and when he turned the key, we stepped into the loveliest room that reminded me of the kind in the John Wayne Westerns, where Maureen O'Hara worked hard cooking and cleaning until John arrived home. It was freezing, and we both laid on top of the bed, cuddling up close beside each other to get warm whilst our chatting eventually gave way to a reluctant sleep. True to his word, the young farmer woke me early in the morning with a cup of tea and a slice of scone bread.

"I know ye have to go back home to Derry, but I was hoping that you would come down to Mullingar again and keep in touch. I think ye are lovely."

I was chuffed to hear it all but was too worried about Brendan to dwell any further on the matter. So I gave the wee farmer my address, we said our good-byes, and I invited him to write to me.

Brendan had a desperate night's sleep and nearly froze to death but he didn't seem to mind. We headed back to Derry, listening to Rod Stewart All the way home, "I am sailing, I am sailing 'cross the dark sky far away ..."

Back home from Mullingar a couple of weeks and I felt inspired that life really did exist outside Derry. So there was nothing else for it, I had to do something, as I couldn't stay here much longer. I wished with all my heart that I could go to America. I tortured Dadai to think of some far-off relative whom I could go to in the US but there were none as far as we knew. We must be the only friggin' Irish family on the planet who don't have American relatives. So the next and only option was England. I told me mi'ami and dadai that when it was my turn to pick up my money from Maryanne's Club, I would buy a ticket for England. My aunt Joyce agreed to me coming to live with her and Mi'ami did everything she could to convince me to stay. I couldn't bear to think of how her world was shrinking around her, as her weans, whom she spent the best part of her life loving and protecting were leaving her behind so I put it out of my mind, and I could no more look her in the eyes.

I was now eighteen, and I could leave home. A couple of weeks after the jaunt to Mullingar, Tommy and his girlfriend Helen arrived home for the weekend and as quick as she could without anyone else noticing, Helen ushered me upstairs to the bedroom where she handed me a letter from the Mullingar farmer. Well right enough it was a lovely letter, the kind that I would have been showing off to my friends had I been in contact with anyone of them. He wanted a photo of me and talked of how he longed to see me again and of how he would love me to come down to Mullingar and stay with his family. It was a pity I thought that he lived so far away but in any case, I just couldn't get Frank out of my system and I had my heart set on going to England. Helen tried to convince me that the farmer was a good lad from a good family. He had great prospects and was likely to take over his father's very successful farm. I wrote back and thanked the lovely rosy-cheeked farmer but declined his offer of a visit any time soon. No sooner had my letter to him gone off when another one arrived from him to me. He was obviously smitten and if I wasn't mistaken, he was practically proposing. I might have been tempted but I had just met the most gorgeous fella I had ever clapped eyes on.

He was Moya's cousin from Yorkshire, England. He had come over to Derry for his cousin's wedding, and he offered to hook up with me when I arrived in England. There was no doubting his good looks but the added attraction was that he also happened to be Frank's first cousin and I immediately felt close to him. So between the jigs and the reels, I had no option to move out, away, and on. I would have either lost my mind or got killed or pregnant if I had stayed two minutes longer in Derry. Mi'ami, with the help of Maryanne, came round to the notion but I tried not to think that I might be sticking a knife in her heart.

Whilst I was packing my bags on the day before my leaving, I was compelled to talk to my mother just to say something.

"Mamai… I can only do this because I am me mother's daughter. If you weren't able to do everything that you did for me and for all of us, then I wouldn't be able to do this now."

Again sniffing up her tears before they saw the light of day, she said, "Well daughter, I only got a wee lend of ye that's all. You were never mine to keep and I have no right to hold you here. You go and watch yourself, make sure ye get to a phone. Sure if God's good, you won't be there until you're back and if ye're in any bother, contact me straight away. Make sure you write, let me know if ye need anything, ye're never too big te need yer mother. Now make sure ye watch yerself."

Dadai couldn't come to the airport, he wasn't feeling too good. The journey in the car was stuffy and awkward as Mi'ami and I were seated beside each other in the front seats. We chatted about the weather and the misty Glenshane Pass and hoped that we would get a good safe run up to Belfast airport without being stopped at an army checkpoint that might keep us late for the flight. I really didn't want to be going to Rochdale in England, of all places... England! The very country that had a good hand in the reason that I was escaping from Ireland in the first place and strangely it seemed to be the only place to turn. But my conscience wasn't giving me too great a time about going to England. I couldn't help but think that I was bailing out on my own country.

But what was I doing thinking that? My own country hardly knew I was there for eighteen years, and I was neither use nor ornament to the cause so it wouldn't be missing me. I just couldn't find a place for myself in my own country. But I was not just turning away from a country that hardly noticed me, I was escaping a place in a family where I was noticed, watched, and depended on far too much. I was escaping the troubles all around and those sitting right beside me now in this car, where Mi'ami tried her best to keep our conversation going.

Just beneath the froth of our civil conversations, we were in a stew that boiled and bubbled a sickly smell of loss, abandonment, escape, and hurt, and it brewed between us in the moments of unspoken words. Aunt Eileen and David sat in the back seat and provided some desperately needed fresh air, as they chatted and joked.

Mi'ami tried not to cry, as I picked up my suitcase and readied myself to walk through the departure gates. With nothing else to say, she stroked my hair in the way that people do when they don't know what to do. I knew, without looking at her face, that she was now teary. She urgently searched for some intimacy between us by dusting down my shoulders, fixing the collar on my coat, and I could feel her scanning my face for some kind of connection in my eyes. But I couldn't look into hers. I couldn't bear to see what I might be doing to her, I couldn't stand the thought that I might be ripping the heart out of her and that I too was leaving, just like Tommy and Liam, I would soon be gone. I didn't want to know that she had noticed my Teflon-coated parting hug. No tears were shed until I was seated in the plane and looking out of the window. I saw my mother's concerned face in the distance, waving and trying to smile for me through her tears, reminiscent of that first day at school. Only then could I allow myself to know something of the depth of her love for me, for all of us, and that it was the kind of love that involved a lot of suffering. A mother's love; a Northern Irish mother's love; a troubled love but a love that I carried with me for the rest of my life; a love that grew and softened over the passing years; a love that I depended on; and a love that picked me up when I fell.

Well just as dying wasn't an option for me then when I was eighteen years old, it wouldn't be an option for me now at forty-six years. I had too much to live for and no doctor was going to tell me that my body was riddled with cancer. Just because I had a lump in my breast didn't mean that I had cancer. My mother didn't go through all that she did for me to be told to lie down and die. I would change the course of my own history, if it killed me stone dead. There was nothing else for it, I would get up and run on because I am my mother's daughter.

"I am glad to say that I got it wrong. You have a large benign cyst, and I do hope that you haven't been too distressed. Thankfully, sometimes we do get it wrong!" the breast specialist concluded, following about a dozen tests, where my breasts had been subjected to being squashed, flattened, scanned, scrutinized, pummelled, and drawn on.

"Distressed!" Well I think that was a wee bit of an understatement but I was too relieved and exhausted to be angry or to get into any discussion with him and watched as he inserted the long needle into a huge syringe and then pierced the lump in my breast whilst proceeding to suck out the thick milky coloured puss.

Caroline Owens

"The tragedy of N .Ireland may be contextualized and understood by pointing to; the conflict and its antecedents and the conflict and its aftermath. It is well established that poverty and illness are two sides of the same coin. Prior to "the N. Ireland troubles"; political, religious, structural and systemic discrimination with oppressive practices were the undisputable constants for generations, effectively propelling the conflict. This conflict got right into the hearts and minds of the people and communities and emotional and psychological instability was passed through the generations. The transgenerational nature of the related unprocessed trauma has elevated the rates of psychiatric morbidity in N. Ireland now has among the highest rates of PTSD, depression, psychosis, substance use/misuse, self-harm and suicide in the world. It is possible that we are yet to witness more profound spikes in these elevations of psychiatric morbidity and the community will most definitely require more substantial funding to process these psychological consequences of trauma in the aftermath of the conflict".

Dr Mark Owens.

10. The importance of timing, especially in relation to the risk of the recurrence of violence, is difficult to exaggerate. It has only become possible for some people affected by the troubles to begin to address what has happened to them when the cease-fires were announced. Maintaining a relative absence of violence is crucial to the task of addressing the situation of those affected by the troubles. Should there be a return to violence, it will not be possible to take this work forward in the same way. People who have been drastically affected by the troubles often live with high levels of fear. It is only when this fear is reduced, and when an atmosphere of increased safety is in place that it is possible to work constructively with the issues of coming out of violence. This is not to say that people do not have needs when violence is ongoing, but rather to point out that substantial progress can only be made in the absence of violence. Therefore the peace process and progress therein is at the heart of creating services and measures to address the needs of those affected by the troubles.

THE LEVEL OF NEED

11. The assumption that people "get over" such things in time is not true. In the case of physical disablement, this is visibly not the case. One study we conducted showed that roughly 50% of people still had symptoms of emotional distress and things like sleep disturbance over 20 years after they had been bereaved in the troubles. This means that the scale of the problem may be very large. If we count only immediate family members, there could be over 41,400* people in the population whose immediate family death or injury in the trouble has directly affected, and who suffer distress or emotional disturbance as a result. This figure does not include all the eye-witnesses, neighbours, friends, extended family, co-workers and so on who have been affected by deaths and injuries in the troubles. Not all of this 41,400* need or require, for example, counselling. However, the public acknowledgement of their suffering, and the provision of supportive networks or services for those who need them is an important part of our recovery as a society.

12. The converse of this is that some people who have been affected by the troubles have developed their own way of coping with their situation, and have found ways which work for them. Some of these ways involve not talking about what has happened, or distancing themselves from anything which might require them to think too deeply about what has happened, or to look at the issues from another angle. This must be recognised, and people's right not to participate must be recognised and supported.

13. Many of those affected by the troubles complain about their lack of control over the use of television or still photography of the circumstances of their loss of injury. The reprinting or broadcasting of such material can be very distressing for families and those close to such incidents, and currently little recognition is given to the distress caused by their use without consultation with those closely involved. Many of those who have been disabled have often been made dependent on benefit, and removed from the job-market. Services for the disabled are often inadequate to their needs, and can leave them bitter about their circumstances. Poverty is also another by-product for many that have suffered in the troubles.

14. There is a particular need for the provision of an effective pain management service to cater for those in chronic pain as a result of gunshot and shrapnel wounds.

2. There is also a need to support carers of those with disabilities acquired as a result of the troubles. We estimate that around 100,000 people in Northern Ireland live in households where someone has been injured in a troubles-related incident.

The above is an extract from a Submission by Marie Smyth to the Northern Ireland Commission on Victims of 'the troubles'.

PEOPLE AFFECTED BY THE TROUBLES - WHAT IS THE SCALE OF THE PROBLEM?

Since 1969, 3,585 people have been killed in Northern Ireland. This means that at very least 6,800* people have the experience of one of their immediate family - parent or sibling - being killed in a troubles-related incident.

1. According to the official figures over 40,000 people have been injured in the troubles, although this is likely to be a conservative figure. There is not readily available data on how many of this 40,000 suffer from major disability as a result of the troubles. If we take deaths in the troubles as an indicator (it is likely that injuries and trauma follow the same pattern as deaths) we find:

2. 91% of those killed were male;

3. 37% were under the age of 24, 53% were under the age of 29, and 74% were under the age of 39;

4. Civilians - those without affiliation to the security forces or paramilitary organisations - constitute the largest group amongst those killed - 53%. Security forces from outside Northern Ireland are the next highest percentage - 14.5% followed by Northern Ireland security forces - 14.3%. Within the Northern Ireland security forces, the RUC account for almost 300 deaths, almost 50% more than RIR/UDR deaths. Republican paramilitaries account for 12.5% of those killed, and Loyalist paramilitaries for just over 3%;

5. More Catholics than Protestants have been killed. The death rates for civilians are 3.01 per 1,000 population for Catholics and 1.26 per 1,000 for Protestants. If we include RUC deaths, the rates become 2.5 per 1,000 for Catholics and 1.9 for Protestants. If we exclude those killed by paramilitaries on their own side (Catholics killed by Republican paramilitaries and Protestants killed by Loyalist paramilitaries) then the rate becomes 2.3 for Catholics and 1.4 for Protestants;

6. Republican paramilitaries have killed almost 59% of the total killed 704 of whom were civilians, Loyalist paramilitaries have killed almost 28% of whom 818 were civilians, and the security forces have killed just over 11%, 204 of whom were civilians, with the British army accounting for over 9% of that total;

7. Over 41% of those killed lived in postal districts BT11, 12, 13, 14, 15, 48 and BT35. Over 48% of those killed in the troubles were killed in those same districts - North and West Belfast, Derry Londonderry City and South Armagh.

8. There is some overlap between the "victim" and "perpetrator" categories: some victims go on to join paramilitary organisations, at least partly due to their experience of victimhood. If we can generalise from all this, we conclude that the troubles have been a killer of young males from North and West Belfast, Derry Londonderry or the border areas, and who are rather more likely to be Catholic. This is also the group, which is among the most likely to become perpetrators of acts of violence.

APPROACHES TO THE ISSUE

9. All discussions about "victims" of the Troubles run the risk of becoming politicised in the following ways. Acknowledgement of the damage done to a particular grouping or community can seem to some as an admission of defeat, which will gladden their enemies, and so is to be avoided. Conversely, acknowledgement of such damage can be a way of highlighting the wickedness of those who are responsible for the attacks, and so can become a political weapon. All of this runs the risk of compounding the damage done to those who have been hurt. It is of crucial importance that all discussion about "victims" or people affected is shifted onto a humanitarian basis, based on an inclusive concern about the human needs and the resources required to meet them.